Spitfire into Battle

ORDE
18 Aug 1941.

P/O. W.G.G.D.SMITH. D.F.C.   611 SQUAD

SPITFIRE
INTO BATTLE

Group Captain W.G.G. Duncan Smith

DSO DFC RAF(Ret)

JOHN MURRAY · LONDON

© W.G.G. Duncan Smith 1981

First published 1981
by John Murray (Publishers) Ltd
50 Albemarle Street, London WIX 4BD

Typeset by Inforum Ltd, Portsmouth
Printed in Great Britain by
The Pitman Press, Bath

British Library Cataloguing in Publication Data
Duncan Smith, W.G.G.
Spitfire into battle.
1.   World War, 1939–1945 – Aerial operations, British
2.   Spitfire (Fighter planes)
I.   Title
940.54'4941092'4   D784

ISBN 0–7195–3831–9

FOR MY SONS
Barrie, David, Iain

The thundering line of battle stands,
And in the air death moans and sings;
But day shall clasp him with strong hands
And night shall fold him in soft wings.

– from 'Into Battle' by Julian Grenfell,
in *Men Who March Away*, ed. Ian Parsons
(reproduced by kind permission of Burns & Oates Ltd)

Contents

Illustrations

35   D.S.'s Spitfire Mk VIII at Ravenna

ILLUSTRATION SOURCES

Front and back endpapers, frontispiece, 3–5, 8–10, 14–16, 18, 20, 22–4,
26–34: Trustees of Imperial War Museum; 1, 2, 6, 7, 11–13, 17, 25, 35: the
Author; 19: Caproni Aircraft Co; 21: Italian Ministry of Defence

AUTHOR'S NOTE

I would like to thank Louis Jacketts and Eric Turner of the Ministry of
Defence (Air Historical Branch) for their advice and assistance during my
researches. I would also like to thank my friend David Scott-Malden, whose
suggestions were a great help in furthering my story.

Foreword

BY JEFFREY QUILL OBE AFC FRAeS

There is a massive literature covering the air warfare of 1939–45.

Fighter operations have, quite rightly, occupied a significant proportion of this literature and have been approached from many points of view; those of professional or official military historians, of senior commanders giving their personal accounts, of scientists and engineers discussing the aircraft and other technical developments which played such vital parts in the struggle and, last but not least, the accounts written by the fighter pilots themselves.

The sheer volume of the literature and the diversity of treatment involved has perhaps tended to confuse rather than to clarify. This makes it difficult for the ordinary reader, especially for the young, to get a clear idea of what fighter operations were all about, how they changed and developed during the course of the war, how men really fought against each other in the air, what was the relationship between the man and his aeroplane and how could control and discipline and coherent tactics be established and maintained in the fluid, fast-moving and three-dimensional situations which were endemic to fighter operations.

Finally what sort of men the fighter pilots and those who led them in the air really were, as opposed to the stereotyped images which have emerged inevitably with time.

Spitfire into Battle is not a treatise designed to answer these questions. It is the strictly personal account of one of the greatest of British fighter pilots and fighter leaders of the Second World War. Yet it answers the foregoing questions more clearly and more vividly for the discerning reader than any more analytical or technical treatment could hope to do.

Foreword

Group Captain Duncan Smith DSO and Bar, DFC and two Bars ('Smithy' as so many of us will always remember him) flew and fought in front-line operations almost from the very beginning to the very end of that long and arduous war with a minimum of interruptions for staff duties or 'operational rests'. He fought in Fighter Command at home and in the offensive operations over France, Belgium and the Netherlands which followed the Battle of Britain and by which Fighter Command moved from a defensive to an aggressive role. He fought also in the great air battle over Dieppe, in Malta, in Sicily, in Italy, over the Anzio landings and in the south of France invasion. He took part after the war in the fighter operations in Malaya where he was awarded a second Bar to his DFC. In fact, he led his Wing of Spitfires on the occasion, on 21 May 1951, when that famous aeroplane fired its guns in anger for the last time against the enemy. Altogether he served with twenty-three Squadrons, of which he commanded two as a Squadron Leader and eleven as Wing Commander (Flying); four more as Group Captain in command of No. 324 Wing in Italy; and three more when he was Station Commander and Wing Commander (Flying) at Turnhouse. And Duncan Smith's idea of commanding a Squadron or a Wing was leading it in the air.

Truly, he rode on the wings of the storm. It happened that, from first to last, the Wings were those of the Spitfire for which now legendary fighting aeroplane he developed, as so many others, a strong and lasting affection. With a natural and inborn talent for leadership and a steadfastly aggressive spirit towards the enemy the combination of Duncan Smith and his Spitfire was a formidable one and a powerful factor in his brand of leadership, which was by example.

It is impossible to read this book without becoming aware of a sudden shedding of light upon what is to so many an apparently obscure, confused and frequently over-dramatised subject. The book has undoubtedly gained in maturity and perspective by being written now rather than in the period immediately following the war. Everyone, young and old, who wishes to gain a clearer understanding of British fighter operations and fighter pilots of the Second World War should read it.

Dramatis Personae

'Duke' Arthur: Squadron Leader C.I.R. Arthur, DFC and Bar

Arne Austeen: Major A. Austeen, DFC. Royal Norwegian Air Force. Killed in action

George Barclay: Squadron Leader R.G.A. Barclay, DFC. Killed in action

Roff Berg: Lieutenant Colonel R.A. Berg, DFC. Royal Norwegian Air Force. Killed in action

'Barney' Beresford: Air Commodore B. de la P. Beresford, DSO DFC and Bar

'Birk' Birksted: General K. Birksted, DFC. Royal Danish Air Force

Jim Boothby: Squadron Leader J.R.M. Boothby, DFC

'Bitters' Bitmead: Group Captain E.R. Bitmead, DFC

Harry Broadhurst: Air Chief Marshal Sir Harry Broadhurst, GCB KBE DSO and Bar DFC and Bar AFC

Pete Brothers: Air Commodore P.M. Brothers, DSO DFC and Bar

'Mary' Coningham: Air Marshal Sir Arthur Coningham, KCB DSO MC DFC AFC. Killed in air crash

'Doc' Corner: Wing Commander H.W. Corner, AFC MD CHB MRCP. Killed in action

Jackie Darwen: Group Captain J. Darwen, DSO DFC and Bar. Killed in action

Peter Dexter: Flying Officer P. Dexter, DFC. Killed in action

'Dickie' Dickson: Marshal of the RAF Sir William Dickson, GCB KBE DSO AFC

Teddy Donaldson: Air Commodore E.M. Donaldson, CB CBE DSO AFC

Dramatis Personae

Mike Donnet: Lieutenant General Baron Michel Donnet, DFC. Royal Belgian Air Force

'Cocky' Dundas: Group Captain H.S.L. Dundas, DSO and Bar DFC

Simon Elwes: Captain S. Elwes. Royal Norfolk Regiment

'Hannes' Faure: Lieutenant Colonel Johannes Faure, DSO DFC and Bar. South African Air Force

'Pussy' Foster: Air Chief Marshal Sir Robert Foster, KCB CBE DFC

Denys Gillam: Group Captain Denys Gillam, DSO and two Bars DFC and Bar AFC

'Mac' Gilmour: Flight Lieutenant M. Gilmour, DFM. Killed in action

'Sheep' Gilroy: Group Captain G.K. Gilroy, DSO DFC and Bar

Colin Gray: Group Captain C.F. Gray, DSO DFC and two Bars

John Hallings-Pott: Group Captain J.R. Hallings-Pott, DSO AFC

Barrie Heath: Wing Commander Sir Barrie Heath, Kt DFC MA

Richard Hillary: Flight Lieutenant R.H. Hillary. Killed while night flying

Pete Hugo: Group Captain Peter Hugo, DSO DFC and two Bars

'Hunk' Humphreys: Squadron Leader P. Humphreys, DFC. Killed in a flying accident

Ralph Hutley: Pilot Officer R.R. Hutley. Killed in action

'Jamie' Jameson: Air Commodore P.G. Jameson, CB DSO DFC and Bar

Alan Johnston: Pilot Officer A. Johnston. Killed in action

'Taffy' Jones: Group Captain J.I.T. Jones, DSO MC DFC MM

Don Kingaby: Wing Commander D.E. Kingaby, DSO AFC DFM and two Bars

Brian Kingcome: Group Captain C.B.F. Kingcome, DSO DFC and Bar

Air Vice-Marshal Trafford Leigh-Mallory: Air Chief Marshal Sir Trafford Leigh-Mallory, KCB DSO. Killed in air crash

'Tiny' Le Petit: Squadron Leader Le Petit, OBE

Eric Lock: Flight Lieutenant E.S. Lock, DSO DFC and Bar. Killed in action

Dramatis Personae

George Lott: Air Vice-Marshal G.E. Lott, CB CBE DSO DFC

Johnny Loudon: Wing Commander J.M. Loudon, DFC

Tim Lucas: Major T. Lucas, MC and Bar. 60th Rifles

Jimmy McComb: Squadron Leader J. McComb, DFC

Richard McCreery: General Sir Richard McCreery, GCB KBE DSO MC

'Tink' Measures: Wing Commander W.E.G. Measures, AFC

Willie Merton: Air Chief Marshal Sir Walter Merton, GBE KCB

'Zulu' Morris: Air Marshal Sir Douglas Morris, KCB CBE DSO DFC

'Doggie' Oliver: Group Captain J.O.W. Oliver, CB DSO DFC

Keith Park: Air Chief Marshal Sir Keith Park, KCB KBE MC DFC AFC

'Polly' Pollard: Flying Officer P.S.C. Pollard. Killed in action

Peter Powell: Group Captain P.R.P. Powell, DFC and Bar

Jeffrey Quill: Lieutenant Commander J.K. Quill, OBE AFC FRAeS. Chief Test Pilot, Vickers-Armstrong Ltd, Supermarine Works

'Dagwood' Rees: Right Honourable Merlyn Rees, MP MA

David Scott-Malden: Air Vice-Marshal F.D.S. Scott-Malden, CB DSO DFC and Bar MA

'Stan' Skalski: Squadron Leader S. Skalski, DFC and Bar. Polish Air Force

Sir John Slessor: Marshal of the RAF Sir John Slessor, GCB DSO MC

Eric Stapleton: Air Vice-Marshal F.S. Stapleton, CB DSO DFC MA

'Tommy' Thompson: Air Commodore J.M. Thompson, CBE DSO DFC and Bar AFC

Stan Turner: Group Captain P.S. Turner, DSO DFC and Bar

Adrian Warburton: Wing Commander A. Warburton, DSO DFC and two Bars. Killed in action

Lance Wade: Wing Commander L.C. Wade, DSO DFC and two Bars. Killed in a flying accident

Tommy Williams: Squadron Leader T.D. Williams, DFC

Chris Wren: Captain C. Wren, Argyll & Sutherland Highlanders

John Whitford: Air Marshal Sir John Whitford, KBE CB

Eagle in the sun

The great shadow sailed across the hillside, floated over my prone body, unsighting me. Startled, I rolled onto my side, eyes sweeping the sky, trying to focus against the deep blue. I let go my .22 rifle and, shading my eyes, squinted into the bright light. At last I saw him, a golden eagle, wheeling, his head tucked into his body, soaring with effortless ease on widespread wings, bright spots of light glinting on the feathers.

Quickly I resighted the rifle on the hare, thirty yards in front and slightly below my hidden position. It was going to be a race between us, for the eagle had seen the hare too and was now getting into position for his attack. I wanted the hare as much as he did.

The hare wriggled deeper into the grass, ears flat along his back, trying his best to melt into the colours of the hillside. He had not seen me, but he had seen the winged enemy wheeling above and knew what was in store if he so much as moved a whisker. His only chance of survival was absolute stillness.

The eagle marked the spot and, half closing his wings, dived. I held the sights of the .22 steady on the hare's back, raised them a fraction to allow for bullet-drop and squeezed the trigger. There was a spurt of dust short of the hare. Realising I had missed, I frantically tried to reload, but it was too late. The smack from the bullet had made the hare jump up and at full speed he was off down the hill, jinking as he ran.

Fascinated, I watched the race for survival. The golden eagle seemed to spin round in his own length. Still diving at incredible speed, his legs dropped rigid, the huge talons wide stretched on his feet. He snapped up the hare with almost casual ease, talons digging into the flesh, and with one swift movement zoomed back into the blue sky, the struggling hare dangling, kicking for dear life. . . .

1

The eagle's flat, powerful head rose upwards with his razor-sharp beak poised; then with a vicious stroke he hammered it into the softness of the hare's neck. He made the kill as surely and painlessly as any well-aimed bullet would have done.

Carrying the limp body the more easily now, the eagle swung in a great arc, climbing for the upper heights of the crags which crowned the steep hillside. I watched motionless as he disappeared, every detail of the scene etched on my memory by the professionalism of that technique.

The hot sun of high summer beat down, the bright light emphasising individual colours across the landscape. I stretched out on the grass, chin cupped in my hands. Away to my left and a thousand feet below, I picked up the outline of the coast road winding past Loch Duich towards Glen Sheil. Beyond I could see the distant Cuillins rising from the shoreline of Skye – Blaven, stark against the shimmering blue. The air, friendly and warm, encouraged me to imagine I could reach out and run my fingers over the contours of the hills, so near did they seem. I watched idly as a boat nosed its way from Kyleakin through the narrows of the dark waters of Lochalsh towards Glenelg. On the mainland by the shore at Balmacara stood my mother's family home, Reraig.

I realised suddenly, that to soar, zoom and strike, like a golden eagle, would be wonderful. I promised myself that, though I was still a prep school brat, come what may I would learn to fly.

CHAPTER ONE

Starting with Miles

On an evening in late May 1939, I climbed into my battered sports car with Ralph Hutley and motored over to the Bull at Sonning. It was a Saturday and we were all set for a party with other friends who, like ourselves, were based at Woodley, near Reading; we were budding Royal Air Force Volunteer Reserve (RAFVR) pilots carrying out 'ab initio' flying training.

We flew Miles Hawk and Magister dual-control monoplanes; our instructors were a mixture of RAF and civilian pilots. A couple were test pilots with the Miles Aircraft Company whose factory spilled across one end of the aerodrome. The Chief Flying Instructor, Squadron Leader James Moir, looked rather like Basil Rathbone in the film *Dawn Patrol*, in which David Niven and Errol Flynn played dashing RFC pilots of the First World War, shooting down rows of Germans over the battle-torn fields of Flanders. I saw it four times.

Though we were a mixed bunch of individuals from many different ways of life and social background, the thread that bound us was a love of flying. It did not matter who you were, what your job was or whether your family was well-heeled or not, so long as you were keen to fly every free moment you had. We had no illusions as to what was in store when war came. Most of us, I believe, looked forward to it in much the same way as preparing for an important rugger or cricket match. We tended to stick together almost to the point of being called cliquey, and were rather limited in our horizons – we enjoyed being so, especially if it upset others not blessed with the same outlook. We had no interest in politics and, for that matter, had never been taught anything about the subject, much less attended any political meeting. We were amused by our posturing politicians and their promises of fixing Hitler and his jackbooted followers – that there would be 'peace in our time'. We knew perfectly well that war would be upon us sooner than later and, although outwardly complacent, we felt dissatisfied and frustrated with the way things were going. A spectre loomed which heightened our frustration: the thought we might be still untrained pilots and the war over before we got a crack at fighting in a front-line squadron.

Ralph Hutley was a particular friend. Clever, he wrote poetry and possessed a sharp sense of humour that tended at times to be sardonic if the company was not to his liking. He usually flew from White Waltham but, because of overcrowding that summer, arranged to do his annual training with me at Woodley. Patriotic like the rest, he was sincere in his belief that the European dictatorships had to be slapped down, but hoped it could be done by diplomacy and not by war. He once remarked: 'I shall go to war believing I am fighting against oppression and devilry but I expect I shall die like many other misguided chaps because we should never have tolerated the ineptitude of gutless politicians for so long.' He rather despised the middle-class society to which he owed his upbringing and education, believing war, with its wanton loss of life, to be an offence to common sense. 'We'll be at war in weeks rather than months,' he continued. 'Let's make sure we become fighter pilots, learn skills to engage in man-to-man combat – clean honest-to-goodness stuff – kill the other fellow or be killed but, pray God, not as a bomber pilot working out how to blast unseen people to smithereens on the ground. I couldn't live with that. No thank you – I will fly Hurricanes or Spitfires.'

Ralph and I, at any rate, were convinced that when the time came we would welcome a crack at the Germans. We had experienced what it was like to be caught in a crowd of young Nazis on the rampage for, during the previous summer while visiting Germany and Austria, we had seen how brutal they could be to their own kind, just for the hell of it.

Arriving at the Bull, we joined a circle of friends at the top end of the bar. As the evening progressed, the beer flowing, the laughter loud, we talked about the high moments of flying experiences and the insensitivity of some instructors in their jaundiced determination to pass on a doctrine created in the aftermath of the First World War: that the bomber was much more important than the fighter; that the bomber pilot was a professional and the fighter pilot an amateur not to be taken seriously.

My first instructor, Flying Officer Collins, having a forthright ability to communicate, taught me patience and that airmanship had to be learned, not assumed. He believed that a number of short flights was more important than longer ones so that time could be spent usefully on the ground hammering out mistakes and brushing-up on airmanship and the theory of flight. Thus, the next flight would be more productive.

I learned the basic skills: how to taxi, handle the controls and engine, straight and level flight, medium turns with and without engine, stalling, climbing, gliding, approaching and landing, spinning and recovery. Although we got along fairly well, I never felt completely at ease with him. He tended to be cautious while I wanted to fly with a degree of robustness that obviously did not appeal to him. We had words at a time when I was eager to go solo after seven hours of dual flying – I knew I was ready yet he gave no sign of encouragement, no sign that he thought the same. Luckily, the Chief Flying Instructor (CFI) noticed something was adrift between us and I found myself one morning flying with a remarkable man, Flying Officer Dudley. With a change of instructor I never looked back. I had two flights with Dudley in quick succession followed by a solo test from the CFI lasting fifteen minutes and, without further ado, I was sent off on my first solo. Nothing much happened. It proved to be little different from many other circuits and bumps, but it remains the most exciting personal experience in my flying career because of the empty cockpit in front, the silence in my earphones, and the feeling that at last I was in complete control of my aeroplane. After landing I felt I had been round the moon and back.

Dudley gave me a wry smile. 'Come on,' he said, 'sign the authorisation book and we'll get back into the air – do some aerobatics to celebrate.'

Dudley was an ex-Imperial Airways pilot who had completed many thousands of hours' flying. He never raised his voice, was always calm and yet could be full of surprises. During the second of the two circuits and landings we did prior to my solo test, we were flying on the down-wind leg when I heard him in my Gosport intercom: 'You'll have to make a safe landing this time – look.' At that moment he tossed over the side what I took to be the 'stick' or control column, to give it its correct name. For a moment I was shattered, realising the implication of his action. His voice continued softly: 'There you are – no stick, no hands, too – you'd better land with due care – I don't want to find myself plastered all over the airfield at my time of life.' Placing his elbows on the sides of the cockpit he gazed nonchalantly into the wide blue yonder. It was not until after landing that I managed to peer breathlessly into the front cockpit to find the stick still in place. Dudley smiled, giving me a wink: 'Instructing can be fun – if you know how,' he said, hitching his parachute and making for the flight office.

Not long after, I was back with my first instructor carrying out side-slipping, practice forced landings and aerobatics. All went well until, during the aerobatic practices, I 'hung' a bit in executing 'rolls off the top of a loop' as the saying goes, which drew strong language from him. Again, more oaths burst in my ears while spinning and I caught a further mouthful for ham-handedness. We landed in silence and while climbing out of the Hawk I noticed he did not look at all happy. Thinking the whole flight a bit of a joke, I remarked, grinning: 'Hope it went off well?'

'No, it didn't, you kack-handed idiot, there is nothing to grin about – the aerobatics and spinning were quite bloody. And another thing – it might interest you to know that's the first time I've ever felt sick in an aeroplane – congratulations.'

Kack-handed or not I found it tremendous fun. For all his needling he was a great help and I learned a lot from him that proved useful in the years that followed. But above all it was Dudley who helped and encouraged me to succeed and it was largely due to his influence that flying became the great love in my life. The more I flew the more I wanted to fly. What niggled me was the slowness of the training cycle. It was going to take time and there was nothing I could do about it.

That summer of 1939 wore on with lovely flying weather. On 22 August I flew from Woodley on a cross-country solo flight to

Gatwick and back. Two days later the general mobilisation orders went out and I found myself in uniform with the rest of my friends, reporting for full-time duty to our Town Headquarters in Reading. There was no sign of apathy or anger at the upsets this had on most of us over our work and domestic arrangements. We need not have worried – we were to have all the time in the world to sort ourselves out. Meanwhile we heaved a sigh of relief that the uncertainties were over.

The staff at the Town Headquarters, taken by surprise at the speed of events, did not really know what to do with us. There were a few desultory lectures, a check on kit, some work in the engineering shop. Then on 3 September, I heard the Prime Minister's broadcast telling us we were at war with Germany. I felt no emotion except one of anticipation. I was proud to be British and in the RAF, and I could look anyone in the eye for I was a volunteer.

All flying at Woodley for RAFVR pilots ceased. I drove over there one afternoon to collect my flying log-book, maps and personal flying gear. I said farewell to Dudley, then Moir, the CFI. He said: 'Come back and see me sometime when you've settled in a squadron – fighters I hope.' He smiled, 'That is, if I am still here.'

At the Town Headquarters, we were told to report at two-week intervals to collect our pay, otherwise we kicked our heels in the bars and cafés and in the countryside while the phoney war dragged on. Air-raid sirens wailed occasionally to let us know something was afoot while we envied the bomber pilots attacking German warships at Kiel, Borkum and Wilhelmshaven.

Not until November were we ordered to report to an Initial Training Wing on the south coast. These Wings had been recently formed to receive RAFVR pilots under training in preparation for full-time service in the Service Flying Training Schools located at various places around the United Kingdom. In my case it turned out to be Bexhill, where I was billeted in the Metropole Hotel, a large Victorian building that had been stripped of all furnishings down to bare boards. Ralph Hutley, Tony Whitehouse and I discovered an unoccupied bedroom having three bedsteads with straw-filled mattresses and pillows which we acquired as our own. On the third floor, with every lift in the place unusable, we got to know the stairs intimately. We were always in a hurry going up and down them two at a time barked at by regular NCOs to 'get a move on'.

We marched everywhere, queued to use the bathroom and collect our meals in the dining-room, a gaunt place that echoed every noise tenfold. The promenade, open spaces, car parks were all used as parade grounds. Forming up, we drilled, attended lectures, then drilled some more.

The Warrant-Officer in charge of our squadron was 'Timber' Woods, an ex-Regimental Sergeant-Major of the Grenadier Guards. We came both to fear and love him. He had seen much action in the First World War and elsewhere; a stickler for discipline, he impressed us that in all forms it was a prerequisite in enabling one to beat the enemy, be it with a bayonet or in an eight-gun fighter aircraft. He worked us till exhaustion became a meaningless condition, his eagle eye missing nothing nor his voice its penetration. At morning inspection he would stand so close while passing down the line that I swore he could count each hair on the back of my neck, his breath tickling till it became impossible not to lean forward to escape the torment. There would be a bark to stun the ear-drums: 'Stand still! Who toldya to move?!'

The Commanding Officer and staff were either First World War vintage or young junior officers in the administrative branch. One, an ex-RFC pilot, gave a talk one day in the absence of a visiting lecturer who had missed his train from London. He explained he had been in the cavalry at the start but had transferred to the RFC in 1916. Using colourful expressions of cavalry origin to describe flying actions, he kept us endlessly amused. 'We spurred and charged the enemy squadron, trotting back to our lines on a loose rein.' The climax came quite suddenly: 'Men, I could ride anything with hair on it in those days.' I shall never forget his puzzled expression while the lecture hall exploded into ribald laughter for several minutes before he finally saw the point. Embarrassed, he stalked from the room amidst renewed laughter never to give us a second helping, which was a pity.

Physical training and sport played an important part in our

programme. I took part in everything including beagling with the local hunt which gave me the chance to get to know local residents; I joined the squash club, playing nearly every afternoon or evening; and by way of a change, I was even browbeaten into taking part in some amateur dramatics for Christmas.

We had weekly tests on the subjects we studied, inter-flight drill, cross-country runs, tug-of-war contests. Although postings to Flying Training Schools had now started to come through only a few lucky ones went off, the rest of us having to start flying all over again. In my case it was No. 7 EFTS at Desford, near Leicester. I was upset by this for I had been on the point of progressing to fly Hawker Hart advanced trainers when I was mobilised. More time wasting but, I suppose, with the numbers involved, the Service Flying Training Schools' intakes were necessarily limited at that time. One of the factors, no doubt, was the severe winter of 1939/40 which handicapped flying to such a degree that the syllabus could not be completed in time to create more vacancies. Many more RAFVR pilots would have been trained, ready to meet the sudden expansion and shortages caused through casualties in the fighter and bomber squadrons from Dunkirk onwards, if central planning to meet these requirements had been better organised from the start of the war or indeed, even earlier. Many of us, therefore, were made to go through the 'ab initio' syllabus again.

At this point I parted company with Ralph Hutley, Tony Whitehouse and several other friends. Most went on to fly Harvards, an American advanced trainer, or Oxfords for those selected to fly bombers. Ralph and Tony were destined to fly Hurricanes in due course with 32 Squadron but Ralph was later transferred to 213 Squadron at Tangmere and towards the end of the Battle of Britain, while flying from Exeter, he was killed in action. When I heard of his death I felt a great emptiness. By then I had learned many things except how to bear the first personal scar of war.

I arrived at Desford, after some leave, to start again from scratch. Here the pattern was much the same as Woodley except that we alternated each day between flying, lectures or the Link Trainer. These little static machines we used for simulated instrument flying, which helped enormously in sharpening accuracy with the instruments and procedural knowledge.

I was lucky enough to have Flight Lieutenant Brett as my instructor, a wonderful pilot and most likeable man. We flew Tiger Moths, the DH 82, a great aeroplane that required to be flown the whole time and found you out if you were wanting in any of the basic skills.

By then the storm had broken in Europe and it seemed nothing could stop the German Panzers from reaching the Channel ports. Listening to the radio became an obsession. At night my sleep was often interrupted by air-raid alerts or through turning out to guard the airfield perimeter against possible enemy airborne attack – though goodness knows what I would have done if this had materialised for I had nothing more than a pen-knife and winged feet with which to react. It was even rumoured that our Tiger Moths were to be armed with small bombs if the Germans showed up for an invasion and would be expected to attack them in a last-ditch death-or-glory attempt to save the day.

My flying progressed smoothly with Flight Lieutenant Brett. He preferred to arrange the exercises for longer periods in the air so I was able to complete a number of different ones during each flight then go over the mistakes after landing. It helped confidence in application and execution which gave me a better understanding of the theory of flight. One morning, after a prolonged and exacting session of low flying with some aerobatics and practice forced landings included, I was delighted to be told he considered I was up to the standard required for fighter aircraft. If I held my current standard of flying I would be recommended for day fighters. Later, having a drink in our local pub, he asked if I had a preference for the type of fighter I wanted to fly. Without hesitation I told him – Spitfires. It was a natural reaction for the simple reason that I had made up my mind from the first moment I saw a Spitfire (after it had landed one day at Woodley) that this had to be my aeroplane. It had been a thrilling first meeting, while the sheer beauty of line and the exciting power in flight reminded me of my golden eagle, soaring up the mountainside with effortless ease after making his kill. Surely a dream come to life.

He gave me a searching look, then laughed: 'I believe you really mean it – well – why not?'

I landed one afternoon to find a message asking me to report to the Adjutant. I found two men in civilian clothes waiting to see me and was startled to learn they were from Military Intelligence or Special Branch. I was obviously in some sort of trouble. It transpired they wanted to know about my relationship with an American diplomat, Tyler Kent. I explained that I had met him some six months previously at a party while I was on leave in London. The contact was, I told them, purely social; also I had bought an American Ford V8 two-seater from him. Had he asked questions of a classified nature, they demanded, questions relating to the Boulton-Paul Defiant, a two-seat fighter which was undergoing some tests at Desford? I pointed out I was in no position to give such facts for the simple reason I knew nothing at all about the Defiant and, in any case, if I had, I would not have discussed the matter with somebody like Kent – the suggestion was absurd. This seemed to satisfy them and I heard no more about the affair. The incident, however, brought home how careful one had to be in the matter of security; and it had a follow-up. A few months later I read in the press that Tyler Kent and his woman accomplice had been arrested for passing secrets to Germany and Kent had been handed over to the American authorities for trial. The car, on the other hand, escaped arrest for not being taxed and proved a great boon to one of my friends who eventually pranged it returning from an all-night session with one of his girlfriends.

A few days before finishing my course, I went through the RAF flying test with an examining officer from the Central Flying School. It went off well and, afterwards, he confirmed that I was being recommended for fighters; also, I had been selected to carry out a specialised course lasting a week, at Ansty, before reporting to No. 5 Service Flying Training School at Sealand, near Chester. I thought this would be a waste of time but it proved well worth while, however, including some night flying. I flew on average five times a day practising advanced formation, aerobatic and instrument flying on Tiger Moths.

Desford and Ansty had been basically civilian, with a handful of regular RAF flying and administrative personnel; but Sealand proved a great change, being a permanent RAF Station with a group captain commanding a large establishment. A new experience was membership of the Sergeants' Mess. As RAFVR pilot cadets we had not seen inside one previously, only cadet messes, nor had we socialised with the older SNCOs, except ground instructors, along the way. We soon discovered these greybeards did not care much for us. A separate dining-room well away from their Mess had been provided and, though we were entitled to use the Mess facilities, when we did so, which was not often, we were expected to be seen but not heard. I think they felt we were too young and irresponsible to hold a rank which had taken each of them so many years of service to reach. Nevertheless, one had to admire their splendid bearing and professionalism and, having broken down barriers and the generation gap, we eventually broke the ice too. No front-line squadron, I discovered later, could function efficiently without these stalwarts. They supervised complicated engineering, led their men with discipline and humour, made the aeroplanes work when others had given up, and toiled the clock round to make sure that in the morning when the bell rang, the squadron could look the world in the eye and say: 'We are second to none.'

Having gone through the reporting procedures and seen the Station Adjutant, I found myself billeted some distance from the main camp in a disused married quarter with Jock Ogilvy, whom I had not seen since Bexhill. Here we were able to come and go as we liked with no petty restrictions on our free time.

We were assigned to 'C' Flight, commanded by Flight Lieutenant Tom Prickett, who gave us a talk on the Miles Master I in general terms and the fighter training we were about to undergo in much more detail. The Master was the newest of the Service's advanced trainers, having been introduced shortly before the war. It was almost a facsimile of the Hawker Hurricane in looks if not in performance. My initial flight in the Master was memorable. At first the numerous knobs, levers and instruments became confusing but checking and memorising, under the watchful eye of my instructor, Sergeant Alexander, I got the hang of the cockpit layout and we took off. Since the Master was fitted with a Kestrel engine of some 750 hp getting airborne was spectacular for, opening up to full power through the 'gate', the kick from the extra power became a thrilling series of swings due to the unexpected engine torque. The steadying hand of my instructor helped contain my head-long dash down the runway before I felt the aircraft lift into the air and, bringing up the wheels, I settled into a steady full-power climb. Levelling out at 5,000 ft I was told to carry out basic exercises while Alexander explained over the intercom the handling characteristics and technique required to get the best out of the aircraft relative to its greater speed. I practised stalling and recovery, noting the sudden dropping of the nose with the resultant loss of height which was much more than I had experienced previously. Presently we returned to the air-field to practise powered approaches and landings, the standard method of landing the Master.

Apart from the Hawker Hart, a biplane, I had never felt such a surge of power before. The take-off was noticeably short, the controls positive with a high degree of manoeuvrability, the high speed thrilling, lending a touch of class to the (by now) dull flying I had so far experienced. The only comparison I could make was with a 499 cc Manx Norton I once rode down the Winchester by-pass, the wind tearing at my face, 100 mph on the clock, and showing a clean pair of heels to the world and the police.

After three hours' dual flying, Tom Prickett tested and then sent me off solo in the Master. Thanks to his example and leadership we became a happy and keen crowd, eager to do our best with few, if any, binding restrictions on our activities. He left us, unfortunately, before the course ended, to join an operational squadron and after the war rose to very senior rank in the Service.

The Master required thorough familiarisation due to having hydraulic, fuel and ignition systems that were new to me. I had to learn also what action to take in the event of fire and the special procedure for abandoning the aircraft in an emergency. But I enjoyed flying the Master tremendously; she was robust, straightforward in handling qualities provided one didn't take liberties, and a splendid transitional aeroplane for the more

13

serious business of flying single-seater fighters.

My first altitude flight took place on a clear day with large banks of cumulus clouds over the Welsh mountains. By the time I reached 16,500 ft (without oxygen this was the limiting altitude) familiar ground features were easily identifiable. From that height the landscape became a fairyland vision of the Mersey, with Liverpool in the distance, Chester and Anglesey tiny blobs of colour, the patchwork pattern of fields intermingling, the roads mere threads of grey and brown disappearing towards distant horizons. I turned the Master towards the cloud banks diving through a great canyon, wing-tips slicing the edge, then, pulling up the nose and opening the throttle, I aimed for the peak of a cotton-wool cluster of billowing whiteness, rolling onto my back over the summit, hurtling down the other side inverted before levelling the wings and diving to the bottom of the cliff, up again steeply and over the cliff-face, a stall turn and I was once more diving through the gaps, the valleys, up, up and over. . . . So it went on. It was breathtaking, exhilarating, spontaneous and free – an experience never to be caught or repeated in the same mood.

Formation flying occupied much of the available time. We were to become fighter pilots; so to stick close to the leader required alert, skilful usage of throttle, stick and rudder. With practice it became second nature and eventually, tucked wingtip to roundel or nose to tail a few feet apart, we could manoeuvre as one unit; taking off, in the air as a section or flight, flying in cloud, or landing. Instrument flying took on a new dimension. I came to realise that nothing less than expert interpretation of the instruments was essential to personal survival in adverse weather, in rain, snow, fog or darkness. I came to understand, too, that in time I would be charged with the responsibility of leading others under extreme conditions and that their lives might depend on the standard of my own flying ability. Solo navigation flights to other aerodromes, triangular blind-flying cross-country tests using the instruments from start to finish, with the navigational instructor keeping up a commentary on progress, helped to develop a sixth sense and trust in the instruments which built confidence rapidly. Low flying, aerobatics, precautionary and forced landing practices

14

followed one upon the other.

By night the enemy bombing of Liverpool and other targets in our area, intensified by the heavy AA guns positioned near our billet, made sleep difficult. Chester did not escape the bombing nor did Sealand. One evening Jock Ogilvy and I were rounded up with others and herded into the cellar of the Grosvenor Hotel in Chester, while bombs and guns crashed continuously. We were still clutching our beer mugs when we found a secluded spot amongst the barrels of beer in the cellar. By the time the 'all clear' eventually sounded we neither knew nor cared, continuing to help ourselves liberally to the excellent ale close at hand. The management, hearing boisterous singing long after the place had closed, investigated and found us happily enjoying the freedom of their cellar. Having been thrown out, we walked with dignity if unsteadily all the way back to Sealand in the grey light of dawn feeling that, after all, air raids were not so bad.

The Wings Examination proved straightforward notwithstanding a few hiccups over the nagivation paper but when I was awarded my Wings, that most coveted of flying badges, I felt ten feet tall. My overconfidence was not lost on my instructor, who promptly took me to task, saying that I had a long way to go before I proved myself. Accepting the point, I moved over to the Advanced Training Squadron, the last lap in the training cycle.

CHAPTER TWO

Spitfire lesson

 At the Advanced Training Squadron I reported to Jim Boothby, Flight Commander of No. 10 Flight. 'Boothers' had served in the Advanced Air Striking Force in France and seen plenty of action. He told us about the Messerschmitt Me 109, the Luftwaffe's principal day single-seat fighter we would soon be meeting. Both he and Squadron Leader Teddy Donaldson, the CO, gave us invaluable help and advice on how to deal with enemy fighters and with the tactics to be used against enemy bombers. They did not spare themselves in flying and showing us in practice what they preached on the ground. Teddy Donaldson was one of the most exceptional fighter pilots in the RAF. One of the best shots, too, he had led his Squadron, 151, brilliantly in the early fighting in France and at Dunkirk. His recent tactical operational experience and excellence in air gunnery helped enormously to condition us for the job of air fighting and he took infinite care in developing our aptitude as pilots. He considered the Germans mediocre and ineffectual, once they had lost their formation leader. He impressed on us that anyone flying a Spitfire or a Hurricane was the equal of five Germans in their Me 109s. 'Just go after them and rivet their backsides to the armour plate,' he said with his infectious laugh.

I confess, the serious aspects of the air battle joined over the Channel had, up till now, been remote and a bit impersonal. The Prime Minister had said following the evacuation of Dunkirk: 'The battle for France is over, the battle for Britain is about to begin. . . .' It meant little to me in terms of personal involvement though the threat of invasion filled the minds of us all. It seemed obvious the Luftwaffe had the task of spearheading the attack on Britain but BBC radio reports regarding Fighter Command's scale of effort and the numbers of aircraft shot down each day sounded somewhat like a round-up of cricket scores rather than a matter of life and death. As the intensity of action increased during the day, and nights filled with the ceaseless drone of enemy bombers and the harsh vibrations of exploding bombs, our attitude changed and we longed to be ready operationally and in the thick of the fighting, alongside friends in a fighter squadron. There was no thought of defeat nor did we realise at the time that an epic air battle was developing which, in the end, would save us from invasion, pave the way for ultimate victory and prove to be one of the decisive battles in all history.

I flew mostly with Flight Sergeant Papworth or Jim Boothby on those exercises that needed particular instruction. In the Advanced Training Squadron there were more single-seat versions of the Master, much more like the real thing, particularly for air gunnery. The flying took on a more urgent practical application to procedures with most aspects related to those practised in an operational squadron, concentrating on air-to-air and air-to-ground gunnery besides more advanced formation, instrument, and other flying such as reconnaissance. We used ciné-camera guns and the results on film were carefully assessed and analysed.

Night flying the Master was carried out at a satellite airfield some distance from Sealand in order to overcome the unwelcome attention of German night intruders. We drove to the site in the back of a three-ton lorry that did nothing to improve the tenderness of my bottom, which had suffered lately from 'parachute piles', as a result of the intensity of the flying programme. When we arrived, the sky was dark with a thin layer of high cloud. I walked over to the dispersal hut hoping my turn would come sooner rather than later. The instructors flew over but arrived late and it turned out that one aircraft had gone unserviceable, leaving us short to complete the night detail. It was, therefore, around one o'clock in the morning before I taxied out with Jim Boothby in the back for take-off. The straight line of light, from the flare-path of goose-neck oil lamps, blinked starkly against the inky blackness with no break between ground and sky. With no Chance light in position to flood the landing approach I would have to rely on the flare-path alone.

We were controlled by a couple of men near the apron of the landing-run, using Aldis lamps and Very lights. Soon a green Aldis stabbed the night giving me permission to move onto the flare-path.

'Right,' said Boothers, 'line her up, run up the engine on the brakes and test the mags.'

Having completed my checks I did what was asked and, at 'Let's go' from Boothers, released the brakes and opened the throttle smoothly to full power. The roar from the engine faded, we gathered speed, bumping on the grass. As I eased the stick forward slightly the tail came up. I kicked the rudder to keep straight, flares rushing past, a final bump and into the air. My head was now over the instruments – no use looking out, I would find no horizon, stick with the instruments; wheels up, adjust revs, watch the speed, altimeter and rate of climb, artificial horizon, turn and bank indicator while keeping a constant heading by reference to the gyro compass – relax – don't freeze on the stick – relax . . . .

At 1,000 ft I levelled off and started my turn to port onto a reciprocal heading. Soon the flare-path showed away to my left, but I still concentrated on the instruments: checking everything, cross-checking the dials, and adjusting the gyro-compass heading against the magnetic now that it had settled following my turn.

'O.K., let's do a complete circuit,' Boothers cut in. 'Keep your height steady at a thousand feet – you keep losing a bit of height in a turn – watch it.'

Round we went, then back onto the down-wind leg. A green light from the ground flashed a welcome – throttle back, undercarriage down, locked, 15° flap, watch the Vertical Speed Indicator, the Indicated Air Speed, altimeter, steady rate of turn cross-wind – now, full flaps – final turn towards the flare-path – level off, wait – the first flares rush past, hold off, nose up a bit, a bit more – wheels touch down with a bump – stick right back – we rumble on, I juggle with rudder pedals and brakes to keep straight and finally turn off onto the dimly lit taxi-way pointing to dispersal.

After a cup of tea and some encouraging remarks from Boothers I go off once more on my own to practise for an hour the procedures, take-offs and landings. Night flying wasn't always straightforward. Apart from sudden changes in weather or technical faults, sound instrument interpretation was essential to survival. The most common error of judgement – except basic handling like 'losing the instruments' while taking off and promptly pranging – was the critical lateral turn soon after becoming airborne. An inexperienced pilot might inadvertently let the nose drop too much for safety while allowing the degree of bank to steepen, then, in trying to recover, make matters worse by applying harsh backward pressure on the stick thus steepening the turn still further, finally toppling the artificial horizon and losing all control of the situation. The same sort of problem arose in the latter stages of landing when, in the final turn or sooner, the aircraft's speed is allowed to fall away rapidly due to rate of turn and nose-up attitude inducing a stall condition and loss of control. Both conditions were easy to get into and without immediate corrective action usually resulted in disaster.

Towards the end of my Advanced Training Squadron course I was given forty-eight hours' leave on 6 September which I spent in London seeing my tailors about new uniforms and other things because I had been recommended for a commission and told to get on with it. Having finished my business I went off to a cinema on the afternoon of the 7th – the first day of the blitz on London which continued all night. At around 4 p.m., due to 'air raid warning red', the show came to an abrupt end and I found myself in the midst of a jabbering crowd on the pavement. Bombs were already falling on the East End and the docks. Gunfire could be heard in the distance, the drone of aircraft overhead, and the dull vibration of exploding bombs. I had been invited to spend the evening with friends and around nine o'clock we left for the Players Theatre near Charing Cross. As we reached the street hoping to pick up a taxi, the sky glowed a dull red while the noise from exploding bombs and barking anti-aircraft guns echoed across empty streets. We caught a bus, but the Players wasn't much fun, so we walked to the nearest pub which was filled to the brim, not surprisingly, with excited folk airing views on buildings that had been hit and numbers of lives lost. I presently elbowed my way out and, from the Embankment, watched flames leaping skywards from the dark mass of warehouses down-river and across in the direction of Tower Bridge and Woolwich. I heard the drone of aircraft and the thud of exploding bombs oscillating on the warm breeze with sickening effect, carrying with it the pungent smell of burning rubber. It seemed nothing could control the inferno; the fire-fighting services, police, wardens and medical teams, above all the people themselves working like beavers to save life, were surely faced with an impossible situation.

Anger filled me. I wanted more than anything to be up there in the night sky seeking the bombers out, ramming the nearest one if that were the only sure way to bring him down. A feeling of isolation engulfed me as I walked back to my hotel in Lancaster Gate to spend a sleepless night, while the pounding guns across the road in the Park heightened my frustration. Towards dawn the air cleared and the guns were silent. I slept with the thought that very soon, with luck, I would be able to enter the ring myself.

The morning passed quietly, while London counted the cost in lives and material damage. As I walked through the Park past Speakers' Corner, now silent and deserted, I couldn't help comparing it to the last occasion I had passed that way, a Sunday morning in May 1939. Then the place had been alive with speakers addressing whomsoever would listen. One disillusioned man was working himself into a lather from the vantage point of a platform, bearing the words 'Communism *is* Democracy': 'We will go down Oxford Street – smash windows, pinch the wireless sets, pinch the clothes, the food, pinch this and pinch that – it all belongs to us anyway – you and me –' his voice overtaken in the mounting tide of shouting and jeering from the crowd as they lost interest and began to drift away. Suddenly he shouted: ''ere, 'ere, wait a minute you lot – 'oose pinched my bike?'

A couple of weeks later I was commissioned in the rank of Pilot Officer and my ATS course ended with a spate of air-to-air ciné-gunnery. Then Jim Boothby told me that I had earned a couple of days' freedom before reporting to No. 7 Operational Training Unit at Hawarden a few miles from Chester, where I would be converting to Spitfires.

Up till that moment I had not been sure, but now I knew for certain and felt elated at the prospect of flying the beautiful and potent Spitfire. To me this wonderful aeroplane was the greatest fighting aircraft in the world.

The period I spent at Hawarden was brief, eleven days in all, but much happened in the time. I reported to 'Tink' Measures, one of the flight commanders, and he lost no time in introducing me to one of his serviceable Spitfires, a Mark I. Equipped with the Rolls-Royce Merlin II engine rated at 1030 hp; a single-stage, single-speed super-charger; glycol cooling; and two-position, variable-pitch (V/P), three-bladed, metal propeller, it had a top speed of 362 mph at 19,000 ft and a service ceiling at 34,000 ft. Climbing initially at 2,500 ft/min she reached 20,000 ft in nine minutes. Once airborne you unlocked the wheels for retraction by a locking device before using a long-handled lever to hand-pump the wheels up by the hydraulic system.

I sat in the cockpit while 'Tink' Measures went through the drill, pointing out various instruments, knobs, levers, the operation of the reflector gunsight and firing mechanism with its fire-safe switch. He tapped me on the shoulder:

'Sit tight and digest. When you think you know it all, do it over with your eyes shut, then give me a shout and I'll see you off. Got it? Right – don't go to sleep.'

This was the moment I had been waiting for so long. The vast array of gadgets stared back as I carefully identified each, checking and cross-checking. I tested the controls, the high-frequency radio, oxygen and fuel states, rolled the perspex hood back and forth getting the hang of it, switched on the gunsight, tested the range bar. I gazed at the gun-button and felt it gently with my thumb. I was ready.

A few last words from 'Tink' – then, with the propeller in fine pitch, I primed the engine, switched on, gave a nod to the airman by the external battery starter and pressed the contact button. The Merlin burst into life.

Looking back on that moment of fulfilment after all these years, some aspects about that flight come back to mind as if they had happened yesterday, clear and exciting. The long nose housing the Merlin stretching away in front restricting forward visibility while taxiing; the powerful slipstream clawing at my face; the snugness of the cockpit. I indeed felt part of the Spitfire, a oneness that was intimate.

The take-off was astonishingly simple. Correcting the initial swing as the power built up, a wing dipping gently to engine torque because of the narrow undercarriage, we bounced on the rough grass a few times then we were up and clear of the airfield while I pumped at the wheels with the hand lever. We proceeded in a series of pitching motions as my hands worked in sympathy with each other – right hand on the lever, left on the stick – it must have looked peculiar, to say the least, but I didn't think of that at the time, being too busy enjoying myself. Climbing into the blue I sensed the tremendous power, the lightness of control. At 19,000 ft I levelled out and practised medium and steep turns, the Spitfire responding to the lightest touch. The forward visibility now excellent, the blind spot behind the tail helped by a rear-view mirror mounted on top of the windscreen. Later, I dived to 5,000 ft, noticing how quickly the speed built up while the ailerons became progressively stiffer the faster I dived.

I chanced some aerobatics and found the aircraft's response sweet and positive. One of the features of the Spitfire I discovered was how beautifully she behaved at low speeds and at high g close to the stall. With full power in a steep turn and at slow speeds she would judder and shake, rocking to and fro, but so long as she was handled correctly she would not let go and spin – surely a unique feature for a high-performance aeroplane. I had to find this out for myself: no one specifically pointed it out, but with continuous practice dog-fighting I came to explore every part of her handling characteristics, till eventually flying her became second nature. I was to bless these qualities when it came to the real thing: they got me out of trouble more times than I care to remember.

Returning to land I pushed the airscrew into fine pitch, slid back the hood, lowered wheels, turned cross-wind and selected 'flaps down' straightening out for the final approach and landing. I came in rather fast, the Spitfire 'floated' on for a bit before

22

touching down on the main wheels. Holding the stick right back brought the tail down and as I lost speed turning towards dispersal, selected 'flaps up'. The Spitfire had a natural tendency to 'float' because of her clean lines with minimum drag. On the other hand, with a powered approach, nose well-up controlling engine power and forward speed with positive use of the throttle, one could land the Spitfire in a very short space.

In the next few days I concentrated on formation flying, dog-fighting, aerobatics and firing my guns. Our main ground activity concerned practice interceptions, pedalling round the parade ground on tricycles equipped with battery-operated radio sets and compasses while 'controllers' vectored us on to an 'enemy' in the shape of another tricycle. The proceedings usually finished in a boisterous free-for-all with the 'enemy' being rammed from all angles.

The instructors were operational pilots supposedly on a rest from fighter squadrons. They passed on their experience, preparing us, it was hoped, for combat flying in Fighter Command. They did not mince words, and looked tired having had a bellyful of action; and they hated being nursemaids. Because of our limited experience, I don't believe they thought we would survive for long, but they tried their best and flew often, giving us the benefit of their practical knowledge. We picked up some useful tips but mostly we were bewildered by it all and by the lack of any sort of unit spirit, brought on, no doubt, by a feeling of 'here today gone tomorrow'. We felt unwanted. We still had to prove our mettle, not least to ourselves. For all the talk, in the end it would rest on personal ability, guts or whatever else was needed to survive and become acceptable warriors in battle. The important thing now – as we itched to get into action and fire our guns at the enemy – was that we were prepared to work out problems for ourselves.

We had a talk from 'Taffy' Jones, a famous and distinguished fighter pilot of the First World War who had flown with Mick Mannock. 'Taffy' was small, Welsh, highly decorated and of exuberant personality and had many kills to his credit in his war. He told us we shouldn't have any difficulty in doing the same in ours. 'Get them in a "whurzel", boys, then pick 'em off like d-d-ducks – provided y-y-you g-g-get in close – t-t-that's the thing.' We were never quite sure precisely what a 'whurzel' was, but the confidence and exuberance of this old warrior did much for our morale.

Airborne one afternoon, we were ordered on the R/T to investigate a 'bogey' (unidentified) aircraft coming towards Anglesey. There were big banks of clouds lying over the sea and across the Welsh mountains. Levelling off at 10,000 ft we were soon in amongst the dark layers of cloud formations, dipping through gaps then climbing over the tops of fluffy, rolling banks of large ones. The chase became exciting because we did not know what type of aircraft we were searching for. I had started to think the whole thing was a hoax when suddenly I spotted a twin-engined aircraft emerge from a cloud formation about 2,000 ft below. Giving a sighting report, we went after it in line astern. The aircraft meanwhile turned in a wide arc and as we got nearer it banked steeply, having seen us no doubt by this time and, for a moment in clear light, I saw the black cross on the upper wing surface as the Junkers Ju 88 disappeared from view into thick clouds. That was the last we saw of it. Not quite spitting distance but it was a start.

We had a visit one morning from Alex Henshaw, Supermarine's test pilot based at Castle Bromwich, where a couple of months previously a large new factory had started Spitfire production.

By invitation, Alex gave a most excitingly executed flying display of aerobatics, both unique and difficult to perform, including a roll off the top of a loop immediately on taking off and a bunt (downward inverted outside half-loop) rolling out very close to the ground. He started the bunt from no higher than 1,200 ft or so. Incredible.

As we dispersed afterwards, 'Tink' Measures, who had watched it all in silence, said: 'Aerobatics are a fine thing and increase your capability and confidence as a pilot – practise them when you can. Henshaw's shown us what a Spitfire is capable of and this should give you confidence but remember he's a very experienced professional. Don't you get any bright ideas about copying him so close to the ground, expecially the bunt, or your girlfriend will liken you to a pot of raspberry jam, laddie, and she may never touch the stuff again. And don't try

your aerobatics out in combat or some square-head will pin
your ears back, sure as hell. Keep them for clear blue skies. Got
it? Right! And keep your finger out.'

I read the orders in the authorisation book: 'Battle climb. Steep
turns. Maximum rate descent. Time 1 hour.' I signed the book
and looked up.

'Tink' Measures grinned: 'We have only one serviceable Spit
– keep your finger out and for Gawd's sake don't prang or we
will be out of business. You've only an hour so make the most of
it; you'll maybe bless the steep turns you do today for saving
your neck against a Hun fighter in the next week or so. Get
cracking.'

I picked up my helmet and parachute and made my way to
the Spitfire waiting for me not far from the flight office. Buckling on the parachute I climbed into the cockpit and adjusted the
safety harness, then went through the checks, started the
engine, taxied out and took off. Closing the hood I pumped the
undercarriage up and settled into a maximum rate climb, in a
big right-handed arc, reaching for the deep blue of the sky.
Checking the instruments and oxygen state I found everything
functioning normally and at 30,000 ft I levelled out, turning a
couple of times to get a better look at the ground. I could see
Anglesey, then the pattern of hills and fields running towards
the Mersey shoreline and in the distance Hawarden. I stood my
Spitfire onto a wing-tip and went into a steep turn. It was pretty
cold in the unpressurised, unheated cockpit but the steep turns
with plenty of g made me struggle, trying to keep the nose level
with the horizon and soon I began to sweat from the exertions.
Exhaling vigorously, some breath leaked through the oxygen
mask, clouding my goggles. I pushed them onto my helmet. Ice
and frost formed inside the canopy; I tried to rub it off without
much success; I turned, reversed the turn, pulled more g,
blacking out – too harsh with the controls, felt the aircraft
judder under the violence of the turn coming out of the black-
out in time to prevent a spin. I looked down and saw I had
drifted south near the Wrekin. It was invigorating, exciting.
Even at that height the Spitfire handled beautifully – the power
was starting to run out because of the altitude but she

responded to the lightest touch. I had lost some height from the last manoeuvre so climbed back to 30,000 ft and took a breather, heading back towards base. Suddenly I spotted another Spitfire below me crossing from right to left. I swept into a diving aileron turn to bring me into position for a quarter attack. Taking the other Spitfire by surprise and height advantage, I ranged on him closing rapidly. I switched on the gunsight, calculated the deflection half a bar, eased back the stick and fired an imaginary burst from my guns, then broke hard into a steep climbing turn. Looking down I saw the other Spitfire continue on his way without, as I thought, seeing me.

Rather pleased with my efforts I turned towards base to complete the last part of my exercise – a maximum rate descent. Settling back in the cockpit I half-rolled and pulled hard on the stick, diving steeply. I trimmed her into the dive and watched the altimeter unwind rapidly; I swallowed and yawned several times to relieve the pressure and clear my ears. Everything in the cockpit – instruments, canopy, windscreen – clouded over as we got lower into the denser and more humid atmosphere, so I worked continuously to keep small patches free from frost and mist.

At 5,000 ft I eased the Spitfire out of the dive, finally levelling out at 2,000 and throttled back. I still could not see much so wrenched the canopy open to get a better view. Immediately the rushing air clawed my face and mask; I crouched over the controls and looked out sideways: Hawarden was over to my right, and I had arrived by luck in a position to land, as the circuit was right-handed. I still could not see through the windscreen for mist and frost, nor the instruments. I cleared the glass and checked the fuel state: I was taken aback to read there were only a few gallons left. I turned immediately crosswind and lowered the undercarriage, gliding towards the perimeter and slipping off some height, then lowered the flaps, controlling the upward pitch as they went down, pointing my nose at a distant spot on the airfield. Searching up, round and below I found the circuit free of other aircraft; I slipped off some more height and as I crossed the boundary at about 100 ft I was throttled right back gliding straight ahead.

Suddenly the squat shape of an Anson appeared dead in

front, as if by magic, its wings and tail stretching right across the nose of my Spitfire – it was all wings and tail-plane – its nearness smothering my wits before I was stung into action. I slammed the throttle wide open, airscrew already in fine pitch, heaved into a climbing turn to the left. It was too late – there was a sickening shudder, a large object twisted over my head; we seemed to claw at the air for a few moments still juddering and shaking before the Spitfire corkscrewed towards the ground. We crashed vertically, the nose and port wing hitting together. I tried to shield my face with a hand, there was a piercing pain in my leg and I saw the gunsight an inch from my nose.

I came to my senses in the ambulance, flat on my back. I tried to focus: I rubbed my eyes – it hurt like hell and blood oozed from a gash in the eyebrow. I looked across and saw three men sitting on a stretcher, one a medical orderly. I ached all over and wanted to be sick.

At sick-quarters the MO stitched my eyebrow, put a few more in my leg, gave me some pills. Presently I heard the details of the accident. The Anson had crashed in a more ladylike manner. Most of the impact having been cushioned by her undercarriage, which collapsed before ploughing her nose and belly. The navigator was unhurt, though severely shaken while the pilot, a Pole, had a cut face and cracked ribs. Both aircraft had been wrecked. The only reason my Spitfire hadn't caught fire was the lack of fuel. Though the engine had smashed through the bulkhead it had not landed on my lap – due perhaps to the timely intervention of my guardian angel.

Resting afterwards, I tried to reconstruct the sequence of events but they left me baffled. Obviously the Anson and I were on a collision course as we crossed the boundary, the Anson having motored in from a long straight approach, which was not unusual for the type of aircraft; myself in a right-handed gliding turn, thus failing to see each other. Air Traffic Control in those days relied on a 'Duty Pilot' equipped with an Aldis lamp and Very pistol but no radio. He sat in a cold windy hut cursing his luck and wishing, no doubt, he were flying himself.

With the aid of a stick I toddled off to the Mess some time later. 'Tink' Measures's first remark when he saw me was: 'You didn't keep your finger out like I said – still – glad you're in one

piece. Brace yourself, laddie, a signal has come in posting you to
611 Squadron. The Spitfire you attacked before your prang –
surprise, surprise – well, it belongs to 611's forward flight at
Ternhill and the pilot has reported you for dangerous flying. I
doubt if you'll get a champagne reception when you report for
duty – more like a Bath-chair and a couple of aspirins. Never
mind, let's get some beer and I'll tell you how I won my DFC.'
'Tink' Measures knew the details, of course, of the afternoon's
flight because I had spoken to him on the phone from sick-
quarters about the accident.

In the morning life looked gloomy. I had already been told
that the CO wished to see me at nine o'clock sharp. I did not
have to ask the reason. If I had to carry the can I thought, well, I
couldn't wish to have anyone better to sit in judgement.
Wing-Commander Hallings-Pott did not spare my feelings and
left me in no doubt that my accident had been due to careless-
ness, as I had shown a degree of irresponsibility. He was
particularly annoyed over the loss of the Spitfire. Spitfires were
at a premium, he warned, pilots expendable. Then he said
something I have remembered to this day:

'Flying requires keeping your wits about you all the time.
You can never relax completely – something is going on every
second – so you check and recheck and, as you build experience, the checking process becomes automatic. You're going to
discover, soon, there's one more vital check to do – finding the
unseen enemy. Never stop searching or you will be a dead duck.
It's the one you never see that gets you – just like the Anson
yesterday, only the next time it will be red-hot lead right up
your backside.' He paused, swung his flying-booted feet onto
the desk, then looked at me hard, smiling: 'I see you've been
posted to 611 Squadron. Good luck.'

CHAPTER THREE

First bandits

On reporting to 611 Squadron, Auxiliary Air Force, at Digby in Lincolnshire on 12 October 1940, I discovered that the Squadron had been split in two – 'A' Flight, the operational hard-core of eight Spitfire Mk Is based temporarily at Ternhill guarding the Squadron's peace-time base, Liverpool, while 'B' Flight remained at Digby. The Squadron Adjutant, Robin Birley, explained I would have to be passed medically fit by 'Doc' Peock, the Squadron Medical Officer, before being allowed to fly. The cuts and bruises from my accident were still in evidence so the MO had no hesitation the next morning in telling me I was limited to ground duties for the time being. This resulted in a spell of daily 'Orderly Officer' which did not please me at all. My Flight Commander, Ken Stoddart, was more sympathetic and managed to persuade 'Doc' Peock to let me fly a few days later on training exercises and also with the readiness detail for local and airfield defence.

The Squadron was short of pilots, having lost a number to squadrons based in the London and south coast areas. Apart from the Squadron Commander James McComb, the only pilots at Digby were Ken Stoddart, Ian Hay, Jimmy Sutton, myself and Alan Johnston with whom I had shared a room at Hawarden.

The Squadron was equipped at the time with sixteen Spitfire Mk Is, fitted with Merlin III engines, identical to the Merlin II except for the propeller shaft and drive. A new feature consisted of an automatic two-position undercarriage selection box, making it no longer necessary to pump the wheels up by hand.

With the return of aircraft and pilots from Ternhill plus a sudden influx in pilot replacements from Operational Training Units and other squadrons, training and operational flying

29

increased. Jimmy McComb sent for me one morning. An Auxiliary officer, he had led 611 with distinction through the heavy fighting at Dunkirk and all summer. After inquiring if I were quite fit again, he told me he hoped I wouldn't break any of his precious Spitfires and would mix into the Squadron's way of life. I had by then already found they were a stimulating crowd with never a dull moment flying or playing Mess games. Many were pre-war Auxiliaries with some regular RAF who had joined the Squadron at the start of the summer's fighting. With the Hurricanes of 151 Squadron and 29 Squadron's Beaufighters and Blenheims, Digby hummed with activity. Jack Leather, commanding 'A' Flight – an outstanding personality, Cambridge rugger Blue and a fine shot – along with Barrie Heath and Douglas Watkins formed the spearhead of our team when it came to confronting the other squadrons with trials of strength in the more physical Mess party games.

611 Squadron was classified as B category, i.e. a back-up squadron on the fringe of No. 11 Group. The squadrons in Fighter Command fell into three categories:

A. Squadrons in 11 Group covering S.E. England (mostly operational, having the capability of dealing effectively with enemy bombers and fighters alike).

B. Back-up squadrons on the fringes of 11 Group.

C. Remaining Fighter Command squadrons stripped of operational pilots except for four or five necessary to concentrate on local air defence and the training of new pilots. These squadrons were geographically placed beyond the range of enemy fighters.

The UK was divided into Fighter Groups from south to north. Within each Group were a number of Sector Stations with satellite airfields from which fighter squadrons operated. Periodically squadrons were rotated from 11 Group to a more northern group in order to rest, reform and train new pilots before returning to a front-line Sector Station. By December 1940 there were six Groups in Fighter Command deploying seventy-one squadrons. Normally there would be sixteen aircraft with an average of eighteen to twenty pilots on squadron strength.

We used the Sutton Bridge gunnery ranges for air firing on

drogues (a flag like the wind-sock of an airfield) towed by Henley aircraft as targets. At my first attempt I scored zero but thereafter improved by getting the procedure right with the range correctly estimated and thoroughly enjoying the exercises. Having done a lot of big-game shooting in India, as well as duck and snipe shooting in Scotland, I found the experience of firing eight Browning machine-guns with a rate of 1,200 rounds per minute quite fascinating. I realised the sooner I came to terms with it the better, because good shooting was the most vital skill I needed to perfect as a fighter pilot.

The Squadron's aircraft were divided between each Flight. Carrying the Squadron identification letter FY 'A' Flight aircraft were marked A to K and 'B' Flight L to Z. I was given Spitfire Mk I No. X4253 which had N painted on its sides. It flew beautifully and remained my aircraft till the end of February 1941 when the Squadron was re-equipped with Spitfire Mk IIs.

One afternoon, Jack Leather, leading the readiness flight, intercepted a Ju 88 near Nottingham and shot it down. The police later presented us with a black cross from the aircraft's wing which was turned into a score-board.* There had been several single enemy bomber raids of similar pattern in which I was involved. One evening, with Ian Hay leading, we caught a Ju 88 near Boston in diminishing light but before we could get into an attacking position we lost it in cloud. On another occasion the Ju 88 proved to be a Beaufighter of 29 Squadron and we called off the attack just in time. At dusk one evening, I had just landed when a Heinkel 111 popped out of cloud a few hundred feet above me, his bomb-doors open. Obviously he hadn't seen me or the airfield because it was not until he passed that the gunner from the ventral position opened up and sent a spray of bullets kicking up the dirt some yards away from me. He disappeared into the gloom, while the crump of exploding bombs drifted over the airfield, highlighting the nearness of the miss. Just as well, it would have looked silly taxiing back full of holes not having fired a shot. As it was, I had to suffer raucous

---

* Now resting in the Squadron's archives, it records details of all enemy aircraft shot down by the Squadron during the war.

laughter from my friends at dispersal.

Late one afternoon, the readiness section of three aircraft, with Douglas Watkins leading, scrambled to intercept an enemy aircraft heading to attack a convoy 15 miles off Skegness. Climbing to 10,000 ft we crossed the coast above a broken layer of cloud stretching out to sea. Automatically I listened to the ground controller's voice on my radio:

'Bandit, seven miles, angles eight, vector zero-four-zero. Buster.' I was to increase to maximum speed. That meant relaxing into loose formation and I searched the cloud-banks. Soon I sighted the enemy, a Ju 88, through a gap in the clouds.

'Tally-ho!' I yelled. 'Bandit one o'clock below.' Douglas ordered us into No. 1 Attack in line astern, reminding me to give my call sign and diving into the attack in a tight turn as the Ju 88 banked steeply away from us towards cloud cover while jettisoning his bombs. Closing rapidly, I struggled with the controls, keeping station some distance behind the leader as he opened fire, tracer from the Ju 88 streaking past while I closed and opened fire after Douglas had broken off in a steep turn. I fired two short bursts into the Ju 88 from close range, seeing strikes on the centre section and wing root before breaking off into a steep climbing turn. Looking down I could see Leigh, the third member of our section, complete his attack before the Ju 88 popped into a cloud-bank. We were now split, so Douglas told us to carry out individual attacks. Having a height advantage I dived for the far side of the clouds in time to see the Ju 88 burst into the clear. Diving steeply I got into range, steadied my Spitfire and fired a long burst seeing strikes from the De Wilde ammunition (which shows up white when striking the target) hit the enemy's wing root and cockpit area. Firing a second burst I broke into a climbing turn to avoid a collision as the Ju 88 dived towards the lower cloud layer, smoke pouring from the port engine and wing. Reforming, we searched the area thoroughly for some time but did not pick up the enemy again. Later back at Digby we learned that the Ju 88's radar plots had ceased abruptly but we never had confirmation that it was down.

At that time standard attacks and formations were employed in accordance with 'set-piece' practices known as 'Fighting

Area Attacks'.There were five different types of formation attack, good training for formation flying but worthless when it came to effective shooting. Each attack was identified by a number and the leader decided which attack and tactic to use after assessing the strength and disposition of the enemy. A flight consisted of six aircraft in two sections of three aircraft flying a Vic (or 'V') formation. A complete squadron would have four sections of three aircraft, therefore, identified as Red, Blue, Green and Yellow flying in Vic line astern. The snag with these formations lay in the inability of pilots to keep a sufficiently large enough area of sky under constant surveillance because of formation station-keeping thus opening the door for an enemy attack on the squadron from astern.

New formations emerged in autumn 1940 based on an element of two aircraft – a subsection within a formation of four aircraft. Called 'finger four' it established a pair of aircraft as the basic fighting unit. In the event of the squadron or flight breaking up in combat, a pair could still take offensive action or, in a tight situation, give mutual defensive support. These changes became necessary to cope with enemy formations of eight aircraft having two sections of four well spaced apart and used as fighter-bombers in the period following the mass daylight raids by the Luftwaffe on England.

Shortly before the end of October, Jimmy McComb had left to take up an appointment at 12 Group on the staff of the AOC, Air Vice-Marshal Sir Trafford Leigh-Mallory. He was replaced by Squadron Leader 'Bitters' Bitmead, a regular RAF officer with previous service in the Fleet Air Arm, who soon impressed us with his infectious sense of humour and flying skill.

Operational training continued while enemy activity in daylight fell away considerably. Rumours of a move south to the Hornchurch Sector were in the wind, getting us all excited at the prospect. Single raids by enemy aircraft in our area at dusk continued, however, and it was during one of these that 'Bitters', leading a section of four aircraft, caught a Ju 88 near Boston and after several well co-ordinated attacks forced the enemy bomber to crash-land in a field. Out of a crew of four, one was found to be dead and another wounded. We celebrated the victory in appropriate style that evening which included some amusing trials of strength with 151 Squadron ably led by their CO, Hamish West, 'Buck' Courtney and 'Black' Smith, finishing in the wee hours of the morning by forming a 'ladder' and passing up the anteroom furniture to be arranged dextrously amongst the rafters before we trooped off to get some sleep. At breakfast we found a puzzled Clerk of Works gazing at a large leather settee stuck firmly in a space far too small to contain it and muttering he had no idea how to get it down to earth without removing the roof. It was still there when we gathered for lunch to meet the AOC, who had decided to pay a surprise visit to tell us he had been appointed to command No. 11 Group. Without once looking up at the balancing act of the settee perched precariously above him he remarked: 'I'm arranging for 611 Squadron to be moved to Southend shortly. There will be plenty of action and no rafters to divert your attention.' Leigh-Mallory, or L-M as he was affectionately known, took a great interest in the affairs of his squadrons and was never happier than when he could mix with pilots and ground-crews, listening to opinions and discussing operational problems.

At the end of November 1940, Air Chief Marshal Sir Hugh Dowding, Commander-in-Chief, Fighter Command, handed over his command to Sir Sholto Douglas. The news came as a shock to most of us because he had schemed the victory, held Fighter Command together in the Battle of Britain through critical periods and proved himself an all-time great among air commanders. Though he was relatively unknown personally to many pilots, a great bond of affection and respect flowed between them in the knowledge that he was expert in making decisions of far-reaching effect and would go to any lengths to support his subordinate commanders and squadrons. It seemed, therefore, a strange turn of fate, particularly since he had defeated with resounding success the German Air Force in its attempt to destroy Fighter Command. A further puzzling aspect concerned the fact that no immediate honour was conferred on him in recognition of his great achievements.

Within the squadron new friendships were being forged. I became very friendly in particular with Barrie Heath and 'Polly' Pollard. By that time Barrie had taken over command of 'B'

Flight from Ken Stoddart. Trained in the Cambridge University Air Squadron and a pre-war Auxiliary with 611, he had been in action with the squadron from Dunkirk onwards. Tremendously knowledgeable, with a keen incisive mind, he made an instant success of anything he tackled, enlivening proceedings with a remarkably puckish sense of humour. A natural leader, he built a splendid team spirit amongst the pilots and ground-crews which lifted morale and instilled confidence. Having a shrewd sense of knowing what had to be done and how to reach the heart of a problem, his leadership became at once easy to follow and admire.

'Polly' Pollard, a regular, had joined 611 at the time of Dunkirk. I discovered soon after he returned to Digby from Ternhill with 'A' Flight that it was his Spitfire I had attacked on the day of my crash at Hawarden. Though we had a laugh about it, he told me he had watched my dummy attack with interest from start to finish. He concluded: 'If you want to survive, you'll need eyes in the back of your head, the ability to shoot straight and avoid listening to bullshit.' Reserved and not prone to small-talk, 'Polly' ignored anything he didn't wish to hear, which protected him from the interference of his superiors, or extravagant suggestions from the inexperienced regarding the finer points of tactical flying.

There were others too; Auxiliaries, week-end fliers like myself and sergeant-pilots. With the help of Flight Sergeant Pritchard in charge of servicing, also Sloane and Powell my fitter and rigger, I got to know the technical aspects of my Spitfire intimately and appreciate the worth of our ground-crews. The fact that we flew and they did not, getting their hands dirty in the process, drew together rather than separated us. In no way could it be said there was any lack of understanding or sympathy, that one job was more important than the other, that pilots could or would adopt a patronising attitude towards any of them. I never found anything but an easy comradeship, a solid understanding of the value of one to the other. Your ground-crew were the first to pat you on the back when you scored a victory, the first to shoot a line on your behalf when others doubted and the first to console and lift your morale when you made a balls of it.

I was spending some leave with an aunt and uncle at their farm near Bedford when I had a message from Robin Birley, the Squadron Adjutant, to say that the Squadron had been ordered to Southend and I was to go there at the end of my leave. I was in bed with tonsilitis at the time but said I would pick up my kit from Digby and drive to Southend as soon as I was well enough.

Southend, a satellite of the Hornchurch Sector, was a collection of small buildings with one hangar. The domestic arrangements were non-existent. We used the old flying club building as the Squadron dispersal and flight offices while the Officers' Mess was about three miles from the airfield in a large country house with a Great Dane to guard it.

Raids by Me 109s had increased. They used to carry single heavy bombs and were escorted by more fighters or, having dived from altitude, would release their bombs willy-nilly, escaping at low level and leaving the escort or subsequent offensive fighter patrols to join battle with our squadrons. It is not clear what the Germans hoped to gain by these tactics, but at the same time they were tiresome to counter. This was a period of standing squadron patrols over Tenterden, Dungeness, Maidstone and North Foreland. We had to gain maximum altitude, and patrolling was seldom carried out under 30,000 ft, as it was useless to expect to make contact with the enemy with any sort of tactical advantage below this altitude, in the initial stages at any rate. Often we staggered up to 36,000–37,000 ft, wallowing there with little ability to manoeuvre in the rarefied air. The Germans also developed diversionary schemes in which threats would develop in, say, the south coast area; in chasing after these raids we would find that the main attack had been carried out on a target along the Norfolk coast or at low level on shipping in the Thames Estuary.

New formations and tactics were devised. A pair of aircraft, as a fighting formation, had come to stay. It was much more flexible than the old formations of three aircraft, and flying in pairs line astern we could manoeuvre more comfortably and fly at a much higher cruising speed. Enemy bomber formations had left the skies over London and the home counties by day, but their attacks at night had increased. Hardly a night went by without a raid, and the sirens seemed to wail ceaselessly through the long winter nights.

Though our Spitfires were quite capable of fighting the Me 109s we felt we were outgunned. We desperately needed more punch. The eight .303 Browning guns were devastating at close quarters but they were inadequate at longer ranges against manoeuvring enemy fighters, unless a hit was registered in the engine, petrol tank or cooling system. We badly needed cannons of heavier calibre than the Browning guns.

Initial tests on 20-mm cannons mounted in the wings of a Spitfire had proved unsuccessful because of the stoppage rate. The powers-that-be told us this was a temporary setback and that Mk V Spitfires, sporting two 20-mm Hispano cannons and four Brownings, were on their way. We licked our lips and waited. In the meantime we shot down some 109s but a lot more got back to France to fight again.

During a squadron patrol in the Maidstone/Dungeness area on 19 December, we were attacked by ten Me 109s. While turning sharply to counter them a further formation of 109s dived through the mêlée of twisting, turning aircraft before releasing their bombs and escaping. Becoming separated from my flight during the confusion that followed, I managed to shake off the attention of a Me 109, which was firing at me, by turning inside him and as he straightened before diving I gave him two short bursts from my guns, but then I had to break immediately as a second 109 dived onto my tail. He didn't stay, however, continuing his dive towards the coast. I searched frantically for the squadron but the sky was clear with not an aircraft in sight. One moment the whole sky was alive with Spitfires and Me 109s, now nothing remained but vapour trails. Having used up most of my fuel I landed at Manston in Kent. My airborne time had been two hours.

A few days later, in poor visibility and low cloud, 'Polly' Pollard and I were on convoy patrol in the Thames Estuary when a Dornier 17Z bomber suddenly appeared out of the muck. As he turned towards the ships he crossed our line of sight enabling Pollard to close rapidly. The enemy saw us and tried desperately to climb back into cloud, firing at us as he went, but 'Polly' was able to get in a longish burst before the

Dornier disappeared from view. I remained a spectator. Splitting up, we searched the area thoroughly but without finding him again.

I met the new Sector Commander of Hornchurch, Group Captain Harry Broadhurst, for the first time one evening when Barrie Heath and I were having a drink at the bar in the RAF Club in London. I must confess I was a bit overawed because I had heard a lot about him, but meeting him like this, I could think only of his 'tied together' aerobatic team at Hendon which he had led with such skill in the pre-war flying displays. They were a sight to remember. A born leader with vast experience on many aircraft and operations, he had seen active service before the war in the Middle East and the north-west frontier of India, besides commanding 111 Squadron – the first Hurricane Squadron in the RAF.

In his badly damaged Hurricane in France, before Dunkirk fell, Broady was very lucky to get his aircraft down at base in one piece. He was much amused when, later, the *Sunday Dispatch* reported that despite his being hit by cannon-shells that had disintegrated his Hurricane he managed to land back at base!

Now, in the months that followed, he was to lead 611 Squadron on many offensive operations while I, with my heart in my mouth, would try my best to follow him as his number two.

Barrie Heath and I were at readiness early one morning when we were scrambled on an enemy aircraft making towards a convoy assembled in the Estuary. The weather was not at all good, with two layers of thin cloud low down and a thicker layer at about 4,000 ft. This layer was 1,000 ft thick and stretched as far as the eye could see. Above this was a big gap of clear air with a further layer of cloud at 10,000 ft. We were vectored to the Crouch and informed by Operations that an enemy aircraft was coming in from the sea at 5,000 ft. Searching, we could see nothing below, so we climbed and levelled off just under the high cloud layer. We got a new vector from Operations and swung left. Then we saw him. A Dornier 17Z about 1,000 ft below us. I slipped into line astern as Barrie led the way into the attack. His first burst raked the Dornier right along its port wing root, engine and fuselage. The port engine started to smoke and the bomber wobbled about like a drunk. There was intense return fire from the rear dorsal guns with plenty of tracer, but this particular German was a rotten shot. I steadied my Spitfire and as Barrie broke away into a diving turn after his attack, I opened fire. My Brownings chattered and the aircraft's nose dipped to the recoil. I eased back the stick and gave another burst before breaking off my attack sharply upwards in a steep turn. As I fired, many strikes appeared in and around the gunner's position and the return fire ceased. Completing my turn, I looked round in time to see Barrie go in again for a further attack from a nearly head-on position. The Dornier had dived for the lower layer of clouds, smoke still pouring from his port engine. I just had time for another quick burst before the Dornier was engulfed by the cloud stretching below us. We spent the next fifteen or twenty minutes see-sawing below and above cloud, trying to make contact again but without success. Disgusted, we at last returned to base and landed. This was just the type of engagement where the heavier fire-power of the 20-mm cannon was needed for quick results. Later, a Royal Observer post reported seeing an enemy bomber crash into the sea.

The weather over the next few days became unfit for flying. Mist, rain and sleet made me wonder if I would ever see the sun again. Gloomily playing cards in dispersal one morning, Barrie suggested a sortie to London. Bowling along Seven Sisters Road in Barrie's Humber Snipe we suddenly saw Harry Broadhurst's staff car coming towards us. Instinctively I shouted: 'Quick – it's Broady – duck.' We dived under the dashboard until the danger passed, imagining we had got away with it. As Broady reminded us later, however, he couldn't help recognising Barrie's Humber immediately since it stuck out like a sore thumb cruising along with not a sign of anyone in it. 'If you wanted to let me know you were off on a spree to London,' he went on, laughing, 'that was the best way to do it. Still, I suppose you could say it was a case of full marks for initiative but zero for execution.'

CHAPTER FOUR

To France for 'Rhubarbs'

We had known for some time that Trafford Leigh-Mallory was keen to carry the offensive over to France. From October 1940 onwards the Germans had shown little inclination to engage our formations except during hit-and-run raids or occasional offensive sweeps; the AOC was determined, therefore, to bring them to battle over northern France and the Low Countries.

A few days after New Year 1941 Harry Broadhurst invited us to Hornchurch for a special briefing. We all sensed the excitement in the air as we gathered in the briefing room with 41 Squadron. Various pilots put forward theories on the scope of future operations. We wondered what we were likely to meet in the way of opposition over France miles from our home base, with the full measure of the German Fighter force fanned out over the Pas de Calais airfields. The latest Intelligence figures had put this total at around 1,500, about 1,300 of them front-line combat aircraft, which Fighter Command could not hope to equal in numbers.

Broadhurst began his talk by outlining the state of the air war since the close of the Battle of Britain. We had chased the Luftwaffe back to France and the Low Countries, but now the time had come when we had to maintain the initiative and this could be done only over France. We were going to harass the enemy through the use of bombers supported by heavy fighter escorts against specially selected targets; by fighter-bomber attacks and shipping strikes against the enemy's lines of communication at sea and in the network of canal traffic. Rail and road transport, marshalling yards, supply dumps and airfields would be singled out for attacks by day and night. Also, our fighters would carry out as many offensive fighter patrols, sweeps and target support missions as possible throughout the daylight hours, giving the Germans no respite and preventing them from dispensing their fighters and bombers to other theatres of the war.

A special planning staff had been set up at the Group Head-quarters within Fighter Command to co-ordinate these operations and close liaison was to be maintained with Bomber Command, 2 Group (day bombers), the Army and the Royal Navy.

In bad-weather periods special strike missions would be undertaken to attack opportunity targets and these would consist of pairs of aircraft operating within pre-selected areas in northern France. These two-aircraft missions were to become known by the code-word 'Rhubarb'. One way or another, the enemy was never to be allowed to relax. He was to be attacked continuously; attacked in the air and on the ground; attacked on and off duty; attacked while he slept.

We had no army fighting in Europe, of course. The 8th Army in the Western Desert was faced by the Italians. The Royal Navy was busy fighting for control of supply lines, especially in the Mediterranean and the Atlantic. The United States was neutral, and the Soviet Union an unknown quantity. So it was up to the RAF. The odds against us were going to make it an interesting challenge to say the least, the sort of situation that would demand from all of us complete dedication, and from many the supreme sacrifice; but there was not a pilot present that day at Hornchurch who gave thought to the possibility of failure or defeat.

Harry Broadhurst's words left me in no doubt that, in tackling the Germans over occupied France and the Low Countries, we would have to fight strictly as a team. There would be no room for individual heroics. We would have to concentrate our meagre numbers to deliver the strongest punch available at any given point. Leadership and flying discipline would be all-important and second only to expert marksmanship. We were going to plunge into a hornets' nest; there would be no second chances and the enemy fighter formations would have to be destroyed in a limited time due to the range of our aircraft. Unlike the Battle of Britain, there would be no chance of 'walking home' the same day for those unfortunate enough to be shot down. Survival would depend on skill. Then, with a lot of luck, a very long walk home through France and Spain to Gibraltar.

Dunkirk had shown that, as a nation, we were ill prepared for a land battle in terms of armour and weapons. No Air Force can save an Army that is being outfought in guns, tanks and men. What it can do, however, by establishing local air superiority, is to enable an Army to regroup its resources and buy the time necessary for reserves to be called in. The RAF achieved this at Dunkirk by allowing the Royal Navy and the magnificent 'little ships' to operate with reasonable freedom from air attack, thereby enabling an orderly evacuation to England of over 300,000 men, who would otherwise have been swept into prisoner-of-war camps. On this success we were to build our future. We had, in fact, turned the tables on the German Air Force at a time when, with tails up, they had carried all opposition before them. Poland, Norway, France and the Low Countries had been swept aside by the *Blitzkrieg*, the highly organised use of armour deployed in penetrating thrusts supported by motorised infantry. The key to this type of warfare was the use of tactical air forces operating under a protective umbrella of fighters. All had gone well for the Germans till they met the straight left of Fighter Command which, because of range, became effective only when the Panzer Armies were almost within sight of the Channel ports.

In the beginning, our offensive over occupied territory built up gradually, operating at maximum range, and our successes were moderate.

The first 'Rhubarb' had been carried out in the Pas de Calais area on 20 December 1940 without much success. At night, intruder operations were flown by night fighters in an effort to destroy enemy bombers based in France while taking off from their airfields. Though these operations were successful, we nevertheless suffered, on 29 December, the worst-ever night attack aimed at London. About 120-140 enemy bombers hit the City area with incendiary and high-explosive bombs causing very extensive damage.

By early June 1941 over 100 'Rhubarb' sorties had been flown but only about fifteen escorted day-bomber operations mounted on selected industrial and other targets. We had shot down some thirty enemy aircraft for the loss of twenty of our own fighters. But with the German attack developing against the Soviet Union and the withdrawal of Luftwaffe units from northern France during May and June 1941, to support the Eastern Front, Fighter Command stepped up the offensive effort so that from mid-June to the end of July over 8,000 sorties were flown by our fighters covering over 400 flights by our day bombers on suitable targets. We lost 129 aircraft through enemy action, including fourteen of our bombers, and shot down 110 enemy fighters.

10 January was a clear morning, but cold. 611 Squadron was on dawn readiness, but this particular morning things were a bit different. We knew that a large-scale attack was to be carried out by Blenheims of 2 Group against military targets in the Forêt de Guines, near the French coast at Boulogne. In fact the operation was to be the first of many – a daylight bombing raid on the enemy – heavily escorted by fighters. The code-name was 'Circus'. The Hornchurch wing of 611 and 41 Squadrons, led by Harry Broadhurst, was to act as target support and the North Weald wing, led by Victor Beamish, as close escort to the bombers. The other wings had different tasks, and the whole operation was mounted to demonstrate to the Germans that the RAF had no intention of losing the initiative gained during the Battle of Britain.

We encountered heavy flak crossing the French coast and four rather startled enemy fighters took one look at our neat formations and then bolted before we had a chance to engage them. The bombing was right on target and as we swept over it, four Me 109s dived towards the tail of 'A' Flight led by Douglas Watkins. He turned the Flight into the attacking enemy, who promptly rolled onto their backs, diving steeply with our Flight in hot pursuit. Unable to close with the fleeing enemy they pressed on to ground-level and attacked instead enemy troops and installations at Wisant with some success. Meanwhile, the rest of the Wing stayed in touch with the bombers but we saw no further action before returning to Hornchurch. North Weald had better luck, having engaged a formation of Me 109s that tried to intercept our bombers, shooting down four for no loss with Victor Beamish getting one of them himself.

A few days later I was ordered off on my own to fly a patrol line from Maidstone to Dover for the benefit of anti-aircraft guns carrying out calibration tests. Just as the exercise came to an end I was informed on the R/T by the duty controller than an enemy aircraft had been sighted by the Observer Corps; flying at 7,000 ft it was headed south near Canterbury. My height was 15,000 ft and on being given a vector I dived away in hopeful pursuit of the enemy. There were big banks of cloud in my path and slicing through them I levelled out in sight of Dover, immediately identifying a Ju 88 dead ahead about 1,000 yards distant. He was in a shallow dive and I was closing the range rapidly. But it wasn't my day. Suddenly all hell broke loose as every AA gun in Kent opened up, or so it seemed, before I could get into range and open fire. No doubt helped by my exercise in getting their guns properly calibrated, they proved spot-on and the Ju 88 was smartly shot down, much to my astonishment and disappointment.

At the end of January 1941, we moved to Hornchurch and several times each day operated over the Channel and France. On one occasion we crossed the French coast south of Boulogne at 25,000 ft intending to turn towards St Omer and recross near Calais. It was clear and sunny. I looked across at Barrie and got a nod and thumbs-up sign from him. Suddenly four Me 109s dived past us on the left and six more came in on our formation from the right. I slipped into line astern on Barrie as we dived on the enemy formation on our left. Red section led by 'Bitters' disappeared from view. Barrie called me:

'Two 109s below: let's get them.' He dived on the leading aircraft and I took the other one. I saw him open fire and smoke gushed from the enemy aircraft. The 109 in front of me jerked right, bringing me into a good position for a quarter attack and I gave him a couple of quick bursts. I saw De Wilde strikes on the wing root and a piece flew off – the 109 rolled on its back and dived vertically – I broke off and chased after Barrie, not wanting to lose him. Barrie fired another burst and his target 109 steepened its dive, smoke trailing; then he pulled up and swung left in a wide arc. I continued to watch, fascinated, and followed him a good distance behind. The 109 never wavered from its headlong plunge until I finally saw it disappear into a wood and explode. I glanced at my altimeter and saw I was down to 10,000 ft and could see no other aircraft in the sky. Frantically I searched for Barrie. Somehow, in the spiralling turn, I had lost sight of him. I called him on the R/T and he told me to join him at the coast, giving me his height and position.

I started weaving and searching behind. Two aircraft dived on me and as they got nearer I saw they were 109s: I spiralled down expecting them to close on me: I felt very alone and very frightened; but strangely the 109s continued their dive passing over me, heading inland. I straightened out and, still diving, headed for the sea a couple of miles distant. I had already pushed the throttle wide and soon crossed the enemy coast heading for England like a bat out of hell.

Keeping a sharp look-out behind, I gently weaved my Spitfire and searched for Barrie – but there wasn't a sign of life anywhere. Keeping close to the water I held my course until I saw a lone Spitfire ahead and above. Black smoke was streaming from her as I zoom-climbed and caught up with her. I throttled back and adjusted my speed to that of the damaged aircraft. Then I recognised the pilot. It was 'Sadie' Sadler, an experienced ex-Sergeant Pilot from my Flight and he was in a bad way. His canopy was open and a large jagged hole below the port exhaust was emitting flames and black smoke. His rudder was torn and there were more holes along the fuselage. The door of the cockpit was open and placing a hand on this he tried to rise, then fell back into the cockpit. He looked over and saw me. His oxygen mask was unfastened and I could see his face was as white as a sheet. The black smoke and flames increased in volume. I pressed the emergency button on my radio and called 'Mayday', the rescue code, several times at intervals then I went back to the operational button and called 'Sadie'. There was no reply. I kept on trying. I saw that Sergeant Gilegin had come alongside and was keeping station off my port wing tip. I told him to keep calling 'Mayday' while I tried to get an answer from 'Sadie': but it was no use.

'Sadie' now started to lose height rapidly. I could see the English coast – Folkestone only a few more miles – but it was too late. 'Sadie' struggled up in his cockpit. . . .

I shouted at him 'Bale out, bale out – for God's sake, bale out. Roll her on her back – bale out.'

He slumped forward onto his controls, the Spitfire went into a steep dive – I followed in formation. At 100 ft I pulled up and watched in horror – the Spitfire plummeted into the sea in a cloud of smoke and spray.

Climbing up, Gilegin and I called a few more 'Maydays' then switched channels and reported the tragedy to operations. Sadly we turned for Hornchurch, the excitement gone.

I often recalled this episode later when I assumed more responsibility and became in turn a Squadron Commander and a Wing Leader. Leadership in the fighter business needed a special approach.

You trained your team with infinite care. You flew with them, had parties with them and laughed with them, understood each and every one of them, on the ground and in the air. But unlike a rugger team, or a boat crew or a bomber aircraft where the captain was physically in their midst, a fighter team had to be led by example and personality. The team looked to the captain for all the little and big things that would give each one confidence, a sense of belonging, a purpose in life. The captain in his turn had to be capable of putting across his leadership qualities almost in a spiritual way, for he could see, but he could not touch. He was expected to lead a team – big, say three squadrons, or small, a flight or section – and do battle with the enemy at a particular place at a given time. He could look about and see his team grouped around him. He could watch this one wink his eye, that one hold up his thumb or another give him a rude sign. The one thing, however, he could not do was to stretch out his hand and touch each or any one of them. If one fell by the way he could not go to his aid, nurse his head, or comfort him. He flew a few feet or yards away, but for all the nearness each one of them was as remote as a star. This was the invisible thread that bound fighter pilots together, gave them strength and separated them from the rest. It harnessed the opposing forces of initiative and loyalty, individuality and comradeship – each necessary for the job in hand. A fighter squadron was a tightly knit community, yet when death came it was individual and personal.

CHAPTER FIVE

Broady shows the way

Operations over the Channel, France, Belgium and Holland followed one upon the other. We covered bombers attacking German destroyers off Knocke in Holland; attacked E-boats near Calais. Early one morning we pounced on four Me 109s over Dunkirk. Harry Broadhurst was leading the Squadron with 'Bitters' Bitmead flying as his number two. The combat was a model in the art of good shooting at altitude and high speed. At 20,000 ft the Me 109s dived on us in pairs from our left flank. Harry Broadhurst anticipated their tactics, cut the corner, and, as they closed, turned into them. They realised they could not stay with us so they straightened out and dived. Broady immediately reversed his turn and, ranging onto the leading enemy fighter in a fine quarter attack at about 300 yards, opened fire. I saw the spurt of vapour from his guns and immediately black smoke gushed from the 109 which rolled onto its back in a steep dive. It careered down for about 1,000 ft, then there was a vivid flash and it exploded, bits of aircraft flying in all directions. It was a beautiful piece of shooting and took less than a couple of seconds. In the meantime 'Bitters' had got on to the tail of the second 109 and sent it down in flames as well. The other two 109s were engaged by Douglas Watkins. These split, one turning away pursued by Watkins and the other turning and diving past Harry Broadhurst who had now pulled up with Barrie and me covering his tail. Broady lost no time. Again his guns streamed and the 109, badly hit, poured out a mixture of black and white smoke and dived for the ground. After these hectic dog-fights we claimed three destroyed and one 'probably destroyed'.

Harry Broadhurst was, of course, a first-class shot with a skill in air gunnery acquired many years before, at a time when fighter gunnery training had been directed at ground targets. Air-to-air gunnery had been introduced in 1934 when towed targets were used for the first time. There were four methods laid down in the training syllabus: Above, Astern, Quarter and Beam attacks. Trophies were introduced as an incentive to improve efficiency standards; one being a trophy for individual marksmanship and the other for squadron proficiency. Teddy Donaldson won the individual trophy that year but Harry Broadhurst won it for the next three years while his squadron, No. 19, won the other trophy during the same years. As a result of these achievements, Fighter Command asked Broady to instruct selected fighter pilots in his air-to-air gunnery techniques. Later he was sent to Middle East Command to preach the gospel to fighter pilots in that part of the world.

At this time two machine-guns were fitted to fighter aircraft but when the multi-gun fighter came into service a big controversy arose. The theorists believed in and produced a 'spread' pattern for sighting the multiple machine-guns whereas officers such as Donaldson, Malan and Broadhurst (by then commanding 111 Squadron) insisted that 'spot' harmonisation at 200 yards' range was the ideal pattern to adopt and, to their lasting credit, won the argument.

Two days later 'Bitters' got a Do 215 while he was on convoy patrol. Things were looking up. The following day Broady led us again and got two more Me 109s. I got on the tail of a single Me 109 that had not seen me, and after a two-second burst knocked large bits off it, but failed to set it alight. Hastily I had to break off my attack as I was pounced on, but managed to shake the enemy fighter off my tail: then, turning inside him I gave a wide-angled deflection burst and he dived away pouring black smoke.

We were living all this time under constant tension with long, freezing sorties into hostile skies punctuated by moments of combat from which we returned wringing wet and exhausted. Life was hectic, you were in and out, there was no time to watch everything that happened. To survive one had to be alert. My eyes were already as sharp as a hawk's and my senses as keen as a razor's edge.

In the beginning, I had not been sure how I would react

against an armed enemy in a tight corner, against a 109 man to man. Like many others, I had been brought up to believe that Germans were not nice to know. I was told: 'The only good German is a dead one', a phrase coined in the aftermath of the First World War to shock the uninitiated. The German fighting man was supposed to be cruel; I had heard stories of his vile atrocities to prisoners and civilians alike in France and Belgium.

I had had little to do with Germans, except for the young students like myself I met during holidays in Austria, France or Italy. They seemed a decent enough crowd except for their arrogance. Together, I found them noisy and not a little rude. Looking at me they passed remarks in gutteral tones I could not understand, then laughed in an offensive way. Most spoke English well but they bored me. We would talk about shooting but I could not reconcile their method of killing deer with a Zeiss telescopic sight fixed to the rifle, for it largely removed the skill of the stalk to within an acceptable range, and shooting over open sights.

In Innsbruck in 1938 I had a dust-up with a young Nazi over a girl. I didn't have much difficulty, physically at any rate, in seeing him off but had found the encounter disturbing. Now, in the air, their arrogance persisted so long as they held the numerical and tactical advantage; however, man to man the memory of Innsbruck had proved an important lesson that stayed clear.

Nobody could doubt the excellent fighting qualities of the Germans, particularly of their Army. In the air it was different. Their fighter-pilots were treating our Spitfires with a healthy respect, born, no doubt, from their defeat in the Battle of Britain, albeit by a 'narrow margin'. Even so, in the summer of 1941, there was a great deal of dash in the way they engaged us.

At the end of February 1941 the squadron was re-equipped with Spitfire Mk IIs. They were an improvement, having Rotol airscrews and greater engine power resulting in a better rate of climb. The engines were also fitted with Coffman cartridge starters which speeded up starting procedure.

I liked to give the ground-crews a whirl in the Station Magister. One afternoon, with my fitter 'Ginger' Powell in the front seat, I had to carry out a forced landing due to engine failure. As I started my S-turn towards a suitable field, Powell unfastened his safety harness and attempted to get out. I managed to restrain him just in time, before we skimmed over a hedge, missed a flock of sheep and landed undamaged.

'Mick', I said, jumping out of the machine, 'what the hell were you trying to do –?' Rather annoyed I went on, 'You are a clot, "Ginger", we were far too low for a bale-out. Anyway, there was no need for for it –'

'Oh – arr –' he started, 'I thought to go up front and give the prop a flick to get us started,' he grinned. 'Seemed a good idea, any road.'

'Great stuff,' I gasped. 'You had me worried for a moment.'

Before taking off after sorting out the technical problem which turned out to be air blockage in the carburettor, I left Powell in the tender care of the local farmer. Later, back at Hornchurch, I learned the farmer had got him 'prapper pissed', delivering him at the Guard Room like a sack of potatoes. A press-on character, 'Ginger' Powell thereafter never stopped telling the world how I foiled his attempt to get a Magister's engine restarted in mid-air. I have a sneaking feeling he might have done it.

Soon after receiving our new aircraft, Barrie's father, George Heath, who was then a senior director of Rootes Motors, presented a new Mk II to the Squadron. This Spitfire was named 'Grahame Heath' in honour of Barrie's eldest brother, who was killed at the age of eighteen while flying with the RNAS just before the end of the First World War in 1918. It was interesting to note that he was reputed to be the first pilot to take off from an aircraft carrier (HMS *Furious*) and shoot down an enemy aircraft.

I was sad to record, however, that a month after this personal aircraft was delivered, one of our own inexperienced pilots, for some reason, landed away from Hornchurch and, coming in too fast, overshot the runway and crashed into the boundary hedge, severely damaging the aircraft. It was repaired and returned to the Squadron, but by that time Barrie Heath had left us to take command of 64 Squadron.

The change to Spitfire Mk IIs meant parting with my Spitfire X4253. It had been a happy partnership with some morale-lifting successes and not a few frightening occasions when we found ourselves alone and outnumbered by hostile Messerschmitts but, in a crisis, she never let me down. I remember in particular an occasion when the Squadron were heavily engaged one day over Dunkirk by twenty Me 109s during a cover patrol. Though 'A' Flight had all the luck and got three destroyed and a probable, I became separated during the action dodging the attentions of three unfriendly 109s on my tail. Spiralling down with a succession of aileron turns to zero feet I ducked over the coast and escaped by skimming the wavetops with every pound of boost Messrs Rolls-Royce could give me till I sighted North Foreland and the snow-sprinkled fields of Kent beyond. X4253 got me home safely without a murmur though I cannot say the same for myself. Out of breath and exhausted I could not resist giving the engine-cowling a loving pat as I tottered towards our dispersal hut to fight another day.

During the first half of March our defensive operations increased while offensive operations continued. We engaged Me 109s over Dunkirk, Boulogne and Calais while keeping up our standing patrols in the south coast area. At 30,000 ft or more our results were meagre, frustrating and very tiring. On a routine Wing offensive sweep behind St Omer, 64 Squadron lost two Spitfires one day from determined 109 attacks. Normally, unless the enemy had a tactical advantage he refused combat, preferring to dive away inland.

On a 'Sphere' operation of six aircraft – the aim of which was to engage enemy aircraft near or over their airfields at low level – I was flying number two to Harry Broadhurst. Not having any luck, Broady decided to machine-gun Calais-Marck airfield. There were some 109s parked as we dived into the attack in the face of intense flak. One shell burst very close to Broady's windscreen blowing out the side panel and damaging the engine-cowling. Later in the Mess over a beer Broady said, smiling, 'I wish the Huns would get up and fight instead of throwing bricks at us.' Under my breath I replied 'Amen.'

At this time an important change occurred at Sector level: the appointment of a Wing Leader and Deputy to the Sector Commander. With the rank of Wing Commander the Wing Leader's prime duty lay in leading two or more squadrons on pre-planned offensive operations. Previously this function had fallen to the Sector Commander or to the senior squadron commander, but as operations developed and increased it became necessary to co-ordinate tactics and training within the wing besides integrating all flying and ground support activities. Affectionately known as 'Wing-co', the Wing Leader could fly with whichever squadron he fancied and please himself about the type of operation he wished to undertake. In the beginning not all squadron commanders took kindly to letting someone else lead their squadron but in the end we put up with it, like so many other things at that time. Our first Wing Leader was Douglas Farquhar, a Scot and former member of 602 (City of Glasgow) Squadron.

Later that month, finding myself with a day off, I decided to fulfil my promise and visit James Moir, my former Chief Flying Instructor, who was still in charge at Woodley. I flew over in my Spitfire but before landing did a slow roll over the airfield rather low. James Moir lost no time in flying the Spitfire himself and, after landing, gave me a cup of tea, a slice of cake and a lecture on the consequences of indulging in unauthorised aerobatics too close to the ground. 'Your three-point landing on this short airfield was, however, commendable,' he concluded. I returned to Hornchurch as pleased as Punch.

'Ginger' Powell and my rigger, Dick Sloane, grinned their pleasure at my new machine. Both Auxiliaries from pre-war days, they worked like slaves to keep me flying. All the airmen of the Squadron, the NCOs and ground officers had but one thought in their minds – to support the Squadron at all costs; hours of work meant nothing so long as they could maintain 100 per cent line serviceability. Throughout the spring and long hot summer of 1941 they did it, working into the early hours of the morning while the pilots slept. By dawn readiness there would be as many serviceable Spitfires as our strength permitted waiting on the line. Sometimes through damage or major maintenance we would find less aircraft than pilots, but more often it was the other way round.

For relaxation on certain occasions we went to the King's

Head at Chigwell, where we would down much ale and have a hilarious meal. Sometimes Victor Beamish would join us with his pilots from North Weald and we would take over the pub, whatever the locals thought. Broady and Victor were friends of long standing. Both were experienced fighters, outstanding leaders. They had that rare gift of being able to instil into others their own outlook on life.

Broady was strict with us in his insistence on a modest approach to the successes of the moment. At a time when the press were hammering at the doors of all the Fighter Command Operational Stations he kept those of Hornchurch firmly locked. He was too experienced to shun or ignore publicity and was always ready to use it at the proper time, but he never encouraged it, and distrusted those who went out of their way to step into the spotlight that was focused on the achievements of fighter pilots. As far as he was concerned we were in business to win the war; we were not doing our exacting job for the edification of the press or movie-makers. In the same way, the combat victories of members of his wing or his own, as far as he was concerned, were a private matter. So long as claims were genuine he respected each pilot, whether he had a long string of victories to his credit or only a modest few, or even none at all. The great strength of the Hornchurch Wing lay in its ability to fight as a team, and as such, it had no room for individual rivalries or petty jealousies. Being a highly successful fighter pilot himself, he never let publicity affect his own judgement or purpose, and protected his pilots from the attention of certain members of the press, who wrote up day-to-day happenings in a sensational form. He was convinced that personal publicity was bad for the individual, as it would eventually undermine his fighting efficiency.

Most of us agreed that to be singled out as a glamour boy of the press was not a good thing; it usually put a tremendous strain on the individual concerned. Gradually it became necessary to live up to a reputation; the individual had to have successes each time he flew because he thought the press would be waiting for him when he landed and would expect some hair-raising story or other. Then he also had to live with the side glances of other pilots who, good-naturedly but with the directness of youth, pulled his leg and made his life unpleasant.

There were honourable exceptions, of course, who would scarcely glance at a newspaper report about themselves and never let such trivialities affect their main purpose. Unfortunately there were others who let the situation get out of hand and were either killed trying to live up to their reputations or had to be prematurely rested because they could not face their inner selves. In fairness to the press, they had a job to do and could not be blamed for doing it. After all, the British people wanted to know what we were doing and they had a right to know. But, in the end, it involved getting down to individuals and hounding some poor fellow till his life was a misery. They only saw the immediate aim, which was a good story. We saw the other side; we had to live with it.

CHAPTER SIX

Fighting mad

The Hornchurch Wing underwent some changes in the spring and early summer of 1941. 54 Squadron commanded by 'Fanny' Orton replaced 41 Squadron and 64 Squadron moved from another sector to Southend. 611 remained based at Hornchurch.

Soon after 54 Squadron arrived, a very badly burned pilot joined them. He had been shot down in flames during the early part of 1940 flying a Hurricane. I remember the shock in meeting him for the first time in the Mess. His face, the colour of copper, was twisted into a semi-permanent grin; tiny blobs for ears, lidless sunken eyes stared back at me. There were no eyebrows and his forehead was an expanse of scarred tissue. It had never occurred to me that I could ever wind up looking like him. I only hoped that if it ever did I would be able to face life with the same fortitude, humour and sympathy as this extraordinary gentleman. I got to know him quite well but it was short lived for he was taken off operational flying – quite rightly – God knows, he had done more than enough to prove his manhood. To be wounded is one thing, but to be burnt to a frazzle is a sacrifice that cannot ever be repaired.

'Bitters' Bitmead, after an engagement in the Channel area, received damage in his engine cooling system and made a forced landing in a field somewhere near East Grinstead. Unfortunately, he failed to secure his cockpit canopy in the 'safe' position before touching down. The hood slid forward and hit the back of his head. He was badly shaken but apart from a severe headache felt all right. He was picked up and brought to sick-quarters at Hornchurch. After an X-ray it was discovered that he had a fracture at the base of his skull. 'Doc' Davies, the Senior Medical Officer, put him into hospital and it was a very long time before he was fit to fly. In fact he never again regained a full medical flying category.

Eric Stapleton took over the Squadron. He, too, was a regular, a navigation specialist, and a Cambridge University graduate. Eric established himself quickly and became a very popular Squadron Commander. He was an able leader and Harry Broadhurst recognised this later by promoting him to Wing Leader.

The German night offensive entered its final phase during February and for the following three months heavy bombing attacks were aimed at a variety of targets with over 500 bombers attacking on the nights of 10 and 13 May. We were ordered to fly frequently on standing patrols even when there was no moon to help. However, on pitch-black nights with no airborne radar aids, eyesight alone proved inadequate. Also, after a hectic day on offensive operations we were in no state to do justice to night-flying into the small hours, knowing that we would be back on readiness states with fighter sweeps or bomber escorts to follow during the day. Only once was I able to spot a Ju 88, some way below me, against the glare of fires along the Thames. Overcome by surprise, I failed to keep my eyes on it for a few moments while turning to position myself for an attack and lost the target as it disappeared back into the inky blackness of the night. After a fruitless search I returned to base only to find bombs falling between Hornchurch and Romford as I crept towards the glim lamps for a landing.

Usually there was no moon visible due to haze or low cloud and it was difficult to see your hand in front of your face when you took off. Under such conditions with only glim lamps to mark the line for take-off across the grass airfield, you needed extra care to prevent a bad swing developing. If this happened, and unless it was corrected quickly, disaster stared you in the face, as forward visibility in the Spitfire was poor during take-off and landing in the tail-down attitude. Another hazard was the flash from the exhaust stubs which tended to blind the pilot temporarily. As the flare-path disappeared you got your head down in the cockpit and flew by the blind-flying instruments entirely.

To get more night flying practice away from the balloon barrage and the bombing the Hornchurch squadrons took it in turn to go to Debden. Here at last, apart from local flying practices, we did not have to do any day operations. These attachments lasted three or four days at a time.

One night, not being on the night-flying detail, I had gone to bed early to make up for much lost sleep. About midnight Charlie Mears, commanding 'B' Flight, woke me and said that a large bombing raid had developed on the Midlands and that Operations had ordered six of our aircraft to get off the ground as quickly as possible. Muttering with disgust and still half-asleep I took off and switched my radio on to Hornchurch operational control. Ronald Adam, the well-known actor, was controlling and in a few brief words told me what was happening. The German bombers were making landfall between Lowestoft and the Wash. He gave me a vector and said he had a target for me. It was quite a pleasant night; there was some broken cloud high up with a moon riding the sky. At 12,000 ft Ronnie told me to level off and gave me a course to steer towards Peterborough. He gave me one or two further alterations and then settled on a north-north-westerly course.

'Bandit fifteen miles, two o'clock. Maintain height. Buster.'

I kept a sharp look-out in an arc in front of me checking every inch of the sky, as I hurtled along.

'Bandit six miles. You're doing fine.' Then, searching along my left front I saw AA fire bursting in a tight pattern slightly below my own height. I reported this and back came Ronnie's voice:

'That could be a bandit. Look out for friends in your area.'

So it wasn't going to be easy. I closed the gap.

Ronnie's voice reached out to me:

'Your position is approximately fifteen miles south-east, Nottingham.'

The AA fire had stopped while I was talking to Control. I searched some more. Quite suddenly, and very close, there was a flurry of bursting shells and in the flicker of searchlights I saw the dark silhouette of a German bomber. I was rather startled, but without taking my eyes off it I dived straight in for an attack. The next moment I saw long streaks of flame from the guns of a Hurricane night-fighter close behind the enemy aircraft, and almost immediately the mid-section of the bomber went up in flames. There was an explosion and bits of flaming wreckage flew in all directions. I was thoroughly pleased to have witnessed this excellent bit of work but at the same time felt very disappointed at not having the chance to shoot the enemy aircraft down myself, especially after all the 'hard-arse' night-patrolling I had done recently.

Returning to Debden I prepared to land. Debden used the Drem lighting system, which consisted of a series of lights funnelling into the threshold of the flare-path. Somehow, I mistook a row of funnel lights for the flare-path and touched down by them. I remembered thinking: 'That's funny, what on earth is that tree doing on the airfield.' I had a momentary glimpse of a tree, its branches almost on top of me, then realisation came and immediate reaction. I had touched down heavily and that fact probably saved me, for as my Spitfire bounced I slammed open the throttle and climbed steeply back into the night. There was a loud tearing noise from outside the cockpit; then I was clear. I climbed up and tested the controls gingerly – everything seemed all right. I decided to keep my undercarriage down even at the risk of overheating my engine just in case it had been damaged. I selected flaps up and the aircraft lurched drunkenly, so I quickly selected them down again. Thus I went round Debden again at a slow speed and finally picked out the flare-path and landed. My Spitfire swung off the runway and bumped crazily over the grass; I sat tight and waited for the undercarriage to collapse, but it did not; I slewed round in a semicircle and came to rest. I was so fed up with the night's work that I stalked off to the Mess without waiting for anybody to come and fetch me. Then I gave my report by telephone to Operations and went to bed. In the morning I discovered my Spitfire in a sorry state. The port tyre had burst, the port wing and flap had been damaged quite badly by contact with the tree while a small branch, looking foolish, stuck out at a crazy angle from the drooping flap.

Debden at that time was commanded by Walter Churchill, an Auxiliary of 605 (County of Warwick) Squadron. When commanding the Squadron, he had been to France with the Advanced Air Striking Force and, returning to England, went through the fighting over Dunkirk and the Battle of Britain. On the morning following my dismal sortie, we heard him address the whole station over the Tannoy system. He made a practice of this, spurring on his listeners to greater efforts by encouraging them with enthusiasm and humour. He outlined the previous night's flying effort in support of the squadrons and went on to detail the successes of various night-fighter squadrons in Fighter Command. He then said that a particularly good show had been put up by Stevens, a Hurricane night-fighter of great repute from 151 Squadron who had landed at Debden in the early hours of the morning. Stevens had shot down a German bomber near Nottingham and the enemy had exploded; covering the Hurricane with its oil and damaging the wings with debris. No wonder I had little chance to get the German bomber myself. I had been queuing up with a real professional.

Though most of the flying effort was devoted to offensive operations we were required to maintain also defensive states with many convoy patrols, some quite surprising. While operating from Southend in the middle of May 1941, Tommy Williams – leading a formation of four aircraft which included Teddy Reeves, 'Mac' Gilmour and Buys, a Dutch pilot – was surprised on patrol by an attack from six Me 109s delivered at low level. The engagement proved short and sharp. Whether the Germans imagined we sent inexperienced pilots on such patrols or not, they got the shock of their lives. Tommy and his formation shot down three Germans into the sea and damaged a fourth before the survivors fled in disorder.

A few days later Tommy Williams and I were on readiness when we scrambled with another pair to patrol Canterbury at 25,000 ft, to intercept small groups of Me 109s sweeping the south coast area. As we reached Canterbury we saw four enemy crossing in our direction over Dungeness tramlining the sky with their vapour trails. Climbing hard in a tight arc we managed to get above them into the sun without the 109s seeing us. As they closed on our starboard beam we dived into a quarter attack, Tommy taking the right-hand pair while I went into the pair on the left. They were flying abreast about 100 yards apart. Closing rapidly I fired two short bursts at the leader followed by a further longish burst. Immediately smoke streamed from him with bits from the canopy breaking away and sparkling in the sun. As he spiralled steeply I tried to follow but had to break sharply as tracer streamed past my Spitfire from an unseen Me 109 firing from above. Giving my aircraft full rudder and stick I skidded round in a tight turn searching behind in time to see a 109 pull up into a zoom climb and above him the welcome sight of two Spitfires coming into attack. Levelling out of a succession of steep turns I found myself out to sea off Hythe with not an aircraft in sight, only thickening vapour trails still hanging in the sky to remind me of the action. Back at Southend I found that Tommy Williams had also been shot at by a follow-up enemy formation while he was firing at his pair of Me 109s.

Later the same day we had a sweep in the Pas de Calais area and engaged a formation of six Me 109s. Eric Stapleton, Mears, Pollard and 'Mushroom' Smith between them destroyed one, probably destroying three others.

A few days later, on 4 June, George Gribble of 54 Squadron, a particularly close friend who was a veteran with 54 Squadron from the beginning of the war, was shot down into the Channel. With others I searched for hours while escorting a Lysander search aircraft to see if I could find him in his Mae West but it proved fruitless. We were not equipped with rubber dinghies at that time, so searching became more difficult over the choppy sea because a pilot's head looked no bigger than a pin-head under such conditions.

The pace at Hornchurch intensified as the good weather continued. Late one evening Eric Stapleton led the Hornchurch Wing on a sweep over the Pas de Calais area. Off Gravelines we ran into two formations of eight Me 109s. 611 as bottom squadron had a perfect bounce, with 54 and 603 Squadrons guarding from above. Eric's first attack produced a flamer which spiralled down into the sea. Thereafter, the Squadron split and we each singled out 109s for individual attacks. I got on to the tail of one German, who was behaving like a lost sheep on a Scottish mountainside, and closing on him from dead astern opened fire. To my satisfaction his tail-plane disintegrated, bits flying everywhere, whereupon he did a most extraordinary upward corkscrew before spinning vertically down. Fascinated, I followed and watched with wonder as the enemy fighter broke up piece by piece. First the port wing came off, then the starboard wing and the fuselage seemed to tumble through the air as the 109 hurtled straight into the sea. The pilot, I suppose, was already dead but somehow I did not think of him. It was the peculiar antics of his plane that held my attention.

Our final bag was five Me 109s destroyed and two probables. The Me 109s encountered were mostly Mark 'E's but the Mark 'F' version was making itself known more and more. This design had a lot more power and a slight edge on us for speed. We were glad therefore when, quite unexpectedly, we were re-equipped with the Spitfire Mk VB which sported two 20-mm cannons and four .303 Browning machine-guns. Immediately our successes came the more easily for with the more powerful 20-mm cannons most hits became effective.

The change-over in aircraft was completed towards the end of May and I flew two different Mk VBs before choosing one that belonged to a batch presented to the RAF by the Motor Industry. It was named 'Crispin of Leicester' and my first offensive mission proved unusually exciting. It was during a big 'Circus' operation. We were top cover at 28,000 ft to twenty-four Blenheims targeted on Bethune, supported by a gaggle of over 260 fighters. A few enemy appeared over the target area but on recrossing the coast we were bounced by about twenty-five Me 109s. Turning into an attack from four of them coming in over my left shoulder I got behind the last one and opened fire. The muffled boom-boom from the cannons was a welcome new sound but the orange flash from one of my cannon shells, quite vivid as it exploded against the enemy's cockpit cover, even more startling. Closing, I fired a second burst but my Spitfire pitched and yawed away from my line of sight and in a split second the 109 rolled onto its back diving steeply pouring smoke from a hit in the cooling system. It was then I realised one of my cannons had stopped firing thus twisting me side-ways due to recoil from the live gun.

We had to put up with this sort of snag during the early days with the Hispano 20-mm cannons till we sorted out stoppage problems. It was very annoying when a stoppage threw one off-balance because of the sudden change in trim. We eventually got things sorted out and the guns proved most reliable and effective. On the other hand in the meantime, being the pilot of 'Crispin' held certain compensations because I began to receive from kind ladies in Leicester, woollen socks, mufflers, fruit cakes and other goodies not to mention a surprise package containing a long scarf in the colours of Leicester City Football Club with a proposal of marriage!

64 Squadron exchanged with 603 Squadron and went to Drem outside Edinburgh for a rest and the training of new pilots. Barrie Heath's departure did not help my morale, for we had spent a lot of free time together. In the heat of battle a close friendship became important in maintaining a balanced team spirit and without it the job would have been impossibly harder.

603 (City of Edinburgh) Squadron had been based at Hornchurch under the command of George Denholm during the Battle of Britain, and been immortalised by Richard Hillary in *The Last Enemy*. I came to know Richard later on, after he left the famous plastic surgeon, Sir Archie McIndoe's East Grinstead hospital and while he was doing a staff job at Fighter Command. Much has been said and written about him. He bore his terrible scars and injuries with great dignity and extreme patience. What he must have suffered through his terrifying ordeal the rest of us will never fully understand. His gallantry and devotion to duty were outstanding because at heart he was so very sensitive, full of charm and feeling for others. He was a deep thinker but was never irritated if he got no response from others more light-hearted. The experience of talking to him left one full of admiration for his courage.

Before Hillary had fully recovered from his burns, his pride and self-respect drove him back to active duty. He was killed quite senselessly on a night-training mission soon afterwards and it remained a source of grief to Leigh-Mallory that he had allowed him back on flying.

Others in 603 Squadron I knew were David Scott-Malden, 'Sheep' Gilroy and Archie Winskill. 'Sheep' had been with me at preparatory school in Nairn, and still had the florid open-air look of the traditional Scottish sheep farmer. At the entrance to his farm is a notice which says simply 'Beware of Sheep'.

David Scott-Malden had left 611 Squadron just before I

joined. Quiet, dark and very handsome he was also clever and an excellent pilot. When I had joined 611 in Digby I saw a 'Car for Sale' notice in the Mess which was typical of Scotty. Now seeing him at Hornchurch it came back to me:

'Unique Bargain. For Sale: Second-Hand, First-Rate, Almost Incredible Austin 7 Family Saloon in Excellent Condition. Guaranteed fully aerobatic, untaxed, unserviceable. It's the tops! Price £1 or NEAR OFFER. Positively Last Day. P/O F.D.S. Scott-Malden. Late 611 Squadron. *Sic Transit . . .*'

Eric Stapleton had been promoted to command the Wing on the loss of Joe Kayll, who had been shot down within a week of joining while flying number two to Harry Broadhurst. We were deep inside enemy territory when we were attacked by a large formation of Me 109s. In the excitement Kayll left his transmitter switched on and this blanked out everything on the R/T. Broady could give him no instructions nor help him with advice, and he had to fight it out with four Me 109s. Later, we were glad to have news that Kayll was safe, but had been taken prisoner.

As the last sweltering days of June reached new heights in temperatures we seemed to get as many as four offensive sorties a day. One afternoon, with the sun scorching through the canopy of my Spitfire, I flew with 'Polly' Pollard as the Squadron climbed steadily for North Foreland. Our task was to act as high cover to bombers whose targets were the marshalling yards at Hazebrouck. We crossed the French coast at 28,000 ft, the sun glinting on the perspex of our cockpit hoods and long vapour trails streaming behind us. Below, I could see the stepped formations of the lower escort squadrons stretching down to the neatly packed group of twelve Blenheims with their close escort of Hurricanes, at about 12,000 ft. We called it the 'Beehive' because with individual aircraft weaving and jinking the whole affair looked like a swarm of bees.

As we approached Hazebrouck a formation of ten Me 109s, slightly below, came towards us. Eric Stapleton turned into them and started to dive; immediately the enemy formation rolled onto their backs and disappeared past the tail of the 'Beehive'. Almost on top of the target another formation of fifteen Me 109s appeared below and we promptly dived for them. They saw us coming and broke into our attack. I stuck close to 'Polly' as we waltzed around trying to get on to their tails. One group of 109s then broke right with two sections after them, while 'Polly' and I with two others latched on to four Me 109s circling across our left front. Swiftly we turned inside them and got into range. 'Polly' called me: 'Take the right 109 Charlie Two, I'll get the other.'

We were now well placed and the 109s stayed with us in a tight circle. They were staggered, the one on the right slightly above and behind the left-hand one with ourselves in a commanding position behind and a couple of hundred feet above.

I swung my nose across closing fast and as the 109 filled the width of my windscreeen I blasted into the side of his cockpit and engine. Bits flew off and thick smoke gushed; the 109 rolled slowly over and plunged vertically down. As I prepared to follow, tracers steaked past my cockpit and over the top of my propeller. I broke sharply in a right-hand climbing turn. 'Polly's' voice hit my earphones: 'Good boy, Charlie Two. Climb. I'm above.'

Wildly I looked round for 'Polly'. Turning, I saw two Me 109s flash past behind me, then above them the unmistakable wing pattern of a Spitfire. Giving my aircraft every pound of boost I had I rocketed upwards in a tight spiral. 'Polly' saw me coming and nosed towards me.

'Did you get one Charlie Leader?' I called him.

'Think so, can't tell – had to break – attacked by six bastards.' His reply snapped and crackled as other voices cut in.

We searched for the rest of the Squadron but could not see them. Below and above Spitfires wheeled. We were somewhere near the tail-end of the 'Beehive'. I glanced at my altimeter and saw we had lost a lot of height. Smoke and dust clouds were rising from the target area below, and away to our right the bombers were flying homewards, angry black puffs of AA shell bursts following them.

'Let's get right into the "Beehive" and climb up.' 'Polly's' voice was flat. Experience had taught me never to fly straight and level, but to search the sky continually. Now as I searched behind my heart leapt into my mouth. Streaking straight at us in a loose line-abreast formation were – I couldn't believe it – nine Me 109s and they were too damned close for comfort.

'Charlie Leader, break.'

Close together we swung into a tight climbing turn to face the enemy.

It was no good. Three more 109s came at us from ahead. I saw the guns of the leading 109 wink at me and tracers flew past – there was a loud bang somewhere along my fuselage. The next second I was fighting for my life.

Again I heard 'Polly's' voice as I turned my Spitfire in a tight circle, wings shuddering, vision clouded in a grey mist as the blood drained from my head.

'Look out behind – dive for the deck.' My radio was terribly noisy.

I slewed round in my harness and looked behind. I saw a Me 109 slightly above with 'Polly' on his tail firing. I heaved my Spitfire round trying desperately to get behind 'Polly's' machine. Suddenly the 109 which 'Polly' was firing at broke into a red glow; black smoke gushed and it hurtled down. More tracer whizzed past and once again I was corkscrewing out of the way. I caught a glimpse of 'Polly' as he rolled on his back and dived for the ground in a tight spiral, and immediately lost sight of him against the dark pattern of fields and woodland below. Just then the 109 that had fired at me shot past my port wing tip terribly close and I got a glimpse of a black-helmeted head peering out as the enemy dived below me.

I rocketed down after the 109. He was out of range, losing height in a gentle dive. I glanced round behind, above, below – the sky was clear. Fairly close now and over on my left I could see the French coast. Slowly I gained on the enemy still diving and keeping just below his slipstream. Then at last the 109 began to loom large in my windscreen. I held my fire; a quick look behind; I had no intention of fouling it up; I was determined not to open fire until I was sure I could not miss. Now, I was ready to make the kill: I eased the stick forward a little and at close range pulled the nose of my Spitfire up sharply, lined up my sight and opened fire, pouring cannon shells into the enemy's belly. There was a sheet of flame, the 109 flicked over onto its back and dived straight into the ground. It crashed close to the corner of a wood, near a white-washed and neat-looking farmhouse. I circled once clipping the tops of the trees with my wing-tip, watching the column of black smoke belching into the air from the wreck. I felt elated and terribly pleased with myself.

I scrambled somehow back to Manston, hugging first the grey-green fields of France at treetop height, then the uninviting and hostile waters of the Channel. I didn't have much fuel to spare; I got down with about two sherry glasses left, and by now in a thoroughly filthy frame of mind, upset and frightened.

Later, back at Hornchurch, I discovered that between us we had destroyed seven Me 109s and probably destroyed or damaged a further five. As far as I was concerned there was nothing to celebrate for, tragically, 'Polly' had not returned. I hung about dispersal till late in the evening, then paced up and down in my room in a whirlpool of emotions. Operations had tried all the airfields, air/sea rescue units, the Navy. Nothing.

We had flown together many times and I had learned that by sticking together even when separated from the rest of the Squadron we could engage the enemy with success. The strength of the enemy attack this time had forced us apart because, as 'Polly' dived away, I could not follow since I was under attack myself. By then I had the bit between my teeth, against all advice and the known hazards of following a Me 109 diving back into France. But I had done it before and got away with it so why not this time? A cannon shell had hit my radio set and wrecked it. We were no longer in touch – no longer a fighting partnership – and in a matter of seconds lost touch for ever.

The loss of a close friend in war stirs a deeper feeling of personal sorrow because of its abrupt and harsh reality. Though there is no reason to brood on the tragedy the chances are that if his name is mentioned it will recall the happy moments of laughter shared and never any of darkness. Though it makes one aware of the uncertainty of life it also hardens the will to survive and in a strange way the thought of death as the final enemy transforms it instead into an honourable escape.

CHAPTER SEVEN

Wrong formation

On the appointment of Eric Stapleton to Wing Leader, Eric Thomas took over 611 Squadron. An experienced pilot, he had served as a flight commander with 222 and later as CO of 91 Squadron. 611 Squadron was averaging over 600 hours' operational flying a month, while most of us averaged well over thirty combat missions a month. I had done eighty-four flights over to the Continent in two and a half months. In the same period the Wing had shot down sixty enemy aircraft with a further sixty probably destroyed and damaged. Our losses were twenty-five pilots, some of them very experienced. During June and July, 611 Squadron destroyed thirty-four German fighters with a further fifty probably destroyed and damaged, for the loss of eleven pilots. We were all getting to know northern France and Belgium so well that names like Lille and Arras, Hazebrouck and Dunkirk, St Omer, Markdyk and Dieppe became as familiar as the local pubs.

We had regular visits from the AOC, Trafford Leigh-Mallory, who was always keen to hear our views and reactions to the offensive operations. He made a point of putting our suggestions and ideas into effect in a constant effort to keep down losses. He was much upset by casualties, and even during the Battle of Britain was convinced that to operate in Wing strength was the proper way to deal with enemy formations. By this means he believed in getting two or three squadrons into a given area at the same time, making it possible for our squadrons to attack large concentrations of enemy bombers and fighters in depth. He had achieved this with considerable success on several occasions when the Duxford Wing, led by Douglas Bader, played havoc with the enemy's attacks on London. Now, over France the 11 Group Wings were having a marked success using a pre-planned offensive to determine the scale of effort required and the choice of targets. We were, in fact, bringing home to the Germans some hard truths regarding the employment of air forces, and how a properly organised offensive could be carried out successfully. This the Germans had failed to appreciate themselves during their own offensive in the summer of 1940, largely because the Luftwaffe was essentially a tactical air force organised to support armies in the field and not trained for the flexible use of air power. Added to this was the indisputable fact that they had under-estimated the training and efficiency of the RAF, and the superb fighting qualities of our pilots and aircraft despite the fact that Luftwaffe pilots had more combat experience and tactical knowledge gained from the Spanish Civil War and in Poland.

In view of the intensity of continuous offensive flying during the summer, a system of wing 'releases' was introduced. This enabled the squadrons to get off the station for much-needed relaxation and gave ground-crews a chance to catch up on servicing as well as giving them time off from their own very arduous duties. We found the swimming pool of the Chase Hotel, off the Southend road, an ideal place to relax in the sun. It kept us fit and calmed our taut nerves. In the evening we would go to London to meet friends at Shepherd's, where Oscar, a Swiss, and his wife always gave us a special welcome and preferential treatment over other customers. The Wellington Club in Knightsbridge was another favourite Squadron haunt. Wally Wisher, the proprietor, had been our catering officer at Digby, so he made us all life-members. Wally's wife Doris looked after the place in his absence and we always got a very friendly welcome with a splendid dinner not to be found elsewhere in London. Jeanne D'Arcy, the vocalist in the band, used to sing a number called 'If I only had Wings' and do a cabaret act. If we were present one of us would be led onto the floor to help put over the act. With suitable amorous gestures and a bit of all-in wrestling she would sing and act out the scene. Members of other squadrons present were not amused because if we weren't there the act didn't go on. There was no stand-in for 611.

Several experienced pilots joined 611 to make good our losses. Eric Lock took over 'A' Flight. He was a much-decorated ex-member of 41 Squadron and had been shot down and badly wounded just before the end of the Battle of Britain. 'Locky' was a very live wire. In something like nine weeks he had shot down twenty-three enemy aircraft. He had spent nine months in hospital and received specialist treatment at the hands of Sir Archie McIndoe.

Peter Dexter was another who came to us after being shot down and wounded with 602 Squadron. He had started the war in Lysanders in France and had the rare distinction of having shot down a Me 109 while doing a recce for the Army. This was quite an achievement in a Lysander. Getting home after the French débâcle he transferred to fighters and joined 602. A Me 109 got him and he had to bale out. He was wounded, and, in leaving his Spitfire, his boot got trapped between the seat and side of the cockpit. He fell with his burning machine, suspended by one leg; though he kicked and struggled he could not free himself. He fell 15,000 ft before he finally managed to wrench his foot out of his flying boot, just in time to pull the rip-cord of his parachute and land in one piece in a ploughed field. He had six months in hospital and was then sent to the RAF rehabilitation centre at Torquay. However, his damaged leg never recovered fully.

A frequent visitor to Hornchurch was 'Doc' Corner, the Command expert on aviation medicine. He was one of the first – if not the first – 'flying doctor' in the RAF. He usually arrived in a trim-looking Gladiator biplane – a wonderfully manoeuvrable machine that was still in squadron service at the beginning of the war – and used to let some of us fly it for the sheer joy of flying. Aged about fifty, it was quite extraordinary how competent he was in flying Spitfires, and how keen he was to get first-hand information on the flying equipment we used and the effects of high altitude and combat strain on pilots. He flew as my number two on a number of occasions, carrying out exacting missions with skill and verve. On most occasions we tried out better-designed experimental equipment that he brought with him. Oxygen masks and regulators, a Mae West, flying boots, gloves, overalls and helmets were all produced in turn and left for us to test thoroughly. Later he would come back for some more flying and receive our reports on the efficiency of each particular piece of equipment. His formation keeping was superb and he stuck to me like a leech. Several times I put him in a good attacking position on Me 109s but I never saw him fire his guns. Then one day we were escort cover to Stirling bombers over Lille when two Me 109s dived through the top cover to attack the right-hand one of a Vic of three. 'Doc' Corner was right behind me and we were well placed to attack the 109s. I called 'Doc' to take the right-hand one, while I fastened on to the tail of the other. I put in a good burst of cannon and machine-gun fire and saw strikes on the mid-section and wing root. Glycol poured out of him and he did two flick rolls before plunging vertically down. I looked hard for 'Doc' Corner, expecting to see him attacking the other enemy fighter over to my right, but it was now disappearing rapidly in a steep inverted dive and there was no sign of a Spitfire behind it. Then over my shoulder I saw 'Doc' Corner sitting on my tail weaving like mad!

After we landed I asked him why he had not fired. His forehead creased by a puzzled frown, he answered:

'I didn't see any 109s. All I saw from start to finish was your tail, and tail-wheel. Funny how it keeps on going round and round.'

Looking into his eyes I at last got the message. He had no intention of shooting anything down. Although he took frightful risks, and understood the dangers he faced, he concerned himself only with the medical aspects. He regulated his life by the code of the medical profession and the deliberate taking of life was outside the limits he had set for himself.

'Doc' Corner did not confine his flying to the Hornchurch Wing, but flew also with other Wings. In the middle of 1942 he was shot down by an FW 190 off Folkestone and killed. Many pilots owe their lives to the improvements he introduced into the safety equipment for aircraft, not to mention the experiments he conducted on himself to help overcome human problems affecting pilots engaged on continuous operations. Without the efforts of 'Doc' Corner and other 'flying doctors' of those days, the RAF's Institute of Aviation Medicine at Farnborough would not exist as we know it today.

Wrong formation

Jeffrey Quill, the Chief Test Pilot of Supermarines, visited us frequently and, being a friend of Harry Broadhurst, flew with us to get current information first-hand on the performance and capability of our Spitfires. Marvellously calm and a brilliant pilot, he impressed us all with the keen professional interest he took in everything we did. As a member of R.J. Mitchell's original team of experts that designed the Spitfire, Jeffrey had been associated with the development flying from its first flight on 5 March 1936. Moreover, he had taken time off from his test flying in August 1940 to fly with 65 Squadron at the height of the Battle of Britain and, more important, proved himself a superb combat pilot in action. Now, looking for ways to improve the Spitfire's performance in the battles with the improved Me 109s, it was largely due to his personal experience in operations that the Spitfire Mk IX emerged in April 1942 ahead of its time.

The finest aerobatic pilot I ever saw, Jeffrey's trick of lowering his landing gear while inverted in the final approach, rolling out and landing in one smooth operation was a sight I shall never forget.

The summer wore on, with almost continuous offensive operations. Harry Broadhurst led 54 Squadron one day on a Wing escort cover to Blenheims bombing St Omer. Over the target area, about fifteen to twenty Me 109s carried out a determined attack on the bombers. In the following dog-fight Broady shot down one of the Me 109s in flames. The Wing was split up by this affray and Broady and his number two, 'Streak' Harris, became separated from the others. They had to lose height and fight a defensive battle all the way to the coast, where a very determined attack was launched upon them by six Me 109s. No matter which way they turned they were attacked in strength and 'Streak' Harris was shot down and killed.

I heard Broady's voice on the radio – his call-sign 'Taipan' – asking for assistance and luckily some of us saw the 109s and raced to his aid. However, one of the 109s detached himself and made a determined head-on attack on Broady. Two other 109s stationed themselves above and on each side of Broady's Spitfire cutting off any chance of escape. He promptly flew straight at the oncoming Me 109, the guns of both blazing at each other on a collision course. When the 109 was almost on top of him it exploded and Broady flew right through the wreckage. The 109 pilot had scored hits on Broady's wing and along the side of the cockpit, spraying cannon-shell splinters into the cockpit and wounding him in the leg and arm. One of the German's shells had actually gone up the barrel of his Spitfire's port cannon, buckling it like a hairpin and ripping a large hole across the upper wing surface. By this time the rest of us had driven off the remaining 109s, destroying two of them. We all got back to Hornchurch without further incident, much relieved by the outcome of the battle. Broady had had his hydraulic system shot up as well, so he had to carry out a wheels-up crash-landing. His Spitfire was a write-off. The *Tatler* later on stated he managed to fly home despite being wounded and rendered unconscious! It was interesting to note, on examining the Spitfire, that Broady in flying through the enemy's wreckage had had his Spitfire splashed with oil from the enemy fighter. After climbing out of his crashed aircraft he gave strict instructions that the oil-splashed propeller spinner was to be transferred to his new machine when it was ready, to remind him of the fight. We heard later that the intrepid German pilot who had met his end at Broady's hands was one of Germany's leading aces, with a large number of combat victories to his credit.

One morning, after a target support operation to Lille, the Wing was heavily engaged near St Omer by concentrated Me 109 attacks. I became separated from the Squadron after engaging two separate 109s and, finding myself alone and still some distance from the coast, I searched frantically for friends. Suddenly, a large formation of aircraft appeared about 5,000 ft above and to one side of me flying parallel to the coast. Keeping a close look-out behind I climbed after them at full power. Gradually I came up alongside and joined the end section, intent the whole time on watching for danger from behind. I was quite close when at last I looked to verify the squadron markings on the nearest aircraft. To my horror, all I could see were big black crosses and I realised I had joined up with a Me 109 formation. I remember looking across and seeing the nearest German pilot staring back at me. He must have been as surprised and shocked as I was. Somehow the idea of turning into him and blasting him with my guns never occurred to me. The next moment – the German pilot presumably having given the alarm 'Achtung, Spitfire' – the whole formation rolled onto their backs and went hurtling earthwards.

I dived down too, only in the opposite direction. My troubles, however, were not over. I reached ground-level just short of the French coast and at full throttle, skimming the fields and trees, I set my face homewards, crossing the coast somewhere between Gravelines and Calais.

I was within yards of the beach when there was a terrific blast just below my starboard wing-tip as a 40-mm AA shell exploded very close with nerve-shattering violence, nearly blowing me on to my back. The next instant a stream of shells burst all around me. I pressed my back against the seat, trying to hide behind the protective armour plate. Shells – some large ones, others unmistakably tracers from cannon – flashed past me curving a pattern and striking the surface of the sea ahead, spraying fountains of water into the air. I kicked the rudder one way then the other, skidding my Spitfire across the surface of the sea. It seemed a lifetime before the shooting stopped and I realised that I had miraculously escaped with nothing worse than a few shrapnel holes in my starboard wing. Relaxing my tense muscles I looked over my shoulder and caught my breath as I saw a Me 109 over on my right, and screwing round in my seat saw another on the opposite side. I was in real trouble. I called repeatedly on the R/T for help, and flogging the last pound of boost out of my engine, eased my aircraft down even closer to the tops of the waves. The Me 109s opened fire: first the one on the right, whereupon I skidded my aircraft to the left, and watched fascinated as the shells splashed past my wing-tip; then the one on the left opened fire, and I repeated the manoeuvre in the opposite direction. I soon realised that each time I did this it slowed me down, enabling the 109s to close the gap. I saw no way out, for whichever way I turned I was bound to have a 109 right on my tail. There was only one thing left to do: I heaved back on the stick and zoomed up into an off-centre loop to the left. By keeping it as tight as I could I felt sure neither 109 would be able to keep inside me. These were real First World

War tactics. I watched over my shoulder and saw the 109 pull up after me, firing. Harder, I pressed on the stick until I felt the wings starting to judder. Suddenly the 109 flicked and spun – the horizon came back into view above my head and quickly I rolled out into a tight turn.

I looked all around and got a great feeling of relief when I picked out one of the 109s, also in a turn, but circling away from me. There was no sign of the other one. Quick as a flash I reversed my turn and dived once more for the waves – and home. A few minutes later I saw the low level Hurricane patrol ahead (a squadron usually maintained a standing patrol off North Foreland and St Margaret's Bay, to help lame ducks home) and slipped under their protective umbrella. Wringing wet, and shaking with nervous tension, I landed at Hornchurch still unable to believe my luck.

Jack Charles, a pilot of 54 Squadron, told me later that he had witnessed my tussle with the 109s, having recognised my voice and call-sign, as he was heading home above, but he was out of ammunition and short of fuel. However, he confirmed that one of the Me 109s had plunged into the sea, spinning down from a tight turn.

The Luftwaffe was becoming noticeably more cautious and a number of their 109 pilots, once their formations split, acted foolishly. This led us to believe that many were inexperienced. There had been reductions in the total numbers of enemy fighters in the Pas de Calais area, and we assumed that this was due to Germany's attack on the Soviet Union, requiring the withdrawal of experienced squadrons to the Eastern Front. It became increasingly difficult to make the 109s mix it with us; they either avoided combat, or immediately on contact took evasive action. They also flew in much smaller formations, but were usually led by experienced pilots.

To deal with these tactics 'Locky' led the flight operating as a unit of six aircraft, but on engagement we broke up into pairs acting independently. Success came during a high-cover mission to three Stirlings bombing Lille. We were flying at 30,000 ft, and just after crossing the coast took the German formation by surprise as it was positioning itself to attack the escort-cover squadron. Eric Lock got one, 'Mac' Gilmour one and a probable, Peter Dexter got another and I knocked large pieces off the 109 I attacked and promptly flew through the bits. I was so surprised that I took violent evasive action thinking I was being attacked from behind and thus lost sight of him. On landing at base, I found one piece from the enemy aircraft had damaged the muzzle of a machine-gun, while another piece had torn a hole in the undersurface of the wing and was still stuck there – a jagged piece of metal about six inches long by about three inches wide. Peter Dexter confirmed that the 109 I attacked subsequently blew up.

A few days after this engagement I was not flying because I was grounded with a severe cold. However, four 109s dived down through the top cover over the Channel when the Squadron was escorting bombers to St Omer, and Alan Johnston, flying to one side of our formation, was too far out. The Squadron broke into the enemy attack and in the ensuing dog-fights a 109 was destroyed and another damaged. It was not until after the Squadron reformed that Alan was discovered to be missing. I questioned a number of pilots but no one had seen what happened to him.

About the same time Peter Dexter collided over Boulogne with a pilot of 54 Squadron but managed to bale out. Later we heard through the Red Cross that he had been picked up dead in his parachute. Peter was my third room-mate and friend to go in a short space of time, so I talked the Mess Secretary into letting me keep the room to myself, and maintained this arrangement until I finally left Hornchurch a year later.

Bad weather usually meant some respite from operations but one day, with the visibility rather poor and low cloud cover, a German supply ship tried to slip along the French coast to Boulogne. The news did not reach us till late, so we hurriedly took off just after nine in the evening to act as escort to three Beaufort torpedo-bombers and, flying at sea-level, made for the French coast. We found the enemy ship off Berk-sur-Mer and, on sighting us, it put up a terrific AA barrage. We positioned ourselves on either side of the Beauforts to protect them and watched the fun. All three torpedoes missed the target which was not surprising as the flak barrage was heavy and accurate.

Two Me 109s appeared and, on seeing twenty-four Spitfires, turned tail and ran.

Eric Stapleton, who led this affray, wanted to lead us down to strafe the enemy ship with cannon-fire, but our comments on the R/T were lucid and to the point; Eric was persuaded and we flew back to Hornchurch much relieved. Next morning we heard that the Royal Navy had attacked the supply ship successfully with MTBs, and sunk it in the approaches to Boulogne harbour.

At last, I went away on some much-needed leave and I spent first a few days with Barrie and Joy Heath near Drem. Barrie still had 64 Squadron on rest.

Having arrived on the night sleeper, I joined Barrie and Joy for breakfast in their house at Gullane. Scrambled eggs, bacon, coffee and champagne greeted me banishing the overnight hangover which kept me awake. Joy laid on some splendid parties during the next few days with the pilots of 64 also pushing out the boat in the Mess. After a memorable three days I left to spend the remaining part of my leave with my uncle, George Duncan, in Crieff.

Some trout fishing and golf restored my equilibrium while the peace and grandeur of the lovely countryside helped slacken the taut nerves that had held me together too long. I tried to believe there were more important things in life than flying my arse off, day in and day out. Amidst the remote stillness of my glen, though the war seemed far away, I had to guard against a compelling force that tried hard to draw me back to the Squadron, the excitement of action, the fulfilment of a combat well won. While fishing I am usually completely absorbed by its fascination but I was now finding it difficult to concentrate.

I also found conversation with relatives and friends difficult, my thoughts being far away in the cockpit of my Spitfire, my slang responses clipped and unintelligible, making them wonder why I had nothing to say for myself. 'Do you get a bath every morning?' someone asked once. 'Depends on whether I'm on readiness,' I replied. Nobody cared or understood and the conversation changed abruptly.

I was into a good fish one evening but let the line slack for a long enough moment to snag the cast on a rock and I lost him.

Survival, I thought, that was what it was all about. There is this feeling in the pit of your stomach when above you, you see Me 109s like a gaggle of geese wheeling against the crispness of a pale winter sky. You count them automatically – which is it to be when they pounce on you – which one your own – or is it to be the other way round this time – your turn for a slack moment, a wrong judgement and a quick exit? There are so many things that determine survival: height advantage, sun, rate of turn and climb, defensive circle, reflex reaction in seeing the bastard before it's too late. You can take your pick but in the end it all depends on how well you handle your Spitfire – in knowing its limitations and your own – whether you are prepared to fly it to the very edge of its boundary of performance without destroying your own will and determination to survive as well; a steadfast resolve never to let the blood run cold, and break.

I put up my rod and walked along the riverbank in the twilight, back to the world of reality where a clean shirt and good manners confirmed that, after all, a fighter pilot was just an ordinary chap with nothing much to say for himself.

CHAPTER EIGHT

Nine on the loose

The day after I got back to Hornchurch Eric Lock carried out a 'Rhubarb' operation in the Marguise–Montreuil area behind Boulogne. A pilot of 403 Squadron was also in the area and reported later that he heard 'Locky' call on the R/T that he had gunned a column of troops on bicycles and was well pleased with the results. Unfortunately he set off for England right through the Boulogne defences and was shot down into the harbour by intense AA fire. In my opinion, the operation was a waste of effort. At that stage in the war we could ill afford to lose a pilot of 'Locky's' calibre. Experience was becoming a very precious asset and, though losses in combat were inevitable, it seemed senseless to waste valuable experience on 'Rhubarb' operations, which made little difference to the war effort.

During August we had another shock. Douglas Bader, leading the Tangmere Wing, collided with a Me 109 but managed to bale out successfully, although he lost one of his artificial legs in the process. The Germans were elated at taking Bader prisoner and made much of it through their propaganda machine. They also tried to inject into the affair some of the First World War's chivalry among airmen, by informing us that they would give 'safe passage' to one of our aircraft if it brought a new set of artificial legs over to France for him. The offer was not accepted but new artificial legs were delivered by parachute at the end of a routine bombing attack on one of the airfields. Douglas Bader's loss was felt throughout Fighter Command, for his exceptional leadership, fighting spirit and supreme courage directly influenced the morale of every fighter pilot to rise above himself.

At this time I had no thoughts of promotion, but out of the blue I was appointed to take over command of 'B' Flight in 603

Squadron. Naturally I was delighted, though sad at leaving 611. However, the two squadrons were great friends and it wasn't as though I was leaving Hornchurch. 'Sheep' Gilroy had been posted to command 609 Squadron, leaving a vacant spot in 603. A short time later the CO, Hiram Smith, also left the Squadron to go to Group Headquarters, and Johnny Loudon took over. Tall, dark and handsome, Johnny had been lucky enough to survive the almost complete destruction of the ill-fated Defiant Squadron in which he served around the Dunkirk period. I got on extremely well with him from the start, and with David Scott-Malden as the other flight commander we formed a pretty good team.

Almost the first operational mission I flew with 603, however, nearly turned out to be my last. We escorted nine Blenheims, supposedly on a bombing trip to the Lille marshalling yards. I never discovered what went wrong but they proceeded to get lost on the way there, though the weather was quite clear. After crossing the French coast the Blenheims turned south and made for Amiens, where to our surprise they dropped their bombs. We had to stick with them and it soon became apparent we were all going to be very short of fuel by the time we saw England again, and if we had any engagements the position would become critical. As we turned over Amiens my worst suspicions were realised. Flying at quite a low speed we held our station to protect the bombers, and while still turning we were set upon by fifteen Me 109s. I led my Flight in a tight turn to face the attack. Johnny Loudon had also turned with his Flight in the same circle and the 109s for once were keen to mix it. The R/T, after all the preliminary chatter and anxious cries of '109s here' and '109s there', suddenly went quiet, a sure sign that everyone was too busy fighting to pass any further comment.

I found myself in an extraordinary circle which went on endlessly, 109, Spitfire, 109, Spitfire, in a stream which finally disappeared round the back somewhere with everyone shooting at everyone else. I ranged on the German in front of me, who was shooting at the Spitfire ahead of him, and squirted two bursts from close range. I registered hits immediately and he rolled on his back and hurtled down in an inverted dive.

79

Quickly I looked round to see what was happening behind, only to find a 109 firmly stuck to my tail blazing away with everything he had. As I took violent evasive action I heard and felt a couple of sharp bangs as two bullets tore through the bottom of my Spitfire. One of these came in between my legs and smacked into the control column. I discovered that I could not use my guns any more and realised I would not have any flaps or brakes for landing, because these were operated off the same air system. I was thankful to have Griffiths behind me for he shot the 109 off my tail and then proceeded to damage another that also tried to get me.

Twisting and turning we stuck together and slowly managed to pull ourselves out of a very nasty situation and make for the English coast. We kept our height because of the uncertain fuel state. As we crossed over the French coast we saw a Spitfire fly clean through a Hurricane. The Spitfire made it back to Manston but the Hurricane pilot had to bale out. The whole affair was spectacular, to say the least. I was still some distance away from Manston at 9,000 ft when my fuel-gauges registered zero and I sat rigid waiting for my engine to die. Just short of the coast at about 7,000 ft my engine finally gave up the ghost after much coughing and banging, and I started my glide for Manston. The wind helped and I was thankful to put my Spitfire down all right without flaps or brakes.

I joined a crowd of Hornchurch pilots who, like me, were either shot up or out of fuel or both, and we soundly cursed the morning's events. Johnny Loudon had been quite seriously injured in the arm and face, and his machine was in a shocking state with holes everywhere and bits missing. He had put up a fine show by getting home at all. Later I discovered that Eric Stapleton, leading 403 Squadron, and his number two each destroyed a 109. Because of the mix-up and uncertainty, we could claim only one destroyed, four probably destroyed and a couple damaged. But my hero that day was Griffiths.

Towards the end of September we started hearing news of the new German fighter, the Focke-Wulf 190. We were close escort to Blenheims bombing a target near Bethune when we ran into formations of 109s. My Flight was attacked by ten or twelve of them, and as we twisted and turned firing quick bursts at individual 109s, I suddenly noticed a radial-engined aircraft dive through the formation. I thought I was seeing things. On this occasion we all thought the 109s were being particularly hostile.

We managed to dispose of altogether four Me 109s with a further three probables and two damaged. Sergeant McKelvie destroyed what he claimed to be a Curtis Hawk. This intrigued us greatly when we discussed the operation with the Intelligence Officer. One theory put foward was that the Germans were running short of aircraft and therefore had to resort to using old French Air Force aircraft left over from June 1940, since some French squadrons had been equipped with the American Curtis Hawk, a radial-engined fighter of limited performance. What a hope! We very soon discovered we were wrong, as Intelligence reports confirmed the introduction of the FW 190 into service. We were to discover that the FW 190 was a very formidable aircraft, with excellent armament and a splendid turn of speed.

David Scott-Malden left 603 to take over 54 Squadron and 'Chumley' Innes took his place. Scotty had done a lot for 603 during the long time he had been with them and had a very fine operational record. I was going to miss him in the air and on our sorties to Shepherd's and the King's Head. Shortly after Scotty left, John Loudon was sent to the Middle East to pass on to the Desert Air Force fighter squadrons up-to-date information and the current tactics of Fighter Command. He was supposed to be away for three weeks but, as it turned out, he never came back and I was later to join up with him myself in the Desert Air Force. Roger Forshaw, who arrived from Training Command to take over 603, was still lacking operational experience, so I had to lead the Squadron in Johnny's absence.

The added responsibilities and the strain of operations throughout the year had left their mark on me and I found that I easily became tired. I didn't give it much thought at first, but I did notice that any violent steep turns of extra g made me cough and sometimes in the morning I was violently sick. I put this down to nervous tension and said nothing about it to the Squadron Medical Officer because I was worried about being taken off operations and sent to some training job. However, Harry Broadhurst must have noticed signs of my slowing up, because he sent for me one day and asked whether I would like to go to Hawker's for a period under Philip Lucas on production testing. He went on to say that he had been in touch with Philip Lucas, who was prepared to have me if I wanted the job. I didn't want to leave, but the winter was setting in, and I thought that six or nine month's test-flying Hurricanes would be fun, so I agreed.

A few days later I flew over to Langley and saw Philip Lucas. He gave me a grand lunch and showed me round the works. I was very excited at seeing Hawker's new aeroplane, the Typhoon, taking shape. From all accounts it was going to be faster and more heavily armed than anything the Germans had or were contemplating. I also met Sir Sydney Camm, Hawker's Chief Designer, who not only designed the Hurricane and the Typhoon but was, along with R.J. Mitchell and Joe Smith of Supermarines, one of the pioneers of British aviation. If it had not been for such men as Camm and Mitchell the outcome of the war might have been very different. No praise is too high for them and their chief test pilots, Philip Lucas and Jeffrey Quill. Their Spitfires and Hurricanes have assured them of an honoured place in history.

I was accepted for the job, and told to report as soon as possible. I was to work directly under Bill Humble in charge of production testing, and report back to him after the necessary formalities were completed. Then I ran into a snag.

Harry Broadhurst was sent on a 'goodwill' tour of the United States, where he was to give lectures in order to impress the Americans with the determination of our war effort. Eric Stapleton, who assumed command of Hornchurch in his absence, agreed to my going to Hawker's but insisted that I should not go until Roger Forshaw became operational. Since I was determined to get Roger fully operational as quickly as possible I made him fly first as my number two, and then as a flight leader. He was quick on the uptake and, being a natural pilot, learned easily and readily. But he wasn't there yet – so I waited and got on with the job.

We had two particularly good low-level operations escorting Hurricane bombers led by Denys Gillam on targets at Fécamp and Le Touquet aerodrome. In the first mission we shot up a sailing barge heavily armed with flak, and sank it; in the second we gunned enemy troops and AA batteries on Le Touquet golf course and airfield. This particular operation had an extraordinary sequel a year or two after the war was over. The Germans were known to have a Headquarters and Officers' Mess in P.G. Wodehouse's villa by the golf course. The Hurricane bombers duly attacked the villa marked as the target and we all straffed the area. The target was well and truly hit and destroyed. Then we moved on to the airfield and shot it up. When Le Touquet golf course was in use again after the war, I played in a match there with a retired Brigadier from Thompson's Falls in Kenya, while we were both on holiday. As we passed the wrecked villa, the Brigadier said: 'That used to be my place before the war, but the RAF knocked it down.' I replied that he must be wrong as it was supposed to belong to Wodehouse. 'No,' he replied, 'the one next door is the one belonging to Wodehouse – your chaps blasted mine – the wrong one. Anyway, how do you know the details?' My face went red as I replied: 'I'm sorry to say my Squadron escorted the Hurri-bombers when we knocked it flat. I would like to apologise if some of my cannon-shells broke any of your windows.' I had little difficulty in winning the match after that.

Returning from a convoy patrol I blacked out after landing at Fairlop, a new Hornchurch Satellite airfield. The Squadron doctor put me to bed and the next day, 21 November, I was carted off to Rush Green Hospital at Romford. Here I was put under the care of two civilian doctors, Tommy Thompson and Ian Duncan. I don't remember a great deal about the first few days I was there, but eventually I was informed I had double pneumonia; in fact it was so bad, I had not been expected to live.

The doctors filled me with new drugs – one was called M and B – which had a peculiar effect. It made me want to vomit at the sight of food and sometimes I imagined seeing spiders crawling up the wall in formation. My sanity was saved by the nurses, one in particular from Ireland, quite beautiful, with all the charm of her race.

Depression stalked me for a couple of weeks which was not helped by the news that 603 Squadron, during an offensive operation over France, had lost eight out of twelve pilots in a disastrous engagement with Me 109s and FW 190s. It was withdrawn from front-line service and sent to Dyce, near Aberdeen, to regroup.

Soon after arriving Roger Forshaw was scrambled to intercept a Ju 88 off the Aberdeenshire coast and never returned from the mission. I struggled with my emotions for I felt I should have been with the Squadron and not lying flat on my back in bed.

David Douglas-Hamilton, brother of the Duke of Hamilton, also in the RAF, assumed command and soon afterwards the Squadron left by sea to strengthen the air defence of Malta.

One bright spark penetrated the gloom. I heard on my bedside radio that, following the Japanese attack on Pearl Harbor, the Americans had entered the war. With their great resources there was no doubt left now regarding the final outcome, only the time it would take.

After being discharged from hospital in early January 1942 followed by two weeks' sick-leave, the Hornchurch doctors examined and passed me fit for duty, but I still had to be seen by the famous chest specialist Sir John Conybere at the RAF Hospital, Halton. This turned out to be a pleasant experience and after a few days of examination tests, and helping the great man in his garden, I reported back to Hornchurch. First I was told that, due to the time factor, I had lost the Hawker job, then that I was to go to Southend as Station Adjutant. It was a shattering thought, but at least I had the consolation of knowing I was to stay in the Hornchurch Sector.

I had a surprise visit one morning from George Barclay. George joined 611 as a flight commander following the loss of Eric Lock. We became firm friends; however, after I left to join 603 Squadron, George was shot down over France during a fighter sweep. I was particularly upset about the way it happened and not knowing if he had survived. It was, therefore, with a tremendous feeling of joy that I greeted him. Looking lean and sun-tanned, he told me the story of his escape.

Having survived a bad crash-landing, he evaded immediate capture by German troops already out looking for him through the help of some French patriots and finally found shelter in the house of a schoolmaster named Salingue and his wife. He was given clothes and a new identity then passed along the 'life-line' of the French Resistance through occupied France, Spain and finally to Gibraltar before flying back to England. It had been a hazardous experience, specially getting over and through the Spanish frontier, which could have led to disaster but for the bravery and loyalty of his helpers.

I spent some of my convalescent leave with George and his parents in Norfolk but I learned some weeks later that he had been posted to a Hurricane squadron in the Western Desert where he was killed in action during the summer of 1942. After all he had been through, there seemed no justice left, only a scar to remember a brave friend and resourceful fighter.

Southend was commanded by Cyril Gadney, the famous rugger referee. I think he was a bit nervous of having such an inexperienced character in a key position, so he appointed a warrant officer to act as assistant adjutant and from that moment I never looked back. I took time off to fly with 411 (RCAF) Squadron and in fact managed to get posted to them as a flight commander for a few weeks.

On 20 March 11 Group informed me I had been promoted to command 64 Squadron who were already based at Southend. I was very happy to find that Clive Mellersh (Intelligence Officer) had transferred from 611 to 64. 611 had changed places with 64 at Drem at the end of November just after I had gone into hospital. Now it was like old times again. During the months that followed, packed with hard, intense operational flying, I came to understand and appreciate the tremendous worth of Clive Mellersh as a friend and adviser. After all these years I cannot think about 64 Squadron without remembering Clive. Older than the rest of us, he was a lawyer by profession and an excellent games player. His administrative ability and wise counsel were invaluable in the running of the Squadron.

Peter Powell had been appointed Wing Leader while I was in hospital. He was very experienced, having been a flight commander in 111 Squadron under Harry Broadhurst. Full of charm, he had a forthright and attractive manner in dealing with the pilots.

64 had a strongly international flavour. Leon Prevot, a Belgian, was 'A' Flight commander and Don Kingaby commanded 'B' Flight. Don had made a great name for himself in 92 Squadron at Biggin Hill. He already had well over twenty victories to his credit and was something of an expert in fighting Me 109s. At one time we had no less than twelve different nationalities in the Squadron, including an American.

On taking over 64 Squadron, one of the first things I impressed on my pilots was that you did not 'strap yourself in', you 'buckled the Spitfire on', like girding on armour in days of old. I knew it was essential: the Spitfire became an integral part and an extension of one's own sensitivity.

Broady at this stage was attached to 11 Group for a month as Senior Air Staff Officer. The day after he left dawned clear and was very warm. We spent the morning on convoy patrols, then around mid-afternoon we were called to the briefing room and informed we were to carry out a sweep in the Pas de Calais area in support of other operations. The Biggin Hill Wing was to be above us, with the Kenley Wing following on 'mopping up' operations.

We crossed the French coast at 10,000 ft at Gravelines, with 313 (Czech) Squadron, also based at Hornchurch, immediately above us. This squadron was commanded by Jan Mrazek, a likeable Czech officer of considerable renown.

Almost immediately we were set upon by some fifty enemy fighters, most of them FW 190s. I had heard some hair-raising tales about them, but had reserved my judgement. In no time flat I came to the conclusion that everything I had heard was true; but I had never lost confidence in the Spitfire as a fighting lady so, as I swung in a tight circle after an FW 190 that was obviously prepared to mix it, I was sure I had him cold. In three-quarters of a turn I was on his tail – two two-second bursts from my cannons and machine-guns and the FW 190 blew up at the wing root, rolled over and dived straight into the sea. We went down protecting each other with defensive circles as more FW 190s attacked us, but gradually we withdrew in good order at low level to the English coast, then back to Hornchurch. It had been an eye-opener, but a successful mission, for the total bag was two destroyed, three probables and a damaged for the loss of one of my pilots. He had stayed to mix it too long but Donnet shot down the FW 190 responsible.

The boys needed this sort of action to raise their morale which it did and, as a Squadron, we never looked back. We became a fighting team completely dependent on one another, developing tactics that upset and frustrated the FW 190s each time we met them.

In the meantime the Kenley Wing were set upon by a further large enemy formation off the coast and Victor Beamish, Harry Broadhurst's great friend, was shot down. His section got mixed up in a dog-fight during which he got an FW 190, sending it spinning into the sea. Immediately afterwards, the section were attacked by more FW 190s and at some time in this attack he was lost.

This was a great blow to Fighter Command, as Victor Beamish's courage, fighting skill and leadership were an inspiration. Kenley destroyed ten enemy aircraft for the loss of four themselves on that fateful day, but it had been a sad experience.

Soon after, we lost two of our Belgian pilots, Divoy, who collided with a Spitfire from another Wing, and Conard, shot down by an FW 190. Divoy was later reported a prisoner, but we never heard what happened to Conard. They were both excellent pilots and Michel Donnet was much upset by the losses. He was a particular friend of Divoy, as they had been involved together a few months before in a daring and ingenious escape to England from occupied Belgium. The story is worth telling in full.

Donnet and Divoy learned there was a reasonably serviceable Belgian SV4b training aircraft in a hangar at one of the German occupied airfields outside Brussels and, working a secret way into it under cover of darkness, they made repairs to the bi-plane. The preparations were carried out over an appreciable length of time and involved much engineering skill and improvisation. The Germans, to prevent any chance of having machines stolen, had rendered them unserviceable by removing major parts. Donnet and Divoy replaced the missing parts by making a number themselves. The most difficult part of the whole affair was to find, or manufacture, efficient blind-flying instruments; for the escape to succeed, they would have to fly off at night, and choose a particularly dark one at that: good instruments were therefore essential.

Their nightly activities, carried out under the noses of the German guards, went undetected and finally after months of patient, exacting work, their aircraft was ready. To undertake the escape meant taking their lives in their hands. Added to this was the uncertainty whether the parts they had made and their other improvisations would work. The aircraft had not been started for sixteen months. They had, of course, checked everything possible but much had to be taken on trust. Finally they were ready to go. They would have to take off immediately into darkness before the engine noise could be detected, or suffer total destruction on the ground from enemy rifle and machine-gun fire. How, they wondered, would a stone-cold engine react to this treatment? They decided to wait for one of Bomber Command's heavy night raids to pass overhead before starting the engine, so that in the confusion they might escape more easily.

They got sufficient petrol for their journey with the complicity of black marketeers who bought it from the Germans themselves. The petrol was carried in cans on the back of bicycles. The same methods were used to get sufficient engine oil.

At last all was ready. Impatiently they waited for darkness to fall. Then, saying good-bye to their families, they set off for the airfield. Timing and slickness were essential to success, and luck had a major say in the whole operation. On reaching the hangar they found that the German guards had changed the locks on the doors. They had to set to and make new keys. The delay meant waiting for another British air-raid to develop and conceal their activity. Once more they were ready, but this time, having wheeled out the biplane, they found on turning the engine over by hand that the petrol leaked all over the place. The petrol pipes and union joints did not fit and no petrol was getting to the carburettor. More adjustments were necessary and more petrol had to be stolen. With infinite patience they sorted out the technical difficulties and were able at last to wheel out the aircraft on to the rough grass. They had predetermined the best take-off run and hoped there would be no unforeseen obstacles in the way. Once the engine started they would have to take off at once, so they eased it patiently beforehand by turning the airscrew over many times with the spark and fuel switched off.

At last they wished each other luck: a friend, Mishe Jansen, swung the propeller – once, twice and at the third attempt the engine burst into life. With Divoy already seated in the rear cockpit, Michel opened the throttle – the aircraft moved forward – more revs – the engine coughed and spluttered, picked up, and hummed steadily – gathering speed they bumped over the rough surface – somewhere over to their left were the Germans hidden in the darkness. Tracers poured in their direction, from an anti-aircraft gun on a platform dead in line with their take-off path – a final bump and they were airborne. The cool night air tugged at their skin beckoning them onwards.

Michel, flying on the improvised instruments, kept the aircraft low and swung the nose in a right-handed arc dodging the clutching fingers of searchlights. The Germans, confused and bewildered, were not reacting properly. In a few moments they left the airfield behind, climbing for the coast and freedom. Their ordeal, however, was not yet over: more searchlights and flak met them on the way, but their slow speed helped them, and finally they escaped across the coast. The sudden glint of water reflecting the light from a coastal searchlight told them all they needed to know. They were on their way to fortress Britain to join their brothers-in-arms.

Suddenly, at 9,500 ft the engine cut out completely. They had no idea at the time why it had cut, but later they realised that the poor-quality petrol had frozen. They glided towards the open sea, not knowing what else to do. They had no safety equipment of any kind. If the engine failed to start again it would almost certainly mean a watery grave. They began to accept the situation and prepare themselves for a crash-landing in the sea, when suddenly the engine picked up; hardly believing their luck, they climbed to 2,500 ft and crossed the 150 miles of sea to the English coast. They had deliberately taken a northerly course after leaving Belgium, then swung on to a westerly one. Flying by the seat of their pants, they had no accurate idea where they were. All they were concerned with was getting to England – anywhere – and landing. Around dawn they picked out a suitable field in the heart of Essex, and much to the surprise of the local farm workers, two tired, cold but happy Belgian officers floated out of space into their midst. The local police arrived as if by magic, pencils at the ready, and carted Donnet and Divoy off to the local police station.

It was a great achievement, full of initiative, courage and dash. Soon after taking over 64 Squadron I was able to fly their aeroplane. It was superb. The work these two had put into it had to be seen to be believed.

The loss of Conard brought in its wake a singular problem for it meant that his lovely blue roan spaniel Vicky needed a new master. He was still very young, about five months old, so I decided to adopt him myself. He proved a fine little chap with bags of character and as we were already on the friendliest of terms I hoped he would not miss his old master too much; anyway, I made a big fuss of him and he soon settled down with me. It was extraordinary how he got to know the sound of my Spitfire's engine, even with other aircraft in the circuit. Squadron pilots told how he would listen intently lying in a chair at dispersal, then rush out only when he recognised the sound of my engine and trot up to my aircraft's parking revetment to await my arrival. He had a special chair in my room on which he slept wrapped in a sheepskin coat. In the morning he would watch me dress, never moving till I had buttoned my tunic and opened the door then he would follow me out into the Mess garden for a stroll no matter what hour of the day or night. I always gave him his food but this had its snags, as I discovered, because if I got stuck somewhere for the night or stayed out late without him, he would not take his food from anyone else. Leaving him to be looked after till my return from overseas in 1943, he died from a kidney infection about three months after my departure. There have been five spaniels in my life but Vicky was the last. Other breeds of dogs yes, but never another spaniel.

Each day now we had engagements with FW 190s but they were always ready for us and extremely difficult to engage. Many dog-fights broke out, and though I fired my guns on numerous occasions I had no luck at all. Escorting Bostons bombing Bruges one afternoon, I managed to get a quarter head-on attack on an FW 190. I had the satisfaction of seeing strikes on his tail-section, and a large piece fell off. This might have been part of the tail-plane as the 190 spun viciously and seemed out of control.

Our tactics consisted of flying in a loose 'finger four' squad-ron formation almost line abreast, keeping up a high cruising speed with the sections slightly stepped. Depending on the sun, the stepping and formation pattern would be changed to suit the conditions. If my reader looks at his right hand with the fingers outstretched he will see what I mean. If the sun was, say, on the port beam or quarter, the section looked like fingers with the palm of the hand upwards and the leading and starboard sections like the back of the hand. The starboard section was stepped up, and the port stepped down slightly. In this way four pairs of eyes were continually watching an arc round the sun, and a total of six pairs of eyes was able to cover the sky above, behind and below. It was impossible to suffer a blind spot provided everyone kept well-disciplined station. Another advantage was that in the event of a surprise attack we could turn and manoeuvre rapidly either way without the risk of colliding with each other, and were also able to slip into line astern without juggling. We cut out weaving and maintained a high cruising speed. This enabled us to accelerate quickly to maximum speed for attacks on any enemy formations sighted below, or zoom climb into any attack from above.

The real worth of these ideas lay in the fact that we took much pleasure in luring Germans into attacks with us. Having sighted them, we would hold our positions steady waiting for them to get into range. The enemy fighters would think we hadn't seen them and commit themselves to an attack; then, just as they were about to open fire, I would give the order to break into the attack; the top section, usually led by Don Kingaby, would break in the opposite direction climbing hard. To do any good the Germans would be forced to stay and turn with us, which suited us as our Spitfires could out-turn them. In the meantime Don Kingaby and his merry men would get above and behind the Germans, taking them by surprise and swooping down like eagles on a chicken-run. We had a number of successes using these tactics.

Jeffrey Quill invited me one day to join Jamie Rankin, the renowned Wing Leader at Biggin Hill and a New Zealand Flight Lieutenant for a visit to the Supermarine Works to talk to the factory workers about our experiences in fighting the Germans in our Spitfires. It was a great idea and we all thoroughly enjoyed ourselves. We stayed at the Polygon Hotel in Southampton as Supermarine's guests and were handsomely entertained by Jeffrey and George Pickering, a former test pilot.

We set off each morning to visit the main works and various 'shadow factories' talking to the workforce both collectively and individually. I was most impressed by the great interest the men and women took in our flying experiences and many varied questions were asked and answered. The visit lasted about four or five days and soon after we returned to our respective home bases, I learned that the New Zealand officer had been killed in action the day following the visit. The news was broken to the factory workers by Jeffrey and to their enduring credit, they collected a large sum of money for a suitable memorial.

We moved back to Hornchurch at the end of April, and soon afterwards I was told that 64 Squadron was to be the first squadron to be equipped with the new Spitfire Mk IX aircraft. I had already flown the first one built, when Jeffrey Quill brought it over to Hornchurch for Broady to fly, and afterwards I was allowed to take it up. It had been an exhilarating experience and full of interest. It was fitted with the Merlin 61 engine, a new Rolls-Royce development for high-altitude performance. It could climb at 4,000 ft/min, fantastic for those days, and had a top speed of over 400 mph. The armament remained the same: two 20-mm cannons and four .303 Brownings, but the aircraft could now reach a height of 43,000 ft. This was achieved by fitting a two-stage, two-speed supercharger into the 1600 hp engine, giving the aircraft a complete range of power from ground-level to over 40,000 ft. Negative g carburettors – which did not cut out when the stick was pushed forward with any force – were also a feature.

The increased size of the engine involved a lengthening of the fuselage and the introduction of an additional radiator mounted under the port wing to house the intercooler as well as the oil cooler. Individual ejector exhausts were fitted and a four-blade Rotol constant-speed airscrew was designed to absorb the extra power developed by the engine at high altitudes. The curvature of the cockpit hood was also increased slightly.

Harry Broadhurst, of course, was tickled at the prospect of Hornchurch getting the new Mk IXs. The day Jeffrey Quill brought the prototype over, Broady lost no time in flying it.

It so happened that a Wing target support mission was due to take off just as Broady was getting ready to climb into the cockpit. He turned to Jeffrey and said: 'Why don't you go off in my car to the operations room and watch the progress of the Wing there? You'll hear all the R/T and maybe hear the boys clobbering some Germans.'

Jeffrey did what he was told, and by the time he had got to the Sector Operations Room, which was some distance away in Romford, the Wing was already streaking across the Channel at 25,000 ft heading for Lille.

Ronnie Adam, the duty controller, welcomed Jeffrey and said: 'You've struck it lucky – there's bags of activity in the target area – we should be making contact with enemy formations any minute now.' They watched the progress of the operations for some time in silence.

Suddenly Ronnie Adam inquired of his subordinate controller: 'What's that single plot I see on the table approaching the target area?'

'We don't know – it's flagged as an unidentified – must be a hostile I think, as it's been plotted steadily at 35,000 ft plus – we've nothing up that high.'

Jeffrey winced, then looked at Ronnie Adam: 'I hate to tell you this, but I believe that plot is your Station Commander, flying a highly secret, unique prototype Spitfire, and I hope to God nothing happens to him.'

By the time they looked at the plot again the flag formation showed it at 40,000 ft plus. They watched as the plots of the Wing and the single converged. Combats had broken out in the area and they listened rather apprehensively to the chatter coming through the loudspeaker.

Ronnie Adam turned to Jeffrey: 'Are the guns loaded in that new aircraft?'

'No – I'm not particularly worried about that – I don't think anything can get up to him or catch him. I am worried, however, about the oxygen state – I hope to goodness Broady was topped up before he took off!'

Through the loudspeaker a pilot's voice came through loud and clear: 'Look at that aircraft up there – he must be as high as heaven.'

'That's no aircraft,' another voice chipped in. 'It's a bleedin' angel.'

Eventually the plots started moving back towards the French coast, then in small clusters streamed back across the Channel.

By the time Jeffrey Quill got back to Hornchurch the Wing was coming in to land in groups of twos and fours. One of the last to land was Broady in the precious Mk IX. Climbing out he grinned at Jeffrey: 'It's a magnificent aeroplane – get us as many as you can, as quickly as possible. By the way, you might have told me the guns weren't loaded.'

Jeffrey wiped his brow and held his peace.

We didn't get them as quickly as all that, of course; indeed many months were to pass before a substantial number of squadrons in Fighter Command were equipped with them, but by the time Spitfire Mk IXs were eventually phased out of service, over 5,000 had been built. They lived up to our highest expectations – they were thoroughbreds in every way.

In the meantime, we continued operations in our Mk Vs using the new aircraft for training pilots in handling and building up experience. I was determined not to be rushed into operating our new aircraft against the Germans in penny packets. I was convinced that the only proper way was to build up to squadron strength, then go over to France and surprise the FW 190s with a sizeable force.

A fairly large proportion of our strikes in the Mk Vs were on flak-busting in support of the Hurri-bombers of 615 Squadron, led by Denys Gillam. Gillam was an incredible character, full of guts and razor sharp in his reactions. On one occasion he flew over to Hornchurch for a Mess party, staying up with the rest of us till the bitter end, and was off back to Manston at dawn. We rendezvoused with his squadron on a shipping strike immediately after, and by ten o'clock he was in the sea having been shot down by flak. He was picked up none the worse, taken back to Dover, and was leading his squadron again the same afternoon on a similar mission.

A typical operation of this type was against a merchant supply ship escorted by four flak ships that looked rather like small tugs. 'Jim Crow' (91 Recce Squadron) had reported the position of the enemy ship soon after dawn. We flew down to Manston, and after briefing took off with the Hurri-bombers, 122 Squadron acting as escort. I had decided, for this operation, to put a section of three aircraft on each flak ship to enable the Hurri-bombers to have a clearer run into the main target. I briefed the other section leaders to carry out simultaneous attacks, breaking outwards on completion. The target lay a few miles east of Dunkirk, and we flew in line-abreast formation at sea level and to one side of the fighter-bombers. At a signal from me, on approaching the target, we opened up to full power and leaving the Hurricanes behind, converged on the flak ships. They were taken by complete surprise and were only able to get off a few rounds at us before we pounced on them. All four flak ships were sunk and the Hurri-bombers, with nothing to deter them, hit the supply ship with all their bombs, causing it to explode and sink. By the time we had regrouped and were ready to leave there was little left to be seen on the surface of the sea. A few days later I was delighted to receive from the AOC the following telegram: 'Have seen 64 Squadron films of recent shipping attack. Many congratulations on a magnificent attack. Leigh-Mallory.'

An Intelligence report came up one day that Goering was visiting front-line units in an armoured train, parked at a place called Sesqueux. We took off with 313 (Czech) Squadron acting as close escort to Gillam's Hurricanes and I was to take çare of any flak batteries that bothered us.

We crossed the French coast near Dieppe at 200 ft, over the Euvermeu – Eu railway line, turned left past Fesnoy till we hit the Aumale–Eu line short of Blangy, then left again and flew to Gamaches. Here the fun started. Though we searched the whole area we didn't find anything that looked like an armoured train. However, at Gamaches railway station we found a goods train unloading. We attacked it, setting fire to the storage bays. We continued on our way silencing a medium flak battery which had become troublesome and attacked an alcohol factory, setting fire to it. On the outskirts of Le Treport we ran smack into a train steaming along the Eu line and in the first attack blew up the engine and two goods wagons probably carrying fuel. We rounded off the sport by rubbing out a number of German officers (clearly seen) while they were gardening at the back of a big house on the cliff near Le Treport. During the attack one of my pilots called me: 'Vaxine leader you have squashed their tomatoes in more ways than one.' We called it a day and flew home. Unfortunately, Goering must have got away with it if he had been there, which I doubt.

A couple of days later we again flew off soon after dawn to act as anti-flak escort to the Hurri-bombers on a target in the Forêt d'Eu. Unfortunately, the fighter-bombers got off course and crossed in at Le Crotoy on the Somme Estuary. Flying at zero feet over the sand dunes, to one side of the Hurricanes, I was startled to see dead ahead on a collision course twelve FW 190s. These were obviously aircraft from Abbeville, one of the largest of the German forward bases. There was no time to take any evasive action, let alone gain a tactical advantage, so we streamed straight through them. How we missed hitting each other I will never know. Snapping my wits together I managed to aim and fire a quick burst into a large radial engine dead ahead and then heaved the stick into my stomach, shut my eyes, and waited for the crunch. The next moment all hell was let loose as everyone fired at everybody else; not to be outdone the German flak posts among the sand dunes, who had kept very quiet till then, started blazing away for all they were worth. It seemed they didn't care whom they hit so long as they got results. Circling, climbing, diving, taking snap shots whenever a target presented itself, we got across the coast and out to sea. The end result was less than satisfactory as we could only claim three damaged.

After a quick breakfast we were off again on a sweep taking in Cap Gris Nez, St Omer and Le Touquet, with the Debden

Wing below and North Weald above. At 18,000 ft between Berck and Le Touquet we were heavily engaged by more than fifty FW 190s. Peter Powell was leading the Squadron, and in the dog-fight that followed he was hit and wounded in the neck and head. All we got out of this were a couple of German planes damaged. I joined Peter with my section and led the way back to Hornchurch. I could see he was in distress and was not sure where he was. His canopy had gone and a large hole behind the cockpit area stared at me bleakly. His wireless was smashed and the rudder tattered and torn.

We landed safely and discovered that one of the cannon-shells had burst just behind his head, spraying splinters into his neck and fracturing the base of his skull. He was put into hospital and, when he was fit again, sent on a rest. In the circumstances he was very lucky but although Peter made a full recovery he did not come back to Hornchurch. For the next three weeks I led the Wing until Paddy Finucane was posted from Biggin Hill to take over as Wing Leader.

About a fortnight before these events, Harry Broadhurst was assigned to Headquarters 11 Group as Chief of the Operational Planning Staff. Before he left Hornchurch, Leigh-Mallory had ordered him to fly less, pointing out that leading the Hornchurch Wing was the Wing Leader's job. He never accepted the idea, though he was bound to respect the AOC's wishes and cut down on his operational missions but he continued to fly with the Squadrons and was therefore able to evaluate tactics, training and operations. He maintained this attitude and principle throughout the war by constantly visiting his Wings even when he later became AOC of Desert Air Force. Harry Broadhurst did not understand the meaning of fear and the stickier the situation the better he liked it. We missed his leadership, his sparkling sense of fun and his companionship; above all, he was always one of us.

Broady's move to 11 Group paid off in an unexpected way. During his lecture tour of the USA towards the end of 1941, he met and became friendly with three USAAF generals – Spaatz, Eaker and Hunter. Now, here they were in England in command respectively of 8th Air Force, 8th Bomber Command and 8th Fighter Command. Later on, I learned that after Broady arrived to take up his new appointment, he had been able to use his friendship with the generals and persuade both Spaatz and Eaker to allow their Bomber Groups (which were still training) to extend their training exercises over France and practise their bombing technique under operational conditions before attempting their primary role over Germany and elsewhere. Fighter Command, he told them, would escort the Flying Fortresses safely. That was how the first Fortress attack on Europe took shape. Not only did Broady personally brief the American bomber crews that took part but he also had a day off from 11 Group to fly with the Hornchurch Wing in a Spitfire Mk IX, which I lent him for the occasion. This operation was to prove of great significance. It emphasised that really large heavy bomber raids could be escorted in daylight with little or no loss, so long as the bombers remained within the range of the fighters. The problem, however, was to extend the range of both RAF and USAAF fighters. Priority, therefore, was soon given for the mass-production of lightweight aerodynamic jettisonable fuel-tanks which, as we know, extended the mass daylight-bombing capability of the Fortresses (with Fighter cover all the way) to the very heart of Germany.

CHAPTER NINE

Dorniers over Dieppe

George Lott took over Hornchurch and at once made an impression on us. He had commanded 43 Squadron, flying Hurricanes during the débâcle in France, Dunkirk, and the period preceding the Battle of Britain. During one of the missions he lost an eye while leading his squadron against enemy bombers over France. A cannon-shell burst in the cockpit close to his head and pieces pierced the eye and wounded him in the face. Nothing daunted, he flew his aircraft back to Tangmere with great skill and courage. He eventually got a glass eye fitted and came back to flying. It could not have been easy taking over Hornchurch from Harry Broadhurst; but his personality, humour, and keen sense of duty soon won us all over. We Squadron Commanders, in particular, owed much to him for his expert advice and I came to rely a great deal on him during the early operations with our Mk IXs.

Both before and during the conversion of my squadron to Spitfire Mk IXs, Jeffrey Quill helped enormously with technical advice and on the aircraft's flying characteristics, also flying with us on some of the early operations. Ronnie Harker, Rolls-Royce's chief test pilot, became a frequent visitor also. This proved a great help to 'Johnny' Johns, my Engineer Officer, in his efforts to get the ground-crews familiar with the new Merlin 61 engines. With an average of twenty-four Spitfires on strength during the period, it was no easy task to maintain a maximum serviceability state to meet operational and conversion training commitments.

We had one good day with our Spitfire Vs against the FW 190s over Hazebrouck at the end of June, when I managed to get a sitting duck; then at midnight on 8/9 July, 64 Squadron was released from operations to complete re-equipment with the Mk IXs and carry out a gunnery practice camp. We flew hard for the rest of the month practising formations, tactics and camera-gun dog-fights.

While we were away Paddy Finucane, leading the Wing, set off with 31, 122 and 154 Squadrons on a low-level operation against a German hutted camp at Etaples. I don't know what success they had, but they met intense medium and light AA fire and lost three pilots. Apparently, from the account I heard afterwards, Paddy was hit in the engine and radiator, was told by his formation he was smoking and advised to get out. He managed to climb to about 1,500 ft, thus giving himself enough height to bale out. He was out to sea eight miles off Le Touquet by this time and had a good chance of being picked up by our Air-Sea Rescue organisation who were past masters at snatching our pilots from under German noses. Strangely, he called on the R/T to say he was going to ditch his aircraft. Under the circumstances this was taking a great risk, as the Spitfire was not an easy aircraft to put down on water and tended to turn over on contact with the sea. This made it likely that the pilot would be trapped in an inverted position sinking, and unable to free himself. This is what happened to Paddy. He hit the water hard, ploughed in on his nose and turned turtle. It was a waste of a skilled and courageous pilot. I didn't get to know him too well during the three or four weeks he was at Hornchurch. All the publicity he had been given before he came to us made him aloof and retiring. I think he felt we were suspicious of him, and tended for that reason to keep to himself. I always found him modest and particularly anxious to avoid publicity.

We went off to Martlesham for a week's intensive air firing confident we would do well. Being the first squadron of Spitfire IXs we attracted attention wherever we went and Martlesham was no exception. We had a great many visitors including some Canadians all trying to get flying out of us. I had politely but firmly to turn them down, making myself rather unpopular with the more senior ones in the process. But I had a programme to stick to and a very short time in which to complete it.

While there I tried out one of the new gyro gunsights in my aircraft. It had not yet been fully developed and was difficult to sight, as you had to get your eye close to a small aperture and squint through it. Another snag was that you had to hold the aircraft steady in a turn without any sudden manoeuvre for three or four seconds to give the gyro time to settle. I came to the conclusion that this would be impossible under combat conditions, and in any case to keep steady for three or four seconds in hostile airspace would be signing one's own death warrant. However, several pilots gave it a trial with varying success. One of my firing attempts on the drogue ended by my shooting it off the towing cable about a yard behind the towing Lysander, much to the surprise and discomfort of the crew, who promptly took violent evasive action, and returned to base immediately. On landing they told me they would never tow for me again if I used my new-fangled sight. When fully developed the Ferranti gyro gunsight proved a superb aid to gunnery and the high percentage of casualties inflicted on the enemy in aerial combat during the Normandy battles were due largely to this excellent sight. It also proved very successful as a sight for firing rockets. It would have been invaluable during the earlier years of the war.

Towards the end of the conversion training programme, we practised squadron high-altitude formation-flying. One of the greatest thrills was having twelve Spitfire Mk IXs in battle formation at 43,000 ft in the knowledge that no German fighter could touch us. Though it proved unnecessary to fly in squadron formation at that altitude during operations, there was great satisfaction in recognising, however, that our aeroplanes could out-climb anything the enemy could send to intercept us. In fact the limiting factor rested in the flying equipment available to do the job because existing oxygen and ventilation systems could no longer be considered entirely efficient to meet the exacting conditions. Without pressurisation at such great altitudes, the physical discomfort from fatigue and pain from 'bends' limited the flight-time we could endure to barely five minutes or so.

We returned to Hornchurch well satisfied with our gunnery results and thoroughly familiar with the flying and operating capabilities of the new Spitfires. But I was cheated of the initial success I was confidently expecting.

We took off on a 'Circus' operation, acting as high-escort

Squadron at 25,000 ft to bombers attacking Abbeville. We crossed the French coast at Le Touquet on the way home and having seen the beehive safely on its way, I turned the Squadron back into France climbing quickly to 30,000 ft. We swept round behind Le Touquet as far as Hesdin, then recrossed at Berck and up the coast to Boulogne. As I expected, we got behind and above the FW 190s that had been picking at the stragglers returning to England, and caught nine just off Boulogne in a loose line-abreast formation. It was a perfect jump with the Germans about 8,000 ft below us. The Squadron opened out and down we went. The Germans failed to see us and I was just about to open fire on the leading FW 190 from slightly above dead astern, when Nigel Seely, who heard my order to attack as he was controlling in the operations room, called: 'Vaxine leader, be careful: your friends are in the area.'

This was to warn me that the Typhoons (which had lately come into operational service) were operating in the Channel, and at a distance looked like FW 190s. Though I had already satisfied myself that we were attacking FW 190s and not Typhoons, on hearing Nigel's message I hesitated for those vital couple of seconds – looked up – then back through my sight, and fired. I was closing on the enemy very fast and didn't have time to steady my aircraft. I missed completely. The 190 looked as big as a house in my windscreen but I missed just the same, and it was too late to do anything about it. I zoom climbed away, the rest of the Squadron following me, for they, too, had heard the R/T message and reacted as I did. All except Don Kingaby. That young tiger bored into the 190 he'd picked for himself and shot it down in flames. He and his number two followed it down and watched it crash into the outskirts of Boulogne. We should, of course, have nailed all nine of them, but, as it was, they scattered like a flock of geese in all directions, and we messed up a golden opportunity. We were to redeem ourselves in the afternoon when we went off again as top Squadron on an operation to St Omer. About half-way between the coast and St Omer we caught up with fifteen FW 190s 5,000 ft below us. I led the Squadron down again in much the same way as in the morning show, and got a 190 from slightly above and dead astern. No doubt this time; he burst into flames, spiralling down in a cloud of smoke. Stewart and Michel Donnet also destroyed one apiece, while two others got probables. Don Findlay, who was doing a staff job at Group at the time, in the Engineering branch, came on the trip with us, and claimed a damaged 190. We got separated as a result of the engagement so Arne Austeen, my number two, a Norwegian, and I flew home together on our own. A few miles off Calais, we found an FW 190 attacking a Spitfire, and since we had plenty of height went after him. We caught him easily, each attacking in turn and sending the enemy into the sea in flames.

The total bag for the day now didn't look too bad, but it would have been outstanding if we had not messed up the morning's affair. The rest of the Wing, however, had not done at all well, having lost eight pilots including Leon Prevot, who had been promoted to command 122 Squadron. We were all delighted when Prevot returned less than two months later, having escaped through France and Spain none the worse for his ordeal. Apparently he even found time to spend three weeks with his family in Brussels on unorthodox home leave.

Daylight operations over the Channel were now stepped up in scale by the arrival of the US 8th Air Force with Flying Fortress bombers, who were preparing to start the systematic bombing of Europe in daylight. The Spitfire IXs were to be used to cover the Fortresses on raids into France within fighter range, until they had gained some experience of daylight operations. I attended several conferences at 11 Group to talk over tactics and formations with the American officers concerned. I was much impressed by the direct approach of the Americans: at last we were going to get the weight behind our bomber attacks which we desperately needed and which had been lacking in the past. These chaps really meant business and one could not help being a bit overawed by the scale of effort that they offered us on a plate, with a twinkle in their eyes and chewing long beefy-looking cigars. They talked a new language without mincing their words or expecting us to do so. The 'jaab' on hand was all they were interested in and all they required from us were the facts. They learned quickly and improved upon what they learned from us. Over the next two and a half years they were to range the skies of Europe with a bombing technique that was new in the history of air warfare. They were to combine with RAF Bomber Command into a team that virtually brought Germany to her knees industrially, even before the invasion of Europe became an established fact.

Their Fighter Command, likewise, would not only share the burden of the fighter offensive with us, but extended the horizon of fighter operations by reaching out with long-range escorts, using Mustangs, Lightnings and Thunderbolts to cover both our bombers and theirs as they smashed at the very heart of Germany. We were to get to know their leaders; Generals Spaatz and Eaker, Anderson and Hunter. 'Monk' Hunter commanded their fighters, working closely with our own Fighter Command. Outstanding among his team of Squadron and Group Commanders were pilots such as 'Gabby' Gabreski, Don Blakeslee and Hub Zemke, who led the long-range fighter escorts with great courage, determination and success, each personally shooting down a great number of enemy aircraft.

Peter Hugo, a tough South African, had replaced Paddy Finucane as our Wing Leader. He was an exceptionally good marksman and perhaps the best leader I ever followed, with the exception of Harry Broadhurst. His anticipation and tactical sense were uncanny, and it was impossible to get him excited or carried away by the stress of the moment. He did not say a great deal either in the air or on the ground, but when he did you sat up and took notice. He had done a great deal of fighting in Hurricanes, attacking shipping and flak-busting, as well as in Spitfires in the straightforward fighter role.

With Peter Hugo we practised the technique of escorting the Fortresses and after some misunderstandings evolved suitable formations and tactics. The Typhoons were used as 'enemy fighters' to carry out dummy attacks and also to give the Fortress gunners 'shooting' practice. We had more conferences: then the great day came on 17 July 1942 when we escorted twelve Flying Fortresses to Rouen. They were to bomb from 22,000 ft. None of us had ever seen any bombing from this height before, and we were all keyed up wondering what it would be like. We didn't think they could hit anything from that height. We need not have worried.

64 rendezvoused with the Fortress formation at Beachy Head, acting as close escort, with 401 and 402 (RCAF) Squadrons above, and 611 as top cover – all Spitfire Mk IXs. Everything went well on the way to the target, with no interference from enemy fighters. We watched the bombing, which was truly a sight for sore eyes. I will always remember seeing the bombs falling from the Fortresses in a never-ending cascade spilling out of these four-engined giants bristling with guns, like peas out of a pod. They hit the Rouen marshalling yards from end to end. It looked impossible to put a sixpence between the bomb-bursts. As huge columns of smoke and dust rolled upwards we swung right and homewards. The first enemy attack hit us about ten miles from the French coast and from there to mid-Channel we were constantly engaged by formations of FW 190s and Me 109s. We turned into and broke up four separate attacks of from twelve to fifteen FW 190s. I attacked four individual FW 190s but observed no definite results. It was a matter of a quick burst and away. But Kingaby and Stewart each got a destroyed and Donnet and Patterson a damaged apiece. No enemy fighters broke our protective screen or got anywhere near the bombers. So ended our first escort mission and, incidentally, the first attack carried out by the Americans on Europe. With the arrival of a new dimension of air attack, combining Bomber Command by night and the US 8th Air Force by day, there was at least a promise of ultimate victory. I went to sleep that night happy, and not a little the worse for beer.

We knew that preparations were being made for a combined operation on occupied France. We guessed it would be on a limited scale and that the main object of the operation would be to test enemy defences along the Atlantic wall. This type of operation would also enable us to test our equipment and techniques for landing forces in strength, a preparation for the invasion of Europe which we all believed must take place fairly soon. How the air forces were to co-ordinate their offensive operations in support of the land and sea forces became vitally important.

Planning for the Dieppe raid (Operation JUBILEE) began in

April 1942 at Combined Operations Headquarters and was aimed at a date during the first week in July. The assault was to be carried out by units of the 2nd Canadian Division. As things turned out the operation was given the all-clear for 3/4 July but the weather was unfavourable and the raid called off. The troops, having been briefed and embarked, were subsequently disembarked and returned to their camps. In spite of the obvious security risks, the operation was remounted and the plan carried out on 19 August.

A revision in the plan made the operation much more difficult for the Canadians. To make the weather requirements less rigid, the paratroops originally earmarked for use in the support role were released from the operation and replaced by our Commandos; also the sustained bombing of coastal defences, centres of communication and strong points, which had been considered a prerequisite, did not eventually take place.

The Canadians and Commandos fought magnificently, as did the Navy and the Air Force, but the casualties were extremely heavy. In particular the Canadians suffered huge losses. Out of a total force of some 5,000 men, the Canadians alone lost over 3,000 of which 2,000 were taken prisoner. This was more than the Canadians lost in prisoners later in Italy or north-west Europe. Their dead at Dieppe totalled nearly 1,000 officers and men. It was a terrible price to pay for some nine or ten hours' fighting.

On 18 August the Station Commanders, Wing Leaders and Squadron Commanders were summoned to 11 Group Headquarters to be briefed by the AOC and Harry Broadhurst on the part the fighter squadrons were to play in the Dieppe operation. It all went like clockwork and we returned to Hornchurch for individual station briefing, bursting with excitement and anticipation.

All communications with the outside world were cut and everyone confined to camp. At six that evening George Lott called a briefing for the Wing in which he and Peter Hugo outlined the tasks for each of the Squadrons. 64 Squadron was earmarked to act as escort for the Fortresses, but this depended on how the operation went and on the general air situation. We spent a busy evening checking on the final preparations of our Squadrons and making sure we would have maximum serviceability in aircraft for the morning. I gathered the airmen in our servicing hangar after dinner and briefed them on the operation, explaining that much of the success we hoped for would only be possible through their individual efforts.

Our day started on 19 August at dawn, when we took over readiness while the other Squadrons were being refuelled. Each of the other Squadrons – 81, 122 and 154 – had been on patrol over Dieppe since before first light, much to our annoyance, as we had to sit around dispersal waiting for the first Fortress bombing raid.

Soon after nine o'clock we took off, picking up thirty-six Fortresses over Beachy Head. 64 were top Squadron at 35,000 ft, with 611, 401 and 402 stepped below, all flying Spitfire Mk IXs. The weather was clear and fine as we set course for Abbeville airfield, which was the Fortresses' target. As we crossed the French coast the neatly packed Fortress formations spread out; I could see the big convoy of ships anchored off Dieppe, the warships shelling, and big columns of smoke rising from the town. One ship anchored off shore was burning furiously.

I manoeuvred 64 across the sun as we approached the target, and sent Don Kingaby with his section to search higher for any enemy formations that might be getting into position to attack. Nothing was seen, though plenty of heavy flak greeted the Fortresses. Looking down on Abbeville airfield, I saw a scurry of dust and picked out two German fighters taking off down the runway. They had gone about half-way along the runway when the first bombs started falling in the target area. The bombs burst in a neat pattern right across the airfield overtaking the enemy fighters, enveloping them in smoke and dust, and smashing into the airfield buildings and camp area beyond. The whole weight of the attack was delivered in the centre of the target area. It was precision bombing at its very finest. Later we heard that the attack had knocked out the forward control organisation of the German Air Force, which resulted in a complete stoppage of vital information reaching their air defence system. Abbeville airfield was so severely damaged that it was out of action for many days to follow.

The attack completed, we wheeled left over the Somme and headed homewards. Two Me 109s appeared above as we crossed the French coast, but before we could make a pass, they rolled on to their backs and dived into France. I could not help wondering if Abbeville was their home base and if so what they would think after they had seen what the Fortresses had done to it. We left the Americans over the English coast and returned to the French side of the Channel in the hope of picking up an enemy formation, but saw nothing.

Returning to Hornchurch we had a quick cup of tea while our Spitfires were refuelled and then took off on orders from Group to patrol over the ships and Dieppe. As we turned over Dieppe we crossed over a formation of about twenty FW 190s, about 5,000 ft below us, and immediately went into attack. I dived on the left-hand one of a formation of four, who promptly tried to out-run me. I managed to turn my aircraft round inside him and blasted him at fairly close range. As I was shooting I had to break off my attack sharply as tracers streamed past me from behind. Screwing my head round quickly I saw three FW 190s in line astern coming in from above and behind. I managed to outclimb them in a steep spiral, my Spitfire IX going up like a rocket.

Reforming, we returned over the anchorage off Dieppe. Glancing down I could see much smoke coming from the town and there seemed to be a lot of air activity, low down over the sea and land. Something made me look over to my right and below, and to my surprise I saw three Dornier 217 bombers in a loose formation heading for the ships. Calling the Squadron on the radio to follow I turned into the attack. I singled out the left-hand Dornier, which had its bomb-doors open, and slid into a fine quarter attack. The enemy pilot immediately jettisoned his bombs and turned steeply left. Closing, I pumped two long bursts into his port engine and wing root. As I stopped firing and broke downwards the wing caught fire. The rest of my section all attacked and we sent the German down in flames; his port engine parted from the wing and curved earthwards. This was more like it. We looked for others, but saw only one with four Spitfires hanging on like terriers.

Dorniers over Dieppe

We landed back at Hornchurch full of high spirits to discover that Don Kingaby had got another of the Dorniers and Thomas a Me 109 out of formation that had come in to attack us, while two others had damaged a couple more. I was, however, very angry and upset to find that McQuaig, one of my sergeant pilots had been shot down and killed.

We lunched at dispersal and were off again at half past two on another patrol over the ships. As we climbed for height I noticed at the coast that cloud was building up over France and the Channel area. We levelled off at 23,000 ft and I ordered the Squadron into a loose formation. There was much chatter on the radio but through it I heard Robert Lea's voice say: 'Vaxine leader, there are twenty plus bandits approaching you from the Abbeville area, angels seventeen.' I turned immediately and searched among the cloudbanks below. Soon we saw them, one, two, three, four, five, Dornier 217s darting between the cloudbanks, but instead of being at 17,000 ft they were only a few thousand feet above the sea. I gave a sighting report and led the way down on to the enemy. Clipping round a big cloudbank, I came up straight behind one of them also in a turn. The pilot flying this machine must have been an ex-fighter pilot for he made his Dornier twist and turn like an expert. Steadying my Spitfire, I caught him in a reverse turn to the left and hammered a good burst into his port engine and wing root from very close range. Large pieces flew off the wing, and the engine, streaming smoke, caught fire. His gunner was shooting at me with great accuracy and I should have had the sense to silence him. Tracer whizzed over my cockpit, but I was determined to get him and worried I might lose him in cloud. From astern and slightly above I opened fire again aiming round the cockpit area and centre section. Suddenly I felt four big thuds – cannon-shells – there was a bang somewhere below the throttle quadrant and I felt a sharp pain in my left leg. Flames licked past the cockpit; quickly I opened the hood and released the door. The next moment I felt the full blast of engine oil on my face engulfing me with its stickiness and intense heat. I could see nothing as my eyes had been uncovered and they were now smarting as if I'd been hit by a squirt of Lea & Perrin sauce. I struggled with the safety harness and rubbed my eyes with my gloved hand, but all I could see was a greyish blur. I realised I was diving fast by the rush of air in the cockpit – I had to get out quickly. Instinctively I released the harness and unclipped my oxygen tube and R/T lead. Then, groping for the side of the cockpit, I heaved myself on to the seat, put a leg over the side and kicked at the stick with the other and I was over and out; tumbling in a mass of arms and legs.

I found and pulled the rip-cord of my parachute – a few seconds ticked by that seemed like an eternity before I felt a terrific thump which nearly knocked all the breath out of my body. I rubbed furiously at my eyes and gradually cleared the film of oil from them. At last the blur took shape and though I still could not see properly at least I was able to recognise my open parachute above and the dark outline of the sea below. I was swinging gently from side to side, still gripping my rip-cord ring in my hand. My number two, Arne Austeen, flew past rocking his wings. On reaching the sea I released my parachute too high off the water and went into it head first. As a result my legs got caught in the shroud lines and I had quite a job freeing myself with the aid of a knife attached to my Mae West. In all the mix-up, somehow my rubber dinghy, attached to the parachute seat, came adrift and I lost it. Bobbing about on the swell like a cork I searched frantically but it was nowhere to be seen. After only a few minutes the chill of the English Channel seeped through my uniform to my bones. If I was not picked up soon I was going to be in trouble. Dimly I could see a coastline in the distance – it must be France, I thought – except for the swish of the wind and the occasional sound of a breaking wave I couldn't hear anything definite.

After about half an hour's suspense, I heard the deep-throated throb of engines. I was chattering now with cold, my thoughts tumbling through my head one upon the other. The noise I heard connected somehow in my brain with an ocean liner – what was an ocean liner doing here? I still could not see anything but the distant shoreline and the water. Overhead the clouds had closed in, scudding darkly across my line of vision.

The throbbing note of engines got louder – I swung round in the direction of the noise and saw the low silhouette of a motor launch approaching. I waved and shouted. Cutting a wide arc

Miles Master flown by D.S. at No. 5 SFTS, Sealand, Cheshire

D.S. in his first Spitfire with 611 Squadron, Digby, Lincs

3 F/Lt Lock briefing 'B' Flight, 611 Squadron, for a sweep over France.
l–r: P/O Johnson, F/O Dexter, Sgt Summers, Sgt Gilmour, D.S., Sgt Townsend

4 Me 109s looking for trouble

5 S/Ldr Stapleton, CO 611 Squadron, with pilots and Squadron Scoreboard taken from a Ju 88

6 611 Squadron, Hornchurch. *l–r*: D.S., F/O Pollard, P/O Lamb, Sgt Leigh, F/Lt Mears, Sgt Feely, Sgt Limpenny

7 Officers Mess, Hornchurch. *l–r*: S/Ldr Thomas, CO 611 Squadron; W/Cdr Stapleton, Wing Leader; D.S.; F/Lt Hayter, RNAF; P/O Campbell

8 Hornchurch: G/Capt Broadhurst, Station Commander, with a visiting South American delegation, shows his spinner covered with the oil from a Me 109 he destroyed in action

9 F/Lt Eric Lock in his Spitfire at Hornchurch shortly before being killed
on a 'Rhubarb' mission over France

10 Pilots of 611 Squadron on landing at Hornchurch after destroying five
Me 109s over France. *l–r*: F/Lt Lock, D.S., F/O Dexter, Sgt Gilmour

11 Me 109 being hit by D.S.'s cannon shells in action over France

12 Locomotive being shot up by D.S.'s cannon fire in France

13 D.S.'s Spitfire Mk
VB, 64 Squadron,
Hornchurch

14 Pilots of 64 Squad-
ron, Hornchurch. *l–
r*: F/Lt Thomas, Sgt
McQuaig, D.S., P/O
Barrow (USA), F/O
Donnet (Belgium),
Sgt Johnsson
(Norway); *kneeling*:
F/Lt Kingaby, Sgt
Rogers

15 Dornier 217, one of the principal German bombers

16 Squadron ground-crew relaxing at Hornchurch

17 FW 190 being shot down by D.S. during Sicily invasion

18 Luqa Wing, Malta. *l–r*: D.S., Wing Leader; S/Ldr Hill; S/Ldr O'Neil; W/Cdr Westmacott; S/Ldr Jackson

19 Italian Reggiane Re 2001, a potent fighter which never attained full production

20 The brilliant German FW 190

21 Italian Macchi 205 fighter with an excellent all-round performance

22 AVM Harry Broadhurst in his Fieseler Storch in Italy

23 G/Capt Brian Kingcome, CO 244 Wing, briefing D.S., Wing Leader, and Major Osler (SAAF), OC 601 Squadron, at Foggia, Italy

24 Pilots of 93 Squadron, 324 Wing, scrambling at Anzio beachhead

25 Italy, 1943. *l–r*: S/Ldr Turner, 417 (RCAF) Sqn; S/Ldr Humphreys, 92 Sqn; D.S., W/Ldr 244 Wing; G/Capt Kingcome, CO 244 Wing; S/Ldr Wade (USA), 145 Sqn; Major Osler (SAAF), 601 Sqn

AM Sir John Slessor, Deputy
Commander Mediterranean Allied
Air Forces

Vasto, Italy. ACM Sir Charles
Portal, Chief of the Air Staff, with
AVM Harry Broadhurst, AOC
Desert Air Force

27 Rimini, Italy. AVM William
Dickson, AOC Desert Air Force,
beside his Spitfire

29 Lt-Gen Sir Richard McCreery,
GOC 8th Army, with AVM
Robert Foster, AOC Desert Air
Force

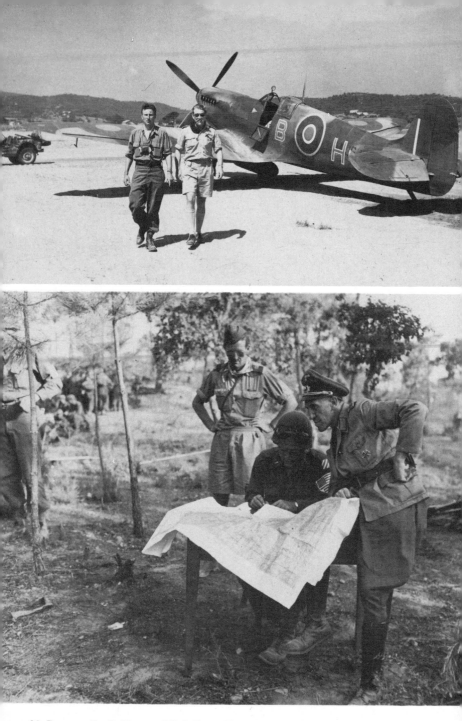

30 Ramatuelle, S. France. S/Ldr Peter Humphreys, OC 111 Squadron, and W/Cdr Barrie Heath, Wing Leader 324 Wing

31 Captured German officer being interrogated by an American officer during S. of France invasion

32 Flying control getting into business at Ramatuelle, S. France

33 The 'Champagne Campaign' had its lighter moments

34 Pilots of 72 Squadron returning after destroying nine Me 109s over Lake Bracciano on 7 May 1944. *l–r*: F/O Hendry, F/Sgt Aspinall, Sgt Bird, F/Lt Blackburn, Lt Van Schalkwyk, S/Ldr Arthur, Squadron Commander

35 D.S.'s Spitfire Mk VIII at Ravenna

with the high stern wave kicking up foam, it circled in my direction. I recognised it as one of ours – the White Ensign of the Royal Navy. For a horrible moment I had thought it might have been a German boat, particularly so close to France. Actually, I found out later I was about four miles off the Somme Estuary.

Without ceremony I was picked out of the sea and tossed onto the deck. Rough hands dragged me below and stripped off my uniform. One sailor rubbed me down with a coarse towel making me cry out in pain. Another handed me a tumbler half-filled with whisky and stood over me while I gulped it down, coughing and spluttering. Quickly the blood began to pulse through my body, a warm glow spreading over me.

An officer came down to the cabin to see how I was getting on and dressed my leg. A few splinters of cannon-shells had splashed into me when my aircraft was hit. There was also a nasty gash in my knee where I had connected with the side of the cockpit. I was given a shirt, a couple of thick sweaters and a pair of naval trousers too big for me.

Later I went up on the bridge. The whisky had made me a bit tight. I was given another glass. I swigged it down. I began to sing. . . . Apparently my rescuers were on their way home, having had a brush with some German E-boats, when they saw our battle going on above them. They had seen me engage the Dornier and confirmed seeing it crash into the sea some distance away. They also saw my Spitfire go in and searched the area for me with no luck. They decided to look further afield. All this took time, but eventually they came near enough to see me waving in the water. Before we slipped into Folkestone the skipper said: 'Well, here's your uniform, my fine-feathered friend, but you won't need these any more –' With that he ripped off my wings and nailed them to the mast, as a souvenir!

Back at Hornchurch the next morning I heard all the details of the day's fighting. Hornchurch had got ten destroyed, one probable and fourteen damaged for the loss of three pilots and four aircraft. 64's share was five destroyed and four damaged. But one of my sergeant pilots – Stewart – had been lost during the same engagement as myself.

The overall picture for the Command was reasonably satisfactory. About 2,400 sorties were flown for the loss of eighty-eight aircraft and fifty-seven pilots. The Command claimed eighty-seven enemy aircraft destroyed, with a further 143 probables and damaged. The Allied Air Force lost eighteen aircraft and thirteen pilots.

The big question was, had the operation proved a success and justified the overall losses of the Army, Navy and Air Force? The answer to this question is that valuable and essential lessons were learned, but it was an extremely expensive way of learning them.

My experience in the sea had left me with severe earache. Two days later I was still rather uncomfortable when George Lott asked me round to his office. I went in and saluted.

'A message has just come in from the AOC saying you have been appointed to take over as Wing Leader at North Weald.'

George Lott's usual broad smile was a bit thin as he went on:

'Jolly good show, and I'm delighted you're being promoted. However, I'm a bit concerned about it, too, as I think you've had enough for the present. I feel it's time you had a rest. I reckon you're a bit punch-drunk – no reflection on you – just that I think a few months off would be a good idea. I put this point to the AOC, but he doesn't agree. You are to go off on leave and then take over the job from David Scott-Malden – he's going to Command on the staff. How do you feel about it?' Now he smiled broadly, studying my face intently.

I didn't know what to think: it had come as a complete surprise. My first thought was 64 Squadron. The very idea of leaving was unthinkable. The team were terrific, my love for them all could not be thrust aside lightly. In their midst I felt confident, happy and on top of the job. In many ways, as most officers would admit, command of an operational squadron is the high point of an RAF career. Promotion may bring wider responsibilities, but never the same satisfaction. Besides, I had been at Hornchurch so long that leaving it would be hard and rather like being turned out of one's own home. North Weald would be another thing altogether, remote and possibly unfriendly. My experience had shown clearly that a Wing Leader was a bit out on a limb. He had a Wing made up of different Squadrons but he could never be an intimate part of any one of them. He was accepted and yet, even if popular, he could never become a permanent part of Squadron life.

I did not feel tired or that I had had enough combat flying. Quite the reverse in fact; my secret fear was that once off operational flying it might not be easy to go back to it, the old keenness might fade.

'I don't want to leave 64, sir, I would like to carry on. I'm feeling fine. After a few days' leave to get rid of this earache I'll be back on the job as good as new. Besides we're just getting the tactics right for the IXs, I don't want to go back to the Vs again. Couldn't you try and persuade the AOC to leave me here?'

George Lott shook his head. Then he picked up the phone and asked to be put through to the AOC. 'The AOC wants a word with you, you tell him.' He laughed. 'I think you need to be taken off operations now, before it's too late. Another experience like Dieppe and you'll have had it for good. Don't get me wrong, you've still got bags of flying left in you, only it's time you took the pressure off for a while. Remember other chaps depend on your skill and judgement – you can't afford to let them down. Maybe North Weald won't be as hectic as a Squadron – see what you can do with L-M.' The phone shrilled. After a few words with the AOC George Lott passed it over to me.

The AOC went straight into the attack: 'Congratulations on getting the North Weald Wing – I'm delighted – you're going off on a spot of leave eh? – good – the Station Commander will give you the details – good crowd North Weald – they'll be getting IXs any day now – up your street – you've had plenty of experience of them – good show – best of luck – see you soon.'

'Yes, sir,' I managed to say, 'thank you very much, I'll do my best –'

'– fine, fine, have a good leave – er, get away from London and get some rest – not too many parties, eh?' His voice chuckled down the line. 'Call in at Group when you get back – good luck.' There was a click and the line went dead.

I looked at George Lott. There was nothing more to be said.

'See you in the bar later – we'll have a drink to the health of the new Wing-co Flying, North Weald. Get the boys together –

it should be quite an evening – I think we'd better go on to the King's Head. In the meantime I'll have a few words with 'Zulu' Morris at North Weald and warn him about his new Wing-co Flying.'

I went back to my room and lay on the bed, thoughts tumbling through my mind. A great feeling of depression possessed me and I suddenly felt very alone. Then there was my aeroplane, one of the best Mk IXs I ever flew and I was most upset by her loss. You get very attached to a particular aircraft – confidence, the heart of the matter, builds up morale and you feel that no enemy can touch you so long as you are together. Now she was at the bottom of the sea and I was on my way to North Weald. Nothing seemed to be going right.

Two days later Tony Gaze took over 64 Squadron from me. Depressed as I was at leaving, I was proud to think I was handing over a magnificent Squadron to his care, sure in the knowledge that it was second to none in the whole Command. They were a wonderful crowd, seasoned fighters with a high morale and full of high spirits, too. Their zest for living had lifted my heart to heights of feeling I had never experienced before. The pity of it was I knew in my inner self that it could not last – nothing lasts for long in war. Flight Sergeant Moon, the Senior NCO of the Squadron summed it up for me when I said farewell to him: 'We must both be thankful for the privilege of having served 64 Squadron.' He was right, of course. Nothing mattered except the job. That was the important thing. I had nearly missed the point.

The following morning I left to go on ten days' leave. I planned to go home to Scotland to spend it with my Uncle Alec Duncan and Aunt Theo, to rest, play golf and do a bit of rough shooting. Before leaving I called on my doctor friend Tommy Thompson at Rush Green Hospital, because I was still suffering from severe earache. Previously 'Doc' Davies the station MO at Hornchurch confirmed I had damaged the ear-drum when I baled out into the sea and the ducking I received was responsible for the subsequent pain as it had become badly inflamed.

Tommy was just about to leave to join the Army as an MO. He took one look at my ear and gave me a note to a consultant surgeon he knew in Harley Street. That worthy confirmed there was nothing seriously the matter, gave me pills and ear-drops, wished me luck and charged me ten guineas.

I caught the night sleeper to Gleneagles. I got no sleep so, rather tired and depressed, I arrived at 7.00 a.m. to find my uncle waiting for me.

'You look rather the worse for wear, laddie,' he said as we climbed into the car. 'Expect Theo will order you to bed.' And she did.

I woke to the smell of bacon and eggs. Theo was standing at the foot of my bed, a breakfast tray poised, and a large smile lighting her eyes. Putting the tray down beside me she laughed: 'You look much better. You might like to know you've been asleep for over twenty-four hours without moving.' The earache was gone. Ever since, I have never ceased to get excited when I smell bacon and eggs cooking.

British and German Groups and airfields, Sept. 1940

Mediterranean Theatre of Operations

117

CHAPTER TEN

Into the drink

'Zulu' Morris was a tough, rugged South African who had fought in night-fighters before taking over command of North Weald a short time previously from Tom Pike, who had also made a name for himself as a night-fighter pilot during the blitz. The Squadrons were 331 and 332 of the Royal Norwegian Air Force and 124 Squadron of the RAF. The Norwegian Squadrons were equipped with Spitfire Mk Vs when I arrived, but soon afterwards they were given the Mk IXs that were now coming off the assembly lines at a good rate.

124 had Spitfire Mk VIs. These were special high-flying aircraft with pressurised cockpits. The cockpit cover was placed over the pilot before take-off, and he locked it by means of four clamping levers. Once locked it could not be opened in flight except in an emergency, when it could be jettisoned. These aircraft were hurriedly produced to cope with the Ju 86Ps, a German high-altitude photo-recce aircraft.

331 Squadron was commanded by Birksted, a Dane, and 332 by Mohr, a Norwegian. Tommy Balmforth had 124. Tommy had been based in Malta when Italy came into the war and was one of the pilots who flew the famous trio of Gladiators known as 'Faith', 'Hope' and 'Charity' on the island.

Birkstead and Mohr ran very efficient Squadrons. The Norwegians were a fine crowd and dedicated to winning the war. A lot of them had got away from Norway after the German invasion and occupation; most of them had hair-raising tales to tell about their escapes. David Scott-Malden had been a very popular and successful Wing Leader and I had my work cut out trying to follow him. However, they received me with great friendliness.

It took some time to adjust as a Wing Leader; however, I was

118

fortunate to have Squadron Leader Hogben as my Chief Intelligence Officer. A Scot and former First World War pilot, 'Hoggie' helped to make me realise advantages in my new appointment.

Co-ordinating operations and training took up much time and I was glad I had already experienced the conversion to Mk IX Spitfires for I was thus able to help 331 and 332 Squadrons convert to the operational role when these aircraft arrived in the Wing. The Norwegians all spoke excellent English and were always keen to fly and fight. I led them often in offensive operations over France, Belgium and Holland, sometimes returning at low level to shoot up coastal shipping. One afternoon we found a 500-ton supply ship off Ostend which we attacked with great accuracy leaving it on fire and sinking. On other occasions we attacked enemy flak posts and installations hidden round the Dutch islands if we had not engaged enemy aircraft beforehand.

I had a shock one dismal afternoon when a Beaufighter crept in to land while the airfield was closed due to severe bad weather. The intrepid pilot turned out to be Diana Barnato, a pilot in the Air Transport Auxiliary. Looking very beautiful in her immaculate uniform she ran a comb through her hair before climbing out of the aircraft to tell me she was short of fuel and had had a very rough flight through thunderstorms. Not the least put out by the weather or the fact that she had made an emergency landing, her only concern was not to be a nuisance or disturb anyone. I discovered later she had flown a considerable distance and that her Beaufighter had not been equipped with any radio or navigational aids while she carried out the flight with only her map and the aircraft's compass. They were an exceptional group of pilots in the ATA and Diana was one of the very best.

North Weald formed a happy band of extroverts and the Norwegians used any excuse for a party, either in the Mess or at the Thatched House in Epping. It was on these occasions I recognised the fact that, as Wing Leader, I was a welcome guest with a foot in the door so to speak, but I could never be the centre of any fun and games in the way that I had enjoyed them when in command of 64 Squadron. It had nothing to do with

119

rank – it was all about team spirit, so I was expected to lead them in the air but on the ground the pilots took their cue from their squadron leaders. Now, that special squadron intimacy was no longer of my making and I did not relish being a wall-flower.

One of the most charming qualities of the Norwegians was the intimate relationship they enjoyed with their Royal Family and senior officers at their London headquarters. King Haakon and Crown Prince Olav visited them regularly and knew the pilots and ground-crews by name. Admiral Riiser-Larsen, head of the RNAF, about whose pioneering flights connected with Polar explorations I had heard and read a great deal, was a constant visitor.

The 2nd American Eagle Squadron, No. 121, also formed part of the Wing but was stationed at Southend. However, before I could get to know them properly they were taken over by the USAAF and went to Debden with the two other Eagle Squadrons, to be formed into a Fighter Group under the command of Petersen. Much has been said and written about the American pilots who joined up in Canada with the intention of getting into the RAF, particularly into Fighter Command. They were a motley crowd and though most of them were tough, rough adventurers, out for what they could get for themselves, they were nevertheless a most likeable bunch of chaps, and I personally counted some very good friends amongst them. There were some, of course, like Petersen, Blakeslee and Lance Wade, who were exceptional leaders, with outstanding operational records.

There was a farewell party at Southend for 121 Squadron when they transferred to the USAAF. I kept going with the rest of them well into the early hours of the next morning. Most of the American Eagles were genuinely sorry to be leaving the RAF. We for our part were very sorry to see them go. One pilot put it to me like this: 'We can't afford not to go: do you realise, Wing-co, as of now, I'm being paid about twice as much as you, if not more – and I'm only a lootenant. Too bad you don't qualify to come with us, your accent would sure be worth every cent of your pay – what, what, old boy.' Having hammered their booze to death, I wended my way back to North Weald in the crisp light of dawn, sad that I would not be flying with them again.

One of the American Eagle pilots, on arriving back at Southend from a forty-eight hours' leave in London, found the Squadron about to take off on a sweep over France. Anxious to take part, he changed places with another pilot and, still dressed in his best uniform, put on a Mae West and roared off into the blue. A degree of stiff opposition was met in mid-Channel resulting in several dog-fights. In the course of this he got shot down, baled out successfully and on landing in the sea climbed into his dinghy. A good fix was obtained on him so about an hour later an Air-Sea Rescue launch came to pick him up. In the meantime to while away the time, he drank a bottle of booze he still had in his pocket that he had brought back from London. He was found by his rescuers waving an empty bottle and singing 'Home on the Range'. Having pulled him aboard they set off for the English coast.

'Say, where's the bar?' he inquired.

The captain of the launch was not amused. 'You had better go below, get out of your wet clothes and get some sleep.'

'Sleep?' replied the Eagle. 'Say, what kinda deal is this. I wanna drink. Wanna drink, savvy – sprechen sie Deutsch? What goddam nationality are you anyway?'

'You are in the hands of the RAF,' replied the captain rather pompously.

'O.K.,' our Eagle friend shouted, 'that does it – why, you son of a bitch, I fly for the RAF – no drink – no fly no more – I'm gonna fly for the other side –' With that he jumped overboard and struck out merrily for the French coast.

The skipper turned the launch, picked up his passenger once more, took him below and dried him out. He then handed him a bottle of whisky. After that, I believe, the Eagle slept all the way to Dover.

Much to everyone's delight we were honoured by a visit to North Weald one day in September by the King and Queen of Norway, on the occasion of an investiture held by the King to present decorations for gallantry at Dieppe. Scott-Malden should also have been present to receive the Norwegian War Cross, but he had gone to the United States on a goodwill tour.

331 and 332 Squadrons between them had destroyed sixteen enemy aircraft at Dieppe, probably destroying and damaging a further fourteen.

85 Squadron, the night-fighters in our sector, equipped with Havocs, was commanded by Raphael. Although for obvious reasons I did not see much of them at the time, later while serving on the staff at Fighter Command, I got to know them well. John Cunningham was then in command and the Squadron flew Mosquitos – that superlative all-purpose aircraft.

John Cunningham was in a class by himself when it came to night-fighting; but after the war his unique contribution to the development of jet flying and, in particular, his personal efforts in proving jet aircraft to be safe, lifted him above the ranks of successful war-time pilots. Quiet-spoken and quite fearless in his actions and decisions, he is completely dedicated to flying. He helped more than anyone else to establish the supremacy of British aircraft and brought into new perspective the operation of long-range jet transports. His work in this field has influenced the design concepts of every major aircraft manufacturer on both sides of the Atlantic. It is a tragedy that successive Governments since the war have failed to capitalise on these achievements; had they done so, they would have placed the British aircraft industry in a position second to none, unassailable by foreign competition. It was open to us at that time to secure the world markets for Britain. Instead all our dreams and aspirations for this great industry suffer one set-back after another, with revolutionary aircraft designs neglected by men without courage or vision for the future. The inventive genius of our race, which could have taken the lead in vertical take-off and variable geometry, seems to have been subordinated to the demands of the welfare state.

Our daylight operations continued at high intensity as the summer of 1942 merged into autumn. During a sweep in the Ypres-Dixmude-Calais area, I was leading 332 when we jumped about fifteen FW 190s. Berg, one of the flight commanders, got a probable and I damaged another. The rest of the enemy formation dived inland so we turned for home rather disgusted with the outcome. Crossing the English coast on the way back we found that the weather had gone sour on us while we had been away. Failing to get a clear homing on the R/T, I overshot North Weald badly and became completely lost in the thick haze and ground mist. We were all short of fuel, and, after searching frantically for an airfield, I took Berg and three others into one of the new American Flying Fortress bases.

I walked over to the flying control tower and tried to get a petrol bowser along to refuel us. A young American officer was very polite but informed me that they would not be able to do a thing until the Forts had been refuelled. We hung about for some time and not till an hour later did an enormous petrol tanker come along with a motley crew of American NCOs and airmen, or rather 'soldiers', hanging on to it. I doubt if any of them had ever seen Spitfires at close quarters before, for they shrieked with laughter when they found out that the Spitfire's fuel capacity was slightly less than one hundred gallons. The crew chief drily remarked: 'Say, Captain (each of us was called Captain), you don't need our tanker – here have my Zippo lighter – there's sure enough gas in it to take care of your Spitfire babies.' More laughter. More remarks to each other like 'Say Al, imagine that – ninety gallons of gas, why my Buick back home eats it up quicker than these babies . . . !'

The refuelling at last over, the crew chief noticed for the first time that our gun patches were off and the wings streaked with powder marks. He inquired if we had been in action. When I told him we had engaged some FW 190s and that Berg had probably destroyed one, he got very excited. Slapping Berg heartily on the back he exclaimed: 'That's great noos Captain – I'm sure gonna tell the folks back home you guys are doin' a swell job over here – here –' he reached into his pocket and pulled out a thick wad of one pound notes. He peeled off three or four of them and offered them to Berg: '– me and the boys would sure like you all to have a drink with us tonight.'

Berg went white round the gills and drawing himself up stiffly gave a slight bow: 'I'm sorry,' he said very quietly, 'I'm a Norwegian officer, I cannot accept your money, please put away your dollars –'

'Sure, sure, we understand – but we mean you to have, on the level – no? O.K. suit yourself –' Slowly he rolled up his wad again and thrust it back into his pocket: 'Just remember, we think you're doing a swell job, and your ships sure look mighty cute – be seeing you –.' They jumped on to the tanker and with cheerful shouts and waves were gone. Much to Berg's annoyance I could not stop laughing for the rest of the evening.

I spent an interesting day soon afterwards with Jeffrey Quill at Worthy Down flying a new Spitfire, a Mk XII fitted with a Rolls-Royce Griffon, 2,000 hp engine. It was quite a machine. If you opened up too quickly, the engine would take charge and you found yourself careering across the airfield at right angles to your intended take-off run. It was really fast at low level – over 400 mph – and though eventually only two Squadrons operated these aircraft they were more than a match for the low-level FW 190s which the Germans were using on tip-and-run bombing and straffing raids against the south coast towns and military installations. Operating alongside the Typhoons, they could catch the FW 190s fairly easily. But to me this was the end of the line: the engine power had outgrown the airframe.

It looked a bit clumsy with its slightly drooping nose but it was great fun to fly and in any case the later version – the Mk XIV – with modifications to the airframe and a five-bladed propeller became a fine combat aircraft.

[After the war I commanded 60 Squadron in Singapore and Malaya during operations against the Communist Insurgents and we flew Griffon-engined Spitfire Mk XVIIIs. They proved to be excellent tactical fighter-bombers with either bombs or 60 lb rockets, very stable and fast. The enlarged fin and tail-plane made aiming and firing rockets or guns much more straight-forward.]

Towards the end of November 'Zulu' Morris informed me that I was being taken off operations for a rest. On the departure of Sir Sholto Douglas to the Middle East Sir Trafford Leigh-Mallory had taken over Fighter Command and at the time a number of officers from 11 Group, the Stations, and Squadrons, had also gone to Command to fill vacancies created by the departure of Sir Sholto's staff to the Middle East.

I was to take charge of the Tactics Branch at Command and hand over my Wing to 'Jamie' Jameson. I can't say I was unhappy about the arrangements, as I felt I needed a rest and with winter well advanced it seemed a good time to make the move. 'Jamie' Jameson, a gallant fighter-pilot, had had a miraculous escape from the aircraft-carrier *Glorious* on that tragic day, 8 June 1940, when two enemy cruisers sank her, killing or drowning most of the ship's company. He managed to get on to a life-raft, saved his Squadron Commander from drowning and also made heroic efforts to save others trapped in the sea around the sinking ship. Out of twenty-seven men that got on to the raft only nine survived the ordeal.

CHAPTER ELEVEN

Rethink on tactics

Not having been a staff officer before, I found life at Fighter Command very strange at first. There didn't seem to be the same urgency about life as one found at an operational station. Most of the decisions that mattered were taken in the higher echelons behind closed doors and I never took part in anything that remotely held world-shaking promises. I worked as Wing Commander Tactics under 'Doggie' Oliver, the Group Captain in charge of the Training Branch. The job was interesting but its attraction lay in the fact that I could visit the Squadrons and stations of the Command from Land's End to John o'Groats and Northern Ireland too. I had a Spitfire V for this purpose and I made full use of it.

On one occasion I visited Eglington in Northern Ireland where an old friend, Findlay Boyd, a famous member of 602 Squadron had command of the station. I flew on several training flights during my visit and discussed tactics and training with the pilots. One afternoon we flew over the border into the Republic's airspace at low level, as a result of poor visibility. Searching for a recognisable landmark I suddenly realised the mistake when I saw a group of irate Irish looking up and shaking their fists at us while waving their national flag. Though we beat a hasty retreat we were reported for a 'border infringement' and in due course I had to write an official apology.

Another time I visited Peter Brothers, one of the Command's most successful pilots and Wing Leader at Tangmere, persuading him to let me fly as his number two on a sweep over France. We saw some Me 109s but were unable to engage them and I wound up getting a rocket from 'Doggie' Oliver when I returned to Fighter Command for sticking my neck out when I was supposed to be doing a staff job. It was well worth it however, since it helped restore my enthusiasm for a return to operational flying. It is true to say: 'The more you fly the more you want to fly.' As a staff officer I became worried that a lack of operational flying might dull my appetite for a return to active operations. I therefore considered that a few flights, like the one with Pete Brothers, were an essential preparation.

A remarkable officer who also made full use of my Spitfire was Group Captain Theodore McEvoy, head of the Operations Branch. Despite suffering from permanent curvature of the spine, he never let it get the better of him, indeed he possessed great charm and an infectious sense of humour. The pain and discomfort were often severe and the handicap in his profession more than most normal officers could bear. But 'Mac' was no normal man when it came to courage and fortitude. He continued to fly many types of aircraft, kept himself up-to-date with current fighter tactics and with inexhaustible patience and humour taught many war-time officers the rudiments of staff work. His personality and example made a deep impression on us all. Acknowledged as one of the best pilots in the RAF he had previously commanded No. 1 Squadron with great distinction.

I had time for reflection now, so I tried to put my thoughts straight on our own tactics and operations and those of the enemy. Being able to discuss things with the Operations planning staff and members of the Training Branch I was able to get a new slant on the facts that were important. Looking back on the previous two years I came to the conclusion that the aspects that most needed reviewing were the training and tactics at Squadron level. Squadron commanders had a tendency to train their pilots in a personal way so that when it came to tactics, most of them being individualists, they were convinced the tactics they employed in their own Squadrons were best. Command directives were issued and manuals provided but hardly anyone took any notice of this bumph, which was usually pushed into a drawer in the Adjutant's desk. Then again no two Squadron Commanders thought the same as to how best to utilise their Squadron aircraft in order to get the greatest efficiency out of them. They arrived at similar conclusions but by different routes.

127

To find oneself completely accepted as boss of one's own Squadron is a cherished experience. It not only lifts you above yourself but also influences your pilots and men to raise their own morale, courage and fighting spirit to new heights. Most fighter pilots are individualistic so a squadron commander must harness the effervescence of the individual to his own way of thinking. Though discipline is the key it must never appear to be so.

What was needed now, however, was a facility where current and potential Squadron and Flight Commanders could be brought together to learn and devise tactics, training and operations under up-to-date operational instructors by actually flying simulated operational missions.

Some of the operations we undertook at that time were also proving unproductive; all they did was to put lives at risk – for instance, the two-men missions known as 'Rhubarbs'. Another was the 'Sphere', the four or six formation of aircraft sweeping round enemy airfields in the hope of picking up easy targets on training flights. Then there was the 'Circus' – a bomber formation heavily escorted by fighters and supported in the target area by wings (two to four squadrons) whose job it was to pick off enemy aircraft trying to interfere with the main formation (the beehive). As soon as formations got split up with pilots separated, individuals made for the beehive for self-protection. This at once took the initiative away thereby bottling up a large number of fighters that either could not or would not return to the offensive because they were alone and unloved in a hostile sky, at extreme range and short on fuel. Thus they became unproductive by putting themselves at risk and those that ventured to be offensive under those conditions usually never lived to tell the tale. New methods had to be found to overcome some of these difficulties.

I became convinced when in command of 64 Squadron that to be really offensive one had to cruise at high speed, maintaining flexibility, but at the same time reforming rapidly after an action, in Squadron strength if possible. If the situation deteriorated then we stuck to the four-aircraft concept or at least the two-aircraft sub-section. If in the end you found yourself alone then the thing to do was to spiral down rapidly to tree-top level and head for home as fast as possible to fight another day. This last tactic did not imply you were running away in an attempt to avoid a fight. Rather the reverse, for if the situation became hopeless it was far better to save yourself than fall easy prey to a German fighter through no fault of your own. Only twice to my knowledge, did I find pilots lacking that combatant spirit necessary to put others before self. It was called 'lack of moral fibre' and it became painful in the extreme to have to deal with it. The ones in question were misfits and should never have been allowed to become fighter pilots but weeded out during their flying training or sooner.

I suspect that some senior commanders and planners tended to get carried away by the idea that Fighter Command had to be offensive at all costs, all the time. Consequently operations were sometimes laid on that did not have a hope of success, either because of the weather or the target or the tactical aspects or a combination of these factors. To get the enemy to fight – that was the all-important aspect. So in the end they hung bombs on us – first on Hurricanes – then later on Spitfires.

After the Germans invaded the Soviet Union and thrust into the Balkans there never were the numbers of Luftwaffe fighter Squadrons in France and the Low Countries as had been present previously. Many of these Squadrons were sent to the Eastern Front and, more particularly, the Germans reinforced Luftwaffe units in the Mediterranean with about 25-30 per cent of the total strength available. The fighting over Malta and the Western Desert influenced the conduct of operations far more than those in France and the Low Countries. But little account was taken of this in the UK presumably because an attack against England of 1940 proportions could not be ruled out. No less than seventy-five Fighter Squadrons with the best aircraft were kept in the UK to counter such a threat, while in Malta and the Western Desert the Luftwaffe were playing ducks and drakes with the out-moded Hurricanes and Tomahawks in the air battles. Not a single Spitfire Squadron was sent to the Mediterranean area until the spring of 1942 – a strange state of affairs when one realises that a year later Malta was preparing frantically for the invasion of Sicily, while in England the invasion of Normandy was still more than two years away. And everywhere the German armies were in retreat.

Close escorting of bomber formations I found inhibiting due to their slow speed. It was not until the USAAF bombers came into action that the picture changed because not only were they faster but also much more heavily armed defensively, so that it became unnecessary to provide a close-escort function, thus leaving the fighter cover Squadrons much more freedom of action.

What was lacking in our training organisation was a place where experienced pilots could be brought together to try out new ideas in air fighting, using up-to-date tactics and formations. We now advocated setting up such a centre with the task of evolving principles of air fighting for the benefit of all Squadrons throughout the Command. The C-in-C agreed with our ideas and finally it was formed at Chalmy Down in Gloucestershire. It was called the Fighter Command School of Tactics, and Paddy Woodhouse was given command of it. His two Squadron Commanders were Peter Simpson and 'Laddie' Lucas, the famous Walker Cup golfer. At the end of the first course Paddy Woodhouse was promoted to another appointment and Brian Kingcome then took over. He proved an excellent choice. He arrived from Kenley where he had been Wing Leader and bang up-to-date, just right for the job. Brian, a very experienced leader with considerable knowledge of offensive operations and a tremendous personal record, had served with 65 Squadron before the war and also with 92 Squadron in the Battle of Britain at Biggin Hill, before also commanding 72 Squadron. His charm and powers of persuasion sorted out the early difficulties at Chalmy Down and soon the syllabus and instruction reflected a pattern of operational concepts, based on his personal experience.

'Doggie' Oliver was equally keen to see the FCST succeed and it was largely due to his efforts that it got off to a good start.

The Fighter Command School of Tactics also ran courses for selected Squadron pilots in the handling of large formations under simulated combat conditions, preparing the way for them to become Squadron Commanders and Wing Leaders. It had an establishment of twenty-six Spitfire Mk Vs with full technical and administrative backing. Visiting lecturers, all experts in some aspect of air fighting or specialist duties, led the discussion periods. Number 2 Group provided Bostons for tactical experience in escort formations and as targets for camera-gun attacks. It was from these small beginnings that the FCST later blossomed into the Central Fighter Establishment, the 'Mecca' of air fighting for all Allied Air Forces. In my capacity as head of the Tactics Branch it became my special responsibility to get it started.

I made friends with a new arrival at Fighter Command who came on to the Training Staff, Derek Walker. He had spent most of his operational career in the Middle East. He fascinated me with his stories about Greece, Crete, and the Western Desert, having campaigned in one capacity or another in these places.

One day I had to visit Boscombe Down and invited Derek to come with me, saying we would go on to Chalmy Down for a night on our way back to Northolt. We took the Proctor, myself flying and Derek doing the navigating. The weather was foul, with very poor visibility forward and thick mist rapidly turning into fog. The weather report indicated better conditions further west so we flung ourselves into the air with gay abandon, and at low altitude headed, as we thought, in the right direction. We had pressed on for quite some time clawing our way through the murk, when I asked Derek if he knew where we were.

'Not a clue, old boy.' He looked at me and grinned.

I peered in front, sideways, downwards, nothing, then over the trailing edge of the wing I caught a quick glimpse of a road meandering past below us. 'Well – we're right ways up,' I said, 'that's something – let's stay with it.'

Then suddenly Derek shouted at me: 'Do you see what I see – there – right in front?'

I looked and to my horror the ramparts and tower of Windsor Castle loomed straight ahead, the flagstaff with the Royal Standard flapping listlessly on it in the damp air, the top half merging into the gloom and murk. I heaved on the stick and kicked the rudder; we skated past missing it by a few yards. Not knowing what else to do, we quickly sat at attention and, giving a smart 'eyes right', saluted as we floated past. We were wearing our Service hats with earphones clamped over the top like airline pilots, so everything was in order and as correct as the Monarch could have wished had he seen us, which mercifully he did not.

As we flew on, Derek said: 'Gives you a big thrill, doesn't it, seeing the old Royal Standard so close?'

'You must be joking,' I looked sideways at him. 'That was too damned close – and another thing – we're not supposed to be within miles of Windsor – it's a forbidden area! We'll catch hell for this if we're reported.'

'Never mind,' Derek said. 'Just as well we didn't prang it – "Doggie" Oliver would have been furious with you. Remember you are in charge of this contraption, I'm just observing – skilfully too, don't you think?'

Shortly after this incident 'Doggie' Oliver explained that, as Brian Kingcome was being posted to the Far East, there was going to be an unexpected gap between Commanding Officers at the FCST and I was to proceed to Chalmy Down and hold the fort until the new CO arrived.

As it happened, the arrangement suited me very well since I had been at Command about four months by then and was beginning to look forward to returning to the fray. Six weeks or so at Chalmy Down, flying hard on exercises, was just the sort of training I needed to get me back with the Squadrons.

While at Chalmy Down I gave a lot of thought to my next tour of operations. On reflection, it didn't take long to come to the conclusion that the year that lay ahead would be much the same as the two previous years as far as the scope of offensive operations across the Channel was concerned. A bigger and better scale of effort supporting more American bombers was certain. Perhaps another raid or two like Dieppe to relieve the monotony, but I thought there was little chance of the much-awaited invasion of France taking place during 1943.

On the other hand the end in North Africa was in sight, and the fall of Tunis was a foregone conclusion. To me this was where the real fighting was going on. Where would the next blow fall? Corsica, Sardinia, or Sicily? It had to be one of these, as a stepping stone to Italy.

'Barney' Beresford had lately visited Fighter Command on

his return from the Middle East. A very experienced tactical pilot and seasoned desert campaigner like Derek Walker, he had fired my imagination with tales of the fighting and the close co-operation between air and land forces in the battles that were taking place. It was obvious that when Rommel had been hit for six out of Africa, as General Montgomery predicted, the Allies would concentrate on knocking Italy out of the war. This was the area to go to, preferably to Desert Air Force.

Many of my friends were already there. Harry Broadhurst was AOC of Desert Air Force. Barrie Heath, John Loudon and Johnny Kent were in various places in the Middle East. Peter Powell was in Tunisia. 'Sheep' Gilroy and Peter Hugo were commanding Wings in support of 1st Army operations. Brian Kingcome was on his way. I decided it was time I joined them. Some 'sand in my shoes' would be a good thing, not to mention the feel of the hot sun across my back.

I asked to see Sir Trafford Leigh-Mallory. He was charming and rather amused at the reasons I gave for wanting to go, but was also kind enough to say he had a Wing lined up for me just as soon as I had finished my tour on his staff. What was all the fuss and hurry about? I explained that though I was grateful for the offer of a Wing in Fighter Command, I had set my heart on getting into Desert Air Force, even at the risk of missing the 'big show' across the Channel. He agreed to do all he could to help and, in the meantime, told me to see Harry Campbell, the personnel staff officer responsible for the likes of me, and ask him to sound the Air Ministry and find out if something could be done.

A few days later Harry Campbell phoned me at Chalmy Down to say the Air Ministry had offered the Luqa Wing in Malta – was I interested? I was disappointed it was not Desert Air Force, but it was a step in the right direction, so I readily accepted.

At the end of the second of the two courses I ran at Chalmy Down I went off on a week's embarkation leave. Returning to Fighter Command to collect my bags, I found that David Scott-Malden and the two American liaison officers with Fighter Command, 'Jake' Stanley and Bob Landry, had laid on a terrific farewell party. It was a fitting end to a memorable period in my life.

One rainy evening in May I took off from St Mawgan in a Dakota for Gibraltar on the first leg of my journey to Malta.

CHAPTER TWELVE

South to Malta

It was in the late afternoon of a hot clear day that I caught my first glimpse of Malta, lying like the shell of a broken walnut across the horizon of an unbelievably blue sea. Peering through the windscreen I picked out the splash of colour and the jagged outline of rock formations that marked the island fortress. As we approached nearer, the pale off-whites and reds of the limestone buildings, and the pattern of stone walls and terracing which divided the cultivated areas like a patchwork quilt, began to take shape. Here and there the great dome and spire of an ancient church towered heavenwards dwarfing everything around it. Dusty roads meandered across the rock landscape, while Valetta and Sliema harbours shimmered in the bright light with warships at their moorings.

Those stone walls and terraces, I thought, would tear an aircraft to pieces if an engine failure occurred on take-off. This was going to be an additional hazard in the days that lay ahead, compared to operating over the green fields of south-east England.

The runway at Luqa was already in sight when we were called on the R/T by Operations and told to turn south immediately and circle out to sea as an air raid was in progress. As we turned and hurried away I saw a splash of bomb bursts near the edge of the airfield followed by two Me 109s which streaked across my vision hotly pursued by angry puffs of ack-ack fire.

We saw no more enemy aircraft, and about twenty minutes later were ordered to land. As we approached Luqa the whole place took on for me the aspect of Devil's Island. My misgivings were heightened, for no sooner had I stepped out of the aircraft to be greeted by 'Tommy' Thompson from whom I was to take over the Luqa wing, than the sirens wailed, and we dashed for cover as a second wave of enemy fighter-bombers dive-bombed the airfield.

I had first met Thompson at Southend at the end of 1940 when 611 moved there from Digby. He had not changed a bit, and his charm and friendliness contributed enormously to the difficult task of adjusting to my new surroundings. The Wing consisted of two Spitfire Mk V squadrons: 126 Squadron commanded by 'Jacko' Jackson, and 1435 by 'Peggy' O'Neil. The Officers' Mess, situated in Sliema, was not very comfortable, so 'Tommy' invited me to move into the flat which he shared with 'Peggy' O'Neil. This worked out well, and I was grateful for the suggestion as it was more comfortable on the waterfront.

After calling on Willie Merton, the Station Commander, the next morning, I met the AOC, Sir Keith Park, and his Senior Air Staff Officer, 'Smidge' Harcourt-Smith. 'Tommy' took me along to the famous Operations room buried deep in a rock face, and known as the 'ditch', where I had a discussion on the current operational situation with the Group Captain in charge, 'Dusty' Miller, and the two senior controllers.

Malta's approach to life differed very much from anything I had come across before. Having held out for so long against fearful odds, the islanders regarded the war as their personal business. The local press each morning gave all the emphasis possible to the previous day's air operations; it was always 'our' fighters, 'our' Navy, or 'our' ack-ack batteries that caught the limelight; foreign news was on the inside pages, and however the tide of war ebbed or flowed on other fronts, Malta at least was thrashing the enemy in the air and at sea. It was a splendid approach which made everyone feel a part of this private war, even though the night-bombing of towns and military targets on Malta by the enemy continued unabated.

The most remarkable of the many personalities in Malta was Adrian Warburton who commanded 683 (Photo Recce) Squadron, equipped with Spitfire Mk XIs. 'Warbie' was moulded in the buccaneer style and his exploits captured the imagination. Immensely brave, he delighted in taking fearful risks, and would go out of his way to embarrass the enemy by the brazen impudence of his photographic reconnaissance missions. Apart from his normal work, which ranged over the whole Mediterranean, he had also a fine record as a fighter pilot. On the streets and in the bars he was immediately recognised and would be greeted affectionately by civilians and servicemen alike.

In the next four weeks I escorted Warburton on several photo-recce missions in connection with the forthcoming invasion of Sicily. We flew together and once or twice I took a Wing pilot along as an extra pair of eyes. We usually ran into trouble. Once 'Warbie' decided to take pictures of Syracuse and without wavering I found myself following him into the harbour at zero feet to be met by the strongest ack-ack fire. We flew up, down and out with everything shooting at us and the only reason we escaped was because the enemy could not depress their medium guns sufficiently – we were so low.

Another time off the toe of Italy, while 'Warbie' was taking his oblique photos, we were pounced on by four Me 109s. I told him to turn so that we could make good our escape out to sea. On the R/T he said: 'Sorry, old boy, got to finish this run – you see them off – you've got the guns.' I had a hell of a time of it with my number two, a sergeant pilot, as we turned into one attack after another, before 'Warbie' called to say he was headed out to sea and why was I not following to protect him. I managed to get one Me 109 and we damaged another but the experience only made Warburton laugh his head off when we landed. I remember a story he told me once. I thought it very funny and typified his outlook on life. His father, a Commander in the Royal Navy, was based in Haifa for a period and, having carried out a routine strategic reconnaissance in the eastern Mediterranean one day, 'Warbie' decided to refuel at Haifa and call on his father before returning to Malta. He finally tracked down his father in the Officers Club where he found him propping up the bar. They recognised each other immediately but made no gesture of recognition. Presently, someone in the circle said: 'By the way, "Warbie", have you met Commander Warburton?' 'How do you do,' the father smiled and held out his hand. 'Nice to know you,' Warbie replied. 'Warburton – that's odd', said 'Warbie's' father, 'wonder if we're related – where do you come from, young man?' The assembled company were, by this time, agog with excitement as father and son gradually checked each other out – through county, town and street till suddenly Commander Warburton exclaimed to Wing Commander Warburton: 'Good God – you don't live in the Cedars, do you –?' 'Yes, I do,' replied 'Warbie'. 'My son,' whooped Commander Warburton throwing an arm round 'Warbie, 'how wonderful to see you.' 'Steady, Father,' laughed 'Warbie'. 'Where the hell have you been hiding all these years – Mother's been looking for you everywhere!'

My favourite story, however, among his many exploits concerned the sortie in which he surprised the Italian fleet in Taranto harbour, taking his pictures from mast-top height. They were of little value from an Intelligence view-point because they were taken too low, but they had great propaganda value as they showed the washing hanging out to dry on the Italian admiral's flag-ship. Having returned to England in 1944 for the invasion of France 'Warbie' was lost on a photo-recce flight over southern Germany. From the report I heard, he was engaged by jet fighters.

The operations at this time consisted largely of defensive patrols, and offensive sweeps over Sicily. To give added flexibility and stimulate German reaction, my Wing had the capability of dropping two 250-lb bombs mounted on racks under the wings. To get the required accuracy we delivered our bombs in a 60° dive from 12,000–14,000 ft, releasing them at about 7,000 ft just above the light flak screen.

This was something quite new to me. I practised hard on the range, which consisted of a few rocks off the south-west coast of the island. There was a standard procedure laid down by the armament experts, but gradually I evolved my own technique with much better results. A typical operation was to form up the Wing with mixed armament, some carrying bombs; fly over to Sicily and bomb airfields, troop positions, road convoys, or factories and warehouses; then tear around fairly low looking for German and Italian aircraft taking off from various airfields.

Luqa was a unique RAF station. Packed to bursting point with many different types of aircraft, even after shedding some of the load to its sister airfield, Safi, it accommodated an astounding number of aircraft packed like sardines, by the time the Desert Air Force Squadrons arrived for the invasion of Sicily.

Willie Merton's job as Station Commander must have been a nightmare. The problems which faced him and his staff were formidable but he was a great organiser, and was always on the move bringing his personality and experience to bear where they were needed most. Each Squadron had its own special task to perform, and the administrative and technical requirements for each one had to be met separately. Excluding the Spitfires of my Wing, the Station was supporting seven other squadrons, comprising Wellingtons and Baltimores on anti-submarine duties and torpedo bombing; Beauforts; Mosquito night-fighters; Spitfire Mk XIs on photographic reconnaissance; and Beaufighters for strikes on enemy shipping.

We had to carry out a number of fighter-bombing missions each day in order to force enemy fighters off the ground. Once they had carried out their strikes on Malta they tended to stay on their airfields avoiding combat. On one occasion, while 126 Squadron bombed, I led 1435 Squadron and swept low round Comiso in the hope of picking up some 109s, but we had no luck. However, we spotted a motor convoy and concentrated on this as a suitable alternative.

If suitable tactics were employed there were ways of catching enemy fighters. Leading 126 Squadron round Comiso, and not finding any enemy fighters, I recrossed the Sicilian coast; then, climbing hard to 12,000 ft, turned the Squadron back inland again. As I expected, the Me 109s were following us out so we had a splendid jump on six of them. I got in two good bursts at the leader, knocking several bits off his tail and port wing, and my number two damaged another. Other pilots destroyed two 109s and damaged two more. This success was the reward of a planned variation in our normal tactics.

The AOC, Sir Keith Park, used to have a Wing Leaders' conference each week, which was known as 'Father's Prayers', to discuss the conduct of operations and give us a briefing on the scope of the following weeks' tasks. All the senior staff officers attended, and the AOC took a dim view if anyone was late. It was usually scheduled for early in the morning.

Most mornings around dawn a German reconnaissance air-craft, usually a Ju 88 or a Me 210, flew over Malta to take pictures and look for signs of activity. Having plenty of height and a high turn of speed he was a difficult target for the readiness flight to intercept. I decided to sit up for him one day. Unfortunately, I picked the morning when the AOC was having his meeting.

The duty controller and I arranged that I would take off and keep low till the enemy was picked up on the radar, whereupon he would let me know position and height, and I would climb at full throttle to a position up-sun of the raider's likely approach. I took off in a Mk IX with Jackson soon after first light. By this time we had received the first batch of Spitfire IXs destined for the Luqa Wing, so getting to altitude quickly presented no problems. We cruised round for some time at reduced power to conserve fuel, and since Operations had nothing to report, I finally decided to climb to 25,000 ft and go over to Sicily on the off-chance of making visual contact there.

It was a lovely clear morning and, picking out Cape Passero soon after leaving Malta, we settled into a full-throttle climb towards the distant landmark. I had just turned on reaching land with the sun at my back, intending to cruise down the coast towards Gela when the controller called me on the R/T and said: 'I don't know exactly what's going on, but there appears to be some activity low down off Gela.' I acknowledged the message and looked down. The sea in the early morning light was a lovely dark blue and against it I saw a sudden long thin streak of white appear, like a cotton thread; even as I looked it was gone. I focused my eyes on the spot and picked out the shape of a largish aircraft. Around it I could see tiny spots – Me 109s. I gave Jackson a thumbs-up sign and down we went like a couple of hawks. With the sun behind us it was too good to be true, and as we approached I counted ten Me 109s escorting a Dornier flying-boat. The 109s were dotted about round the flying-boat in a very haphazard formation.

Sweeping into the attack, I singled out a 109 flying rather wide, and, closing fast, I opened fire giving him two bursts from slightly above dead astern. I saw strikes immediately round the cockpit and a piece broke off the port wing. The enemy winged over and dived towards the sea. I just had time to give another 109 a quick burst before I had to break and zoom climb away. Jackson in the meantime had fired at another 109, observing strikes and damage; but seeing me break, he followed in a tight corkscrew climb.

I wheeled round quickly for another attack, and as I looked down saw my first 109 hit the sea and explode, sending up a huge fountain of spray. The rest of the 109s were streaking for land, having left the old flying-boat (it was an Air-Sea Rescue one) to fend for himself as best he could. To chase them was a waste of time, so I called Jackson: 'Let's tickle up the Dornier.' Overtaking the slow old flying-boat, I throttled back and got into formation, after dropping the undercarriage to reduce speed. The Dornier pilot peered out and although I could not see his face too clearly, or observe his reactions, I reckon if he had had a whip he would have flogged his boat to death. I gave him a rude sign; then snapping up my wheels, turned for home. We didn't shoot down the Dornier because it was obviously on a search and rescue mission, and as we had lost a pilot from one of the other Wings the previous evening (and got a couple of 109s as well) it was just possible it might have been carrying one of our chaps on board.

Landing back at Luqa I just had time to change my shirt before the Intelligence Officer reminded me about the AOC's conference. Quickly I jumped into my old Fiat and tore off to headquarters, arriving about fifteen minutes late.

'Good afternoon,' the AOC chided me, 'I hope you slept well?'

'Yes, sir,' but before I could say anything further, the door opened and a staff officer appeared.

'Excuse me, sir,' he said, looking at the AOC, 'we have just been told by Ops. that a short while ago, Wing Commander Smith and Squadron Leader Jackson shot down some Me 109s out of a formation of ten that were escorting a Dornier flying-boat off Gela.'

Sir Keith Park looked at me and smiled: 'Not bad – not at all bad – now, that's what I call a splendid excuse.'

There were two aspects of life in Malta I never got used to. One was the food – rough to say the least, and, as far as I was concerned, certain to knock me out with tummy trouble if I ate any green vegetables or fruit that had not been cooked. A lot of people suffered with me and the bug was known as 'Malta Dog'. The other nightmare was dust and sandflies. These caused an attack of high fever and an infected throat that put me in hospital for ten days.

Luckily Brian Kingcome, who was on board a ship bound for the Far East, had been diverted to Malta and posted super-numerary to my Wing a week or so earlier, so he led the Squadrons in my absence. By the time I was fit again the build-up for the invasion of Sicily was well under way.

The social life on Malta was pretty basic revolving round the Union Club and its private beach, Charlie's Bar and the Choco-late King; two pleasant night-spots in which we could relax with a few pink gins and a glass or two of wine though goodness knows where they came from. Brian Kingcome and I also kept a boat at St Paul's Bay and we did some sailing when operations permitted. I remember, late one night after a dance, taking a girlfriend to the Union Club beach for a swim, which was strictly forbidden after dark because the place became a restricted area, patrolled by the Army, in case the Germans and/or Italians took it into their heads to send in a raiding party. There was a full moon and nobody in sight so we took off our clothes and dived into the lovely deep water. Not having any-thing with which to dry ourselves, we were lying on a smooth slab of rock when I suddenly felt something jab into my bottom and looking round over my shoulder found a soldier had given me a jab with his bayonet.

'Gotcher!' he cried. 'Hands up – you're under arrest – move.' Taken completely by surprise and furious for having been so rudely interrupted, I got to my feet and shouted: 'What the hell do you think you're doing – you idiot – don't you – don't you know you're talking to an officer –!' Controlling my anger and not knowing what else to say, I glowered at him. At this point my girlfriend shrieked with laughter and, like a silver nymph, took a couple of steps and disappeared back into the sea. The tension broken, the soldier said: 'Sorry sir, I didn't see you had a woman with you – I'll say good-night – some do have all the luck –' he grinned and slinging his rifle saluted smartly and left me in peace. The tact of the British Army has never failed to appeal to me.

142

As a prelude to the invasion Pantellaria was captured almost entirely through air bombardment. This island, so placed that its garrison could observe every movement in the narrow straits off the North Africa coast, had to be liquidated, otherwise no secret preparations for the invasion of Sicily would have been possible. Pantellaria was the Italian equivalent of Heligoland and Mussolini claimed it was impregnable. It supported an aerodrome with underground hangars and living accommodation for 10,000 men. If the Allies wanted to see what air bombardment could do, here was their chance. The effort was left to the Tactical Bomber Force supported by Liberators and Fortresses of the Strategic Air Forces. Altogether some 4,600 tons of bombs were dropped on the island, but before the assault forces could land, a white cross of surrender marked the airfield, and a white flag flew from the Commander's Headquarters. The great weight of bombs had done the trick.

Following victory in North Africa and pending the invasion of Sicily, the Desert Air Force Wings had withdrawn to the Tripoli area to rest and regroup. Now the squadrons of 244 Wing moved into Luqa and to make room I went off with 126 and 1435 Squadrons to Safi. This airfield had been prepared specially to cater for the build-up, and Innes Westmacott, its Commander, was a great help in getting things properly organised for us. Offensive operations continued much as before, but with an increased effort in escort missions to Tactical and Strategic bombers attacking the Gerbini/Catania group of airfields. By the eve of the invasion it was clear that through the systematic bombing of enemy airfields we had gained the initiative. Allied Air Forces could muster some 4,000 aircraft for operations connected with the new campaign, and a direct comparison with the enemy showed that the German and Italian bases in Sicily, Italy, Sardinia and southern France accommodated less than 2,000 aircraft of all types.

Broadly speaking, the RAF provided the fighters, fighter-bombers and maritime aircraft, while the bombers and transport support effort came from the Americans. In Sicily and southern Italy, the enemy effort for immediate operations consisted of 260 German and 200 Italian fighters and fighter-bombers (about seventy-five of these night-fighters) and only fifty Ju 88 bombers; the rest had withdrawn to northern Italy and southern France.

Small wonder that by the eve of the Sicily landings, Allied air power had achieved all its aims. The enemy air forces were scattered and unable to regroup so long as the bombing continued, being driven from one airfield to another until finally they took refuge far afield. The German and Italian fighters were defeated before the land battle took place. A few enemy night-attacks managed to hinder the assembly and dispatch of the invasion forces from the ports of North Africa, but these were on a small scale. The Royal Navy had been prepared for the loss of a good many ships; instead only a few light vessels and an illuminated hospital ship were sunk, while the Americans lost two destroyers, two submarine chasers, and six landing craft. The continuous and effective pounding of the Messina ferry hindered the Germans' attempt to reinforce their combat units in Sicily, by preventing the flow of arms and supplies.

On Malta, Advanced HQ Desert Air Force shared a joint Command Post with 8th Army, but at this stage, in order to preserve unity of air command, the control of Desert Air Force Squadrons was vested in the AOC Malta. Harry Broadhurst, AOC Desert Air Force, had no control over the pre-invasion operations, and although he frequently visited his Squadrons, he did not regain control until the landings in Sicily had taken place and a bridgehead had been established.

This arrangement sounded very odd to me. Sir Keith Park was an expert in air defence matters whereas Harry Broadhurst had all the practical experience of fighter-bomber and tactical bomber operations gained during the recent fighting in North Africa. He was also backed by a splendid system of close support control techniques in calling for and dispensing air-to-ground attacks on battlefield targets. The 8th Army/Desert Air Force team had proved invincible in practice; furthermore, General Montgomery and Harry Broadhurst had worked together closely throughout.

General Montgomery, during the planning stage for the invasion of Sicily, had urged that Harry Broadhurst should be made responsible for all operations in support of the landings. He was, however, overruled.

Inevitably, I suppose, jealousies and in-fighting among some senior air commanders tended to become matters of prestige and led to decisions being taken which were not in the best interests of operations at Squadron level.

Also Malta was defensive minded. I noticed this on taking over the Luqa Wing. The island had fought a very hard defensive battle over the previous two years. Aggressive tactics and carrying the fight to Sicily did not come naturally into the scheme of things. Some of the more senior officers at Air Headquarters needed much convincing, and changing basic defensive attitudes into an aggressive plan was frowned upon.

As fresh units continually arrived on the island I saw more old friends, and met new ones. Jackie Darwen, the CO of 239 Wing, was a desert personality I met for the first time. Small and tough, with the quick movements of a bird and possessing great charm, he led his Kittyhawk fighter-bombers with tremendous courage and success.

Malta was at last coming into its own. The island fortress, which had been preserved through the dark years of 1940–2, was now ready to play a decisive part in the war.

CHAPTER THIRTEEN

A rude visit

How Malta managed to handle and sustain so many extra units preceding the invasion of Sicily was a truly astonishing story of efficiency in supply and organisation. The island had been turned into a gigantic aircraft-carrier supporting twenty Spitfire Squadrons, five night-fighter Squadrons, and a large number of bomber, strike, and reconnaissance Squadrons as well. Added to these were the ground-crews and supporting units of three fighter-bomber Wings whose aircraft were waiting, literally, for enough space on the island to enable them to move in. The spotlight had been switched full on Malta, and we were ready to launch the first large-scale assault into Europe. The 'soft underbelly' of the German-Italian Axis was going to be split open.

About a week before the invasion proper, I landed at Safi late one evening after a Wing escort mission, to find a message from Harry Broadhurst waiting for me, with an invitation to meet him for dinner at his headquarters in Valetta. I had seen him briefly soon after he arrived in Malta, but we had had no chance of a proper talk. When I arrived I found him in the midst of a very lively Desert Air Force crowd. He was looking extremely bronzed and fit, and in excellent spirits.

From the moment Broady joined Desert Air Force as Senior Air Staff Officer under 'Mary' Coningham soon after the battle of El Alamein, he had won acclaim from the Army for his expert direction and understanding of land/air operations. He was a great believer in the fighter-bomber as a battle-winning weapon, and used the flexibility and tremendous firepower of the close-support system to turn the tide of the land-battle by preventing reinforcements from reaching the battle and later turning the enemy's withdrawal into headlong flight.

When he become AOC, just after the fall of Tripoli, his

146

foresight and planning guided the fortunes of Desert Air Force through one of its most difficult periods, for with the formation of the North-West African Air Forces, now dominated by the American contribution, it was touch and go whether Desert Air Force was to lose its identity as a separate and viable force. His theories had been tested and proved to the hilt at Mareth and El Hamma, where, in close co-operation with General Montgomery and the Corps and Divisional Commanders in 8th Army, he used his fighter-bombers to such devastating effect that Monty's divisions were able to break through the German fortified lines with little difficulty. One captured Italian general admitted that the fighter-bombers had destroyed the whole of his divisional transport, making it impossible for him to play an effective part by neutralising his formations. Though the fighter-bomber operations at El Hamma did not pretend to prove that an air force could blast a way along which an army could advance, they did show conclusively that air support, when properly co-ordinated, could completely disorganise enemy units, transport and reserves of armour and enable our own ground-forces to exploit the situation to the full. But it was essential for success that the Army Commander's reaction to the situation was immediate and decisive. There is no doubt that the successes and the lessons were to play an important part later in Normandy. As a result of Desert Air Force's achievements the Americans were quick to appreciate the merit of the British system in calling for and allocating air support, and at once brought their own support system into line with that of DAF/8th Army.

Later that evening, over a night-cap, Broady told me he was trying to find me a spot in one of his Wings; there was a certain reorganisation taking place in Desert Air Force, and he hoped to fix it all up before long. This news pleased me greatly, as I knew that once the invasion had taken place Malta would become exceedingly dull, reverting to a purely defensive role. After all the excitement, I did not fancy being stuck in a backwater.

A few days before 'D' Day,* Sir Keith Park visited my Wing

---

* Here and after I use this term in its correct sense as the day of operations for any major assault landing.

and brought General Montgomery round to meet the pilots and ground-crews. It was the first time I had seen the great man and found him very charming and extremely air-minded. He already knew a great deal about us and our operations. He talked to us about the impending invasion and what an important part the Malta Squadrons had to play in the scheme of things.

My Wing flew out at first light on 10 July 1943 to cover the invasion of Sicily, patrolling with Spitfires from 244 Wing over the immense array of ships and landing craft strung along the Gulf of Noto, where on land the 8th Army was at grips with the enemy. It was a magnificent sight: the shallow waters were packed with amphibious craft and infantrymen wading ashore, while further out a grey shield of warships formed a protective arc, the red flashes of their guns stark against the dawn sky. Our Spitfires were stepped in layers from 10,000–20,000 ft, waiting to pounce on any enemy formations that dared to interfere with the operations on land and at sea. British and Canadians occupied the beaches at the eastern end, while the Americans were establishing themselves at the western end of the invasion front, with the immediate objective of capturing the airfields around Gela.

The previous night, and in the early hours of the morning, the first large-scale airborne assault ever attempted by the Allies dropped on inland strongpoints vital to the overall plan. After a sea-crossing of some 400 miles, 350 aircraft and 130 gliders landed about 5,000 men. The Americans were to be dropped near Gela in order to capture and hold the high ground overlooking the roads leading from the beaches. The British force was to land near Syracuse where they were to hold the canal bridge and railway; also infiltrate into the suburbs of the city.

The Allies learned their first sharp lesson regarding the sensitivity of this type of assault to weather conditions. A terrific wind sprang up while the airborne force was in transit. Gliders were released miles from the intended landing points and came down into the sea. Only twelve landed in the correct area, seventy-five in widely dispersed areas of southern Sicily, and the rest in the sea. The gallantry of the men taking part stands out as one of the great episodes of the war. Eight officers and fifteen men survived and were still fighting off a whole battalion of crack German paratroopers, supported by field artillery, when the force was relieved just in time and the bridge recaptured. Outside Gela the Americans, though surrounded by tanks, were able to prevent enemy reinforcements from reaching the beaches. There is no doubt that their splendid action speeded up the inland advance by days.

Through the combined efforts of the Navies, both British and American, and the Air Forces in keeping seas and skies clear of the Luftwaffe and Regia Aeronautica, in two days 15th Army Group were able to land 80,000 men, 7,000 vehicles, 300 tanks and 900 guns on the beaches of Sicily. During the same period the ports of Syracuse and Licata were captured and used immediately, greatly speeding the build-up and ensuring the ultimate success of the land offensive. Sad and disheartening though the losses were among the airborne forces, the fact that those that got through were widely scattered paid an unexpected dividend. Rumour and uncertainty struck at the hearts of the enemy troops and made them believe that a great airborne armada had landed all over Sicily. Captured Germans were convinced 20,000–30,000 parachutists and gliderborne formations had landed in their midst, and they were seized with panic. Large numbers of Italian soldiers openly deserted, and even whole units gave themselves up. The German High Command reacted swiftly to restore order and discipline through General Hube, who lost no time in ruthlessly dealing with deserters and incompetent subordinate commanders. Under his tough leadership the German army in Sicily regrouped and fought to the bitter end.

With their depleted strength in fighter aircraft, the Germans and Italians could not hope to engage all our formations over the beaches and bridgehead. Consequently, it was not till late on 10 July that I got any joy. Leading 1435 Squadron on patrol, I ran into a mixed formation of Macchi 202s and FW 190s attempting to bomb the ships. We broke up the enemy formation and I latched on to an FW 190, hurtling after him in a steep dive. I gave him a short burst without seeing any result, except that he immediately jettisoned his bomb. I tried desperately to get into a better position but had to break off as the FW 190 flew straight into a wall of AA fire pouring toward us from the ships. As I zoom climbed away, I glanced behind and was surprised to find two Me 109s on my tail, both firing hard, but luckily missing me with yards to spare. Two pilots belonging to 'Peggy' O'Neill's flight, acting as top cover, damaged one of the 109s and destroyed the other.

The next day I had better luck. Soon after getting on patrol I spotted four Macchi 202s immediately below and realised they had not seen us. I went down after them with my number two, and was about to open fire on the lead Macchi when they saw us and broke into our attack, still keeping immaculate formation. Thereafter a hectic dog-fight took place. This Italian pilot really knew what he was doing: apart from giving a splendid aerobatic display, I found that each time he stayed and turned he gained on me in the turn. I looked frantically about for help but there was no sign of my number two. Knowing my Spitfire's capabilities so well, I pulled her up sharply in corkscrew turns into the sun as steeply as I could. I expected to hear and feel the unwelcome bangs of exploding shells in my fuselage but nothing happened until suddenly I felt my Spitfire shake violently and the next instant we were spinning – I caught her after a couple of turns and getting control again looked for the Macchi. Sure enough there he was, slightly to one side and below me asking to be shot down. My first burst caught him in the cockpit area and wing root and he went up in flames, shedding bits as he winged over and dived into the high ground overlooking Noto. He must have thought he had got me when he saw me spin.

I had followed him down, so I climbed up searching for the rest of my patrol. At 15,000 ft I joined up with a group of Spitfires from one of the other Wings and almost at once got mixed up with a formation of eight FW 190s. During the dog-fight I chased after a solitary and managed to damage him, when once more I had to turn hard, on being attacked from behind. To this day I am not sure if the aircraft that attacked me was a Me 109 or a Spitfire. Anyway, it was extremely hostile, and as I was nearly out of ammunition I decided I had had enough; spiralling down towards the coast, I streaked back to Malta well satisfied with life. Later, after the Italian surrender,

A rude visit

I found when I visited Lecce that the Macchi I destroyed that day had been piloted by one of Italy's fighter aces, credited with a large number of our scalps. In general the standard of flying of the Italian pilots was very high indeed, and in encounters with Macchi 205s particularly we were up against aircraft that could turn and dog-fight with our Spitfires extremely well.

Unfortunately, Peter Olver, commanding 244 Wing, was shot down over the beaches the same day, but we heard in due course he was unhurt and was a prisoner. The following day Brian Kingcome took over his Wing. Though I was sorry to see Brian leave, I felt certain I would soon be following him.

Each time I led 126 and 1435 Squadrons on patrols over the beaches on 12 July we ran into FW 190s and Me 109s. I fired several bursts at enemy aircraft without seeing any results, till late in the evening when my Wing caught and attacked a mixed formation of Macchis and Me 109s while on patrol at 15,000 ft between Augusta and Syracuse.

With 1435 following, I had just turned the Wing inland over Augusta, when my attention was drawn to three Macchis that dived across in front of us, then pulled up in a perfect formation loop. The next moment we were jumped by some fifteen Macchis and about ten Me 109s; without further manoeuvring we singled out an enemy aircraft apiece and dog-fights broke out all over the place. Jacques was flying number two to me, and calling him on the R/T to stick close, I pounced on a Macchi, and from slightly above and astern pumped a couple of bursts into him. Immediately smoke poured out and big pieces broke away from the cockpit area with bits of canopy showering and glinting in the bright sun, like drops of rain. The Macchi winged over quite slowly and dived away steeply, out of control. It was obvious the pilot was dead. I looked round for Jacques but he was not there; instead I saw the wicked grey nose of a Me 109 very close pointing straight at me just as he opened fire. There were two enormous bangs behind my back and the Spitfire seemed to double up with pain as the stick was wrenched out of my hand. I heard a high-pitched whine in my ear-phones and my radio went dead. The Spitfire then pitched in a steep nose-up attitude and next thing I remember was that I was spinning. Collecting my wits, I struggled with the controls, and using brute force finally got the Spitfire out of the spin and level again. I had to use all my strength to prevent her from repeating the upward pitch and, testing the elevator trimmer, found it spun uselessly in my hand. The elevator was jammed and the control wires shot to bits. By juggling with the throttle and with the stick pushed hard against the instrument panel I managed to maintain height, my airspeed reading 120 mph.

I had lost a lot of height and was down to 3,000 ft. Looking over the side I noticed that in my exertions I had drifted south of Syracuse and was now inside our bridgehead. I set course for Malta praying for my Spitfire to hold together, for if I had to bale out over the sea, I would not be able to send a Mayday call. I thought about a forced landing on the beach but could not bear the idea of sacrificing my aeroplane. It seemed ages before I picked out the dark smudge ahead that was Malta and dragged myself in on my engine for an adventurous landing at Safi.

The boys were all down, so they rushed over and helped me out of the cockpit. Jacques had seen me shoot down the Macchi and later spin but had not seen the Me 109 that shot me; in trying to follow he had lost sight of my aircraft. There must have been more Me 109s behind me, so I don't know how he managed to escape being shot up. My Spitfire was in a mess. Cannon-shells had blasted a couple of large holes in the side. One had burst against the radio and armour behind my seat. Another, having made a hole the size of a football, had torn the control wires to shreds. The elevator was hanging by one thread of frayed wire and my rigger neatly snapped this with a sharp blow from his fingers. 'You'll not be needing that any more,' he grinned at me. 'It all looks very untidy – doesn't it?' Another cannon-shell had torn big pieces out of the elevator and rudder surfaces. To make up for it, we had one Macchi destroyed, two probables, and three Me 109s damaged.

Malta-based Spitfires had a successful time from 10 July to 20 July 1943: we destroyed fifty-seven, probably destroyed eleven and damaged twenty-six enemy fighters. In the same period our night-fighters destroyed thirty-seven, probably destroyed eight and damaged four enemy bombers. On 25 July, 322 Wing destroyed twenty-one Ju 52 German transport aircraft and four Me 109s, damaging a further three.

A rude visit

Two days after the invasion Harry Broadhurst landed in his Spitfire on the newly prepared strip at Pachino and after a brief inspection was satisfied with the state of the operations set-up, signal units, ground crews and camp sites. He decided that three Squadrons, Nos. 1 (South African Air Force), 92 and 145 from 244 Wing would move in the next day at first light. Thus 244 earned the distinction of being the first RAF formation to operate again from Continental soil since the fall of France in 1940.

After a few days they were off again to a new landing strip at Cassibile that had to be seen to be believed. Hacked out of a vineyard the runway was covered in about six inches of powder-like dust, so that once the first pair of aircraft had taken off the rest followed blind. As 244 moved out, 239 with Kittyhawks and 285 with tactical reconnaissance Spitfires moved in.

Just at this time I had a stroke of luck. Though the Wings that had been operating with the 1st Army in the North African invasion were commanded by group captains, the Desert Air Force Wings were still commanded by wing commanders. Now the Air Ministry decided to upgrade them to group captain status, and to my great joy, on the appointment of Brian Kingcome to command 244 with the rank of Group Captain, Harry Broadhurst got me the Wing Leader appointment under Brian. This was not achieved without some opposition, I believe, from Sir Keith Park, but he agreed to release me in the end. I lost no time in handing over to Tony Lovell, and it was with great excitement that I piled into a transport aircraft and reported for duty to Brian just twelve days after 'D' day.

My first day with 244 saw a section of four aircraft of 1 (SAAF) Squadron intercepting twelve Dornier 17s near Augusta early in the morning, and Van der Merwe got one while two other pilots damaged two more. They were attacked in turn by Macchis and 109s and it was a great pity that no more of our Spitfires could get to the area in time, as we would have had a proper killing. German aircraft were to be seen only occasionally at this stage and when intercepted showed a great reluctance to fight.

Just before the end of July, the Germans were denied the use of the Messina Ferry and the ports of Catania and Augusta, so they tried to air-lift vital supplies of petrol and oil to their armoured units fighting for their lives in central Sicily. They ferried the precious supplies across the sea to a landing strip near Cape Milazzo.

Peter Hugo's 322 Wing, returning from escorting Boston bombers to Messina, espied twenty-one Ju 52 transports escorted by about twenty-five Me 109s and Macchis. Colin Gray, the Wing Leader, could hardly believe his eyes, but from a perfect tactical position led his formation into the attack. The engagement was hectic while it lasted and disastrous to the Germans. They lost all the transports plus four Me 109s and a Macchi. This was excellent work; by the time I arrived on the scene with 92 and 1 (SAAF) Squadrons, all we saw were a number of wrecks still burning furiously on land, and wide areas of blazing sea. We repeated the exercise in the afternoon in the hope that the Germans would try and run the gauntlet again, but in vain.

Most of the Squadron pilots of 244 were veterans from the Desert and a large number were on second and even third tours of operations with their Squadrons. The Squadron Commanders in particular were seasoned campaigners, and presented an interesting cross-section of nationality and temperament. There was Lance Wade, 145 Squadron, an American Eagle, who had come to the Middle East in 1941. He had done brilliantly and had run up a score of twenty-eight enemy kills while serving in Desert Air Force. Dark and balding, he was older than the rest of us, and had been a test pilot with Fairchild in Tucson, Arizona, before coming to England to join the RAF. 'Hunk' Humphreys, commanding 92, was ex-Biggin Hill, also an experienced pilot who had done extremely well in the Desert. He fought hard all the time and was on his third tour of operations. Stan Turner, a Canadian in the RAF, commanded 417 (RCAF) Squadron. He had served with Douglas Bader in 242 Squadron during the Battle of Britain. An expert marksman and brilliant pilot, Stan should have been at least in command of a Wing, but he habitually upset senior officers by his straight talking and blunt manner, so that as soon as he got command of a Wing he would invariably find himself back with a Squadron. But he was happiest among pilots, with his Spitfire pointing in the right direction, preferably towards a Me 109 or a fat Ju 88. Sanitslaw Skalski was a Pole, commanding 601 (AAF) Squadron. I had known him in Fighter Command at Northolt in the Polish Wing. He hated all Germans, was a man of deeds not words, and a killer in the air. He survived the war, went back to Poland and was promptly arrested by the Russians and disappeared into prison for eight years. By the time he was released he was a sick and broken man. I shall never understand why we let him go back. Like many gallant Poles that fought for us so unselfishly, Skalski had a burning desire to return to Poland. Yet we as a nation seemed to wash our hands of him and his compatriots after the war, encouraging them to go home and then leaving them to rot in Communist prisons. It was a strange sequel to our original declaration of war on the Germans because of what they did to Poland. Finally, there was Hannes Faure, commanding 1 (SAAF) Squadron. He took over the Squadron about the time I joined the Wing. A veteran of the fighting in Abyssinia and the Western Desert, he was one of the calmest men I ever knew. Nothing upset Hannes, and the tougher the situation the better he liked it: an ideal type in a tight corner. He reminded me very much of Peter Hugo.

By the beginning of August, the Army was pushing steadily northwards east of Mt Etna. The Gordon Highlanders were in Belpasso, and 78 Division had entered Adrano. Catania had fallen and most of the island apart from the north-eastern tip was in Allied hands. It was time for our Wings to move forward from the bridgehead airfields. The Gerbini group had been severely damaged by bombing and were heavily mined. The airfield engineers got to work on the flat Lentini plain, and prepared a number of fresh landing strips. The plain, low lying and malarial, was well irrigated, supporting small farmsteads. The ground was baked hard by the hot sun, and, provided we did not have rain, was ideal for the operation of aircraft. The malaria, however, was of a serious kind, and having experienced it in India I took every available precaution to protect myself. But casualties were heavy and it took quite some time for our doctors to get it under control.

Our daily operations consisted of escorts for the Kittyhawks and Warhawks and the tactical bombers; battle area patrols; protecting the ports; and occasionally helping out the fighter-bombers with strafing attacks along the roads leading to Messina. We attacked transports, flak posts and troops forward of the bombline.

The end of the campaign in Sicily was in sight. Our attacks increased on Messina and the Straits where the fighter-bombers and light bombers turned their attention to the Siebel ferries, barges and smaller ships evacuating the remnants of the German army to Italy. The Straits became known as 'Flak Alley' and I have never in my life seen such concentration of AA fire of all kinds. We escorted our bombers attacking Randazzo, a major road junction connecting enemy forces in the west to those in the north. We bombed it till it fell apart.

On 12 August 1943 the Germans, feeling they were being cut in half, and wishing to preserve communications through Randazzo to Messina until their evacuation to Italy had been completed, launched a sharp and highly successful moonlight attack on the Lentini landing grounds with a force of thirty to forty Ju 88s. Number 1 (SAAF) had held a party that evening. Brian and I had been invited, and we took along a former CO of 601 Squadron, John Bisdee, who was staying the night. After returning to the Wing we had turned in for the night when quite suddenly the raid hit us. We went outside to watch the fireworks, not realising at first that we were under attack. Huge flares dangling from parachutes hung in the sky, lighting up the whole airfield. Our AA batteries opened up and the tracer shells of the Bofors guns patterned the sky like strings of red beads as they probed for the enemy bombers, now whining their way over us.

Then came the bombs: high explosive, incendiary, and the murderous little anti-personnel butterfly bombs, the size of cricket balls, which showered down all round us.

Just then the phone rang. One of the Operations officers told me that a petrol dump near the Operations caravan had been hit and was burning fiercely and that other bombs were exploding nearby. Suddenly I heard a loud noise on the line and it went dead. Slamming the receiver back I went out to tell Brian that the Operations caravan had been hit, but did not get a chance to do so. A stick of butterfly bombs crackled overhead and we threw ourselves to the ground. The danger past, we recovered from our undignified posture just as the senior administrative officer came along to claim Brian's attention. I decided I had better get to the airfield, so I jumped into my jeep and rushed off down the dusty track weaving my way between the trees. I had not gone far before I heard another shower of butterfly bombs creeping up. Slamming on the brakes I baled out on to my face biting on dust. A figure was standing nearby gazing up into the sky (he turned out to be one of the cooks) so I pulled him down beside me. Luckily, I escaped, but bomb fragments hit my companion in the back. He was badly wounded and as I helped him into the jeep I felt the warm stickiness of blood run between my fingers. Driving as carefully as possible, I got him to Wing sick-quarters and delivered him to the senior medical officer. The wounded were already arriving thick and fast and there was a sickening smell of blood and ether in the hot dusty air.

The airfield was in a sorry state. The Operations caravan had been knocked out and was burning. One of the Operations officers and one of the clerks were dead while the Intelligence Clerk was badly wounded. Huge flames were leaping from the petrol dump, and I could see two parked Spitfires silhouetted starkly against the flames. From overhead came the roar of many engines, punctuated by the sharp crackle of cannon- and machine-gun-fire, and the flat explosions of bombs bursting. The pounding of our Bofors guns added to the din.

Brian rejoined me and together we cleared away some of the debris around the blazing operations caravan, and also managed to carry a pile of ammunition to a safer area. But at this juncture there was little we could do. The raid lasted about three-quarters of an hour. It was obvious that a great deal of damage had been done, but we were not able to assess the full extent of it till morning.

At the height of the raid Dick Atcherley, the Commander of our Mobile Operations Room Unit (the ground control interception organisation for our day- and night-fighters), came to see us. He arrived on a motor cycle he had taken from an army dispatch rider. How he got it away from him I'll never know.

Dick Atcherley told us he had nose-dived his staff car into a bomb-hole on the road outside which he had not seen in the dark. He helped to restore our morale and gave us all an excuse to have a good laugh. His irrepressible good humour was infectious, whatever the shambles around him.

The tally in the morning showed that about thirty Spitfires were destroyed or severely damaged, while eleven men had been killed and forty wounded, twelve of them seriously. 322 and 239 Wings also suffered comparable losses and damage at Lentini East, a few miles distant.

A number of delayed action bombs on the runway prevented us from operating till after midday, and it was some days later before we got the damaged aircraft repaired and were able to function at full strength again. The raid had been highly successful from the German standpoint, yet they never repeated it.

CHAPTER FOURTEEN

Death of a Walrus

On 17 August, just thirty-eight days after the invasion began, Sicily fell. The Germans escaped across the narrow Straits of Messina, leaving in their wake large quantities of stores and equipment, not to mention the battered and burnt-out wrecks of 1,200 Axis aircraft, destroyed by bombing and in aerial combat; more than half of them German.

The shock of this deafeat hit hard in Rome, and made the Italians realise that within a matter of days their homeland would be invaded. Already they had suffered by the bombing of Rome from Strategic American bombers, the targets being the Littorio marshalling yards and the airfield, Ciampino. The Germans retaliated by carrying out sharp attacks by night on the Sicilian ports. They foxed us at first by using slow Ju 87 dive-bombers, which Paddy Green and his pilots in 600 Squadron found very frustrating. However, they adapted themselves to the conditions and shot down quite a few, even though they had to fly their Beaufighters with wheels and flaps down in an effort to prevent overshooting their targets during interceptions.

On 25 August big build-ups of thunderstorms threatened and it was decided as an insurance to put a flight into Gerbini Main for local defence. This airfield had a dumbbell-shaped concrete runway, but otherwise was extremely rough, and certain parts were still heavily mined. 40 (SAAF) Squadron put some of their TAC R Spitfires into Gerbini as well, and in a couple of tents a few yards off the runway we got the phones working and waited for something to happen. The grass area was extremely rough, so I ordered that aircraft taxiing onto the runway were to carry an airman on the tail of each aircraft to insure against the pilot tipping up on his nose, and wrecking the propeller.

159

Death of a Walrus

Suddenly the phone rang and two TAC R Spitfires were ordered off; we were told they would be briefed in the air by the controller. Idly, I watched them start up, then found an upturned box of bully beef handy and sat down to enjoy a cigarette. As the leading aircraft approached down the runway I noticed a peculiar bulge on the tail. It flashed past and the bulge turned into the shocked face of an airman peering down at me, his arms entwined across the sternpost of the Spitfire and with his legs gripping the leading edge of the tail-plane. Already the wheels were up and the nose of the aircraft pointed heavenwards. The South African pilot, having taxied onto the runway, had opened his throttle and taken off at once. He quite forgot about the wretched man sitting on his tail.

My pilots now came out to watch the fun, offering useless advice and taking bets as to whether the airman would fall or whether we would witness a nice messy landing. Strange to relate, neither happened. The SAAF pilot flew his aircraft very skilfully in for a landing. He had seen the man on his tail reflected in the rear-view mirror above his head as soon as he found the trim of his aircraft was haywire; being forewarned he was in a position to use caution tempered with skill. The Spitfire made a perfect three-point landing while I raced over the rough grass in an attempt to intercept him. By the time I got to the startled airman, now standing foolishly on the runway, the Spitfire had taken off again.

'How do you feel?' I inquired.

'I don't know,' he answered dazedly, 'I think I want to be sick.'

His face had gone a peculiar greeny-yellow and his eyes stared into space. The next moment he pitched forward onto his arms and face in a dead faint. Half an hour later he was as good as new again, having had a pint of tea and rum rammed down his throat.

Two days later, we returned to Lentini. Enemy activity continued and a few FW 190s tried dive-bombing shipping in Augusta harbour. Brian thought a couple of Spitfires at Cassibile would be a good idea as the rain was still hanging about. I said I would go, and took a pilot of 417 Squadron with me. While I was airborne a rain-squall hit Lentini, so we spent the night with 600 Squadron. Having spent a quiet evening in Paddy Green's mobile Operations room, watching the activity and listening to night-interceptions going on, I was just about to go off to bed when the news came through that Paddy Green and Desmond Hughes had had successful interceptions, and shot down a couple of German bombers raiding Augusta. Those that were not flying duly celebrated the success with me, so it was with a somewhat thick head that I took off next morning to intercept a further German fighter-bomber attack on Augusta.

There was much cloud along the coast and after following various changes of direction ordered by Operations, round the big banks of rain clouds, I suddenly caught a fleeting glimpse of an FW 190 diving through a gap. Opening up to full power, I chased after the enemy and was immediately shot at by a second FW 190, which dived in over my left shoulder. Tracers streaked past my port wing, and it shot past me very close. The pilot unwisely straightened up giving me an excellent opportunity to open fire on him from slightly below on a fine quarter. I saw strikes on his wing root and the bottom of the cockpit, and with smoke trailing he disappeared into a thick cloud.

We searched round the cloud then spiralled down below and had a look, but there was no sign of him. Chatter on the R/T told me other Spitfires were also in the area, so after searching a bit longer without success, we returned to Lentini.

Arriving at Operations we were greeted with much animated talk from our Army liaison officers, Eustace Elwes and Chris Wren, who informed me that two FW 190s were down in the sea and that the pilot of one of them had been picked up by a rescue launch. I decided to go along and interview the rescued German as I was interested to find out why the German fighter pilots were behaving with such a lack of their former offensive spirit.

Through an interpreter, I found out that the Luftwaffe was in disgrace with Goering, who had ordered that unless there was a marked improvement in combat efficiency, pilots who avoided fighting us would be sent to the Russian front to fight in army units.

Though I had no means of substantiating it, I felt pretty certain that this particular German pilot was the one I had shot at. The prisoner (he was a warrant officer) said he had fired at a Spitfire and overshot it. Before he could escape he had been hit in his fuel tank and baled out in cloud. He had been slightly wounded in the right leg and from the angle I had fired and the hits I had seen on his aircraft it seemed to fit. A few days later a captured enemy Order of the Day was passed from Desert Air Force to Wing Intelligence. Its full text read as follows:

'Together with the fighter pilots in France, Norway and Russia, I can only regard you with contempt. If an immediate improvement is not forthcoming, flying personnel from the Kommodore downwards must expect to be reduced to the ranks and transferred to the Eastern Front to serve on the ground.'

[signed] *Reichsmarschall* Hermann Goering

This piece of information came as no surprise. Lately the German fighter pilots had shown a reluctance to fight. On questioning the prisoner he explained that morale was low, conditions bad and that our Spitfires were more numerous and superior in performance to their FW 190s and Me 109s. He went on to tell me that the only way he and his friends could get away with not being grounded was by firing their guns before returning to base and if that meant into thin air – well, so much the better. He had lost the will to fight; as far as he was concerned it was useless against such odds.

I do not think these sentiments were general but it made me realise that the end of determined fighting by German pilots was in sight. However, at Salerno, Cassino and Anzio, German fighter pilots put up stiff resistance.

During the lull between the end of hostilities in Sicily and the invasion of Italy, we had a chance to relax. Harry Broadhurst used a captured Italian motor launch to go for trips up the coast, and to do some improvised water skiing. Usually, he invited some of us to join him, Claude Pelly, his Senior Air Staff Officer, and John Whitford, his Air Officer Administration. The launch was always well stocked with good things to eat and a large quantity of captured Bavarian beer. We modelled a thirty-gallon Spitfire drop-tank to work as an aqua-plane for towing behind the launch and it did as well as a pair of water-skis. After a certain amount of practice we all got pretty expert.

It was on one of these occasions that I learned about our plans for operations in Italy. Broady, when he asked Brian King-come, Jackie Darwen and myself to join him that particular afternoon, said he had something important to discuss. After some sport with the aqua-plane we cruised into a cove and dropped anchor. We had an excellent meal washed down with iced beer; then he let us in on certain aspects of the forthcoming air operations.

The 8th Army were going to land at points along the 'toe' of Italy on 3 September, pushing up the 'foot' while the American 5th Army with 10 British Corps would be landed on the Salerno beaches with the object of capturing Naples as soon as possible. A British corps was also to land at Taranto and secure the airfield as a top priority.

He went on to explain that other operations were in the melting pot and a final decision was awaited from the Supreme Commander. The Americans wanted to land airborne troops near Rome and, helped by Italian units in the area, seize the city and airfields. Jackie Darwen was to fly two squadrons of Kit-tyhawks into the first airfield captured, and I was to escort him with 417 Squadron, and thereafter provide the local air defence. It did not take long to realise that such an operation was fraught with dangerous possibilities. The Germans would mount an all-out effort to annihilate it, even supposing further seaborne landings were to take place near Rome. A few days later we heard that the operation had been cancelled and breathed a sigh of relief. In the end I was to operate with Jackie Darwen and his Kittyhawks but it was at Taranto that we joined up, after two adventures one of which nearly put paid to my hopes of taking part in the final victory in Europe.

While in Malta, I had received a letter from Anne Walker, a WAAF officer I had known at Hornchurch who later became a pilot in the Air Transport Auxiliary, telling me that she had ferried a Spitfire Mk VIII (a high-altitude variant of the Mk IX with pointed wing tips) painted in Desert Air Force camouflage to a certain airfield for shipment abroad. 'Wouldn't it be funny', she wrote, 'if it was delivered to your Wing? It's the first of its type I've flown so if you catch up with it I hope you'll grab it for yourself.'

Death of a Walrus

Strange to relate it did come to 244 Wing. Seeing it one day parked amongst 1 (SAAF) Squadron's aircraft at Cassibile, I checked the number with the one I had noted in my diary and, as they were the same, had my initials painted on the side. All Wing Leaders were accorded this privilege and as I had no personal aircraft at the time, Hannes Faure was only too pleased to hand it over and get another Mk VIII as a replacement. However, it didn't turn out a lucky machine for me.

I took off in her around eleven o'clock on the day preceding the invasion of Italy on a free-lance mission. I intended to have a look at the first of two remaining forward airfields the Germans were using near Catanzaro, before sweeping on to Crotone where the other one was. After this I planned to return down the west coast, or as it looks on the map, the lower part of the instep of the 'boot'. There had been reports of enemy fighters operating in the area, and taking only one other aircraft with me I hoped we would be able to surprise and pick off a couple of enemy fighters before they spotted us. The Royal Navy, too, were active that day, shelling Reggio with the battleships *Valiant* and *Warspite* escorted by eight destroyers, while our fighters maintained a standing patrol to guard them from air attack, so it was logical to suppose that there might be some enemy reaction.

All went well on the way out, though I was disappointed as we saw no enemy aircraft. We found the two German forward airfields clear of aircraft. We turned and flew across to the other coast, and just as we got over the sea, the auxiliary fuel tank warning light came on, telling me it was time to switch over to main tanks. I reached down and pulled the lever to the 'on' position. It was extremely stiff. We had been cruising at 22,000 ft so I guessed the wire had got 'cold soaked' as it was pretty chilly in the cockpit. I gave the lever a hard pull and it moved about an inch before the wire snapped and the lever went slack in my fingers. The Bowden cable to the cock on the main tank had broken. Frantically I reached under the instrument panel and tried to get hold of the wire, but it had snapped somewhere inside the casing and there was nothing I could do to actuate the main cock. A few seconds later my engine started coughing and banging and finally died for want of fuel. I had already turned south; so I started gliding, pointing my nose out to sea. The best thing to do was to stretch the glide as far as I could, then bale out and hope for an early rescue from a Walrus Air-Sea Rescue amphibian. 'Hunk' Humphreys, on a patrol somewhere in the area with three others, heard me on the R/T and offered advice – then switched to the emergency frequency and called operations and the Air-Sea Rescue Service.

I wondered for a moment whether I would be better off baling out over land or crash-landing in some remote area. I knew our invasion forces would be landing on the beaches early the next morning, so if I were lucky I could hide out somewhere till 8th Army arrived. No, I thought, better to bale out into the sea and not risk being taken prisoner. As I had complete faith in our Air-Sea Rescue units I came to the conclusion they would have me out in a matter of an hour or so.

I looked at the altimeter and saw I was down to 5,000 ft. My number two had been transmitting Mayday signals as well – now he called me and reported a good fix had been plotted.

At 2,000 ft, I baled out. As I went out I seemed to drift against one side of the aircraft, and the next second I hit the tail-plane a crack with my leg.

On hitting the water I released the parachute and promptly disappeared for a while, head first under the surface. When I saw daylight again I pulled the parachute pack towards me by a couple of the shroud lines, reaching for the dinghy I knew must be in the seat. To my horror there was no dinghy. Somehow after I hit the water it had parted company from the parachute harness and disappeared. Having inflated my Mae West I swam around in circles looking for it, but there was no sign. I got very worried. Without a dinghy I was going to be in real trouble unless I was picked up fairly quickly.

I started swimming towards the shore. I recognised the headland as Cape Vaticano, about two miles distant. Better to keep fairly close to land, I thought, in case I wasn't picked up. In that event I could lie offshore and scramble up among the rocks to hide as soon as darkness fell.

I swam for an hour, alternating my efforts with periods on my back. The hot sun blazed down from a deep blue sky, burning my skin with its relentless intensity.

Death of a Walrus

I had taken off from Lentini in a hurry and had not changed into flying clothes. Now I was caught out of bounds, so to speak, in shorts and short-sleeved shirt. My leg ached, and I found a deep gash round the knee-cap which was bleeding badly. An offshore breeze sprang up, and there was a swell running which buffeted my body, forcing me to swallow unwelcome sea water.

Exhausted by my efforts and the swell, I floated on my back for a while to regain my breath and rest. I looked at the shore line and saw that I was in the grip of a strong current which was pushing me further out to sea, and past the sharp point of Vaticano. I redoubled my efforts and ploughed my way through the swell, but made little headway. I looked at my watch. It was half past one. I had been in the water an hour and a half. I kept up a steady stroke towards the distant shore. Another hour went by and there was still no sign of rescue. I heard the drone of engines from time to time, but the aircraft were very high and though I squinted into the bright light, I could not see them.

Suddenly, away in the distance, I saw the low silhouette of a boat, ploughing its way towards the area I had landed in. It was a fishing boat from the mainland. I was ready to give up the unequal struggle and I started to shout and wave. Much better to be picked up by the Italians, I thought, than perish in the sea. But they did not hear or see me.

I was seized with desperation and a great loneliness. Where were my friends? What the hell had gone wrong? Was the war too important to Broady and to Brian, and to the rest of them that they could not spare a few Spitfires to do a search, and send a clapped-out Walrus to pick me up? Surely they must care what happened to me? It could not end like this.

I started swimming again. The sun blazed down but I was cold . . . I started to shiver and found it difficult to breathe. The shivering got worse, then my teeth chattered like a pair of castanets. I tried to heave myself out of the water as much as I could, to get more heat from the sun. The cold sea stung me as I flopped back . . . I looked at my watch; I'd been in the sea well over five hours. The sun was sinking towards the far horizon. When darkness came, what then?

Keep your mind on other things, I kept telling myself –

166

anything – but each time I tried to concentrate, my thoughts wandered, eventually coming back to the sea around me, and the cold . . . I didn't seem able to shut that numb cold feeling out – it gripped my body totally, and I could concentrate only on an arc around my immediate surroundings. Lying on my back, I paddled, no longer caring in which direction my efforts carried me. . . .

At first the sound I heard, when it came, was very loud, then in a few seconds it was gone. I straightened, treading water and tried to rub the stinging sensation of salt from my eyes. I listened for the sound – where was it? – there – what was that? Away in the distance, close to the water? Dots – more dots going round and round. They looked like mere specks of dust floating in a shaft of sunlight. As I strained the sound hit me again, a deep rumble oscillating on the breeze for a few moments; then it was gone once more.

Even as I watched, one of the specks detached itself and came towards me. I kept my eyes glued on it, not daring even to blink. It moved silently at first, but soon I heard the familiar beat of a Merlin exhaust above the hissing of the swell. The Spitfire was quite low, flying on a straight course that would bring it close.

Numbed fingers tore at my Mae West and with difficulty I got one of the small rescue rockets out from under the retaining flap. I ripped the top off and held it firmly waiting for the thing to go off – nothing happened. Damn – I wrenched out another – the Spitfire was almost level – again I tried to fire it, but nothing happened. In an agony of frustration I watched as the pilot flew past oblivious to my frantic waving and shouting. The markings told me it was a Spitfire of 145 Squadron. I watched it sweep past, pent-up emotions tearing at my throat.

Damn and blast – the rescue rockets were all sodden and useless. The yellow Mae West alone would not show up, somehow I must attract attention.

The Spitfire went on for about another couple of miles, then it circled left and flew back again. As it got nearer I started splashing the sea, using my feet and arms, kicking spray high in the air. When it was almost on top of me, I plunged forward threshing the water with my legs and flailing the sea with my arms. I lay back panting.

The aircraft passed, then suddenly wheeled and dived in a steep turn towards me. He had seen the speck of white foam against the deep blue. He passed almost directly above, his wing-tip a few feet from the sea. I caught a glimpse of the pilot peering out, then he waved. In a matter of a few minutes eight Spitfires were circling above, and the deafening noise of their engines was perhaps the sweetest sound I have ever heard.

Another twenty minutes dragged by before the slow old Walrus came into sight and alighted with difficulty on the swell. It taxied across to me – a rope was thrown, and I firmly caught and held it.

I don't remember the next few minutes clearly. As eager hands were reaching to drag me on board the amphibian, I heard several loud explosions, followed by a stinging blow across the back of my neck that spun me round in the water. I felt myself grabbed and hauled aboard. I tried to get to my feet but instead pitched forward onto my face. I lay still – my mind went blank.

When I came to, I found myself covered in a blanket. A man was grinning at me and trying to force brandy between my chattering teeth.

He said: 'You feeling better? Sorry about the mess in here.' He pointed to debris lying about, and about six inches of water swilling along the floor, 'It won't be long before we land at Milazzo. I wouldn't be surprised if the skipper has to crash-land. The old Walrus is in a shocking state.' Then he told me about the rescue operations.

Apparently the first Walrus that had been sent to pick me up had developed engine trouble and returned to base. Due to unserviceability it was a matter of hours before another one was made ready, and because of the distance it had to fly, I had been over six hours in the sea before the second Walrus reached me. Search had been hampered because I had drifted about five miles from the spot where I landed in my parachute. Finally, as I was being dragged on board, we were shot up on the water by three Me 109s, and a gaggle of FW 190s, Macchis, and a Reggiane 2001. The Walrus was badly holed below the water and a cannon-shell had pierced the wing tank, but luckily, though petrol spewed all over the place, the old bus did not catch fire. The blow I felt was from a bullet that tore through the collar of my Mae West grazing my neck before smacking into the Walrus.

We got down at Milazzo safely, after a brilliant landing by the pilot, and I was whisked off to the American field-hospital close by. There they were very kind and after fixing up my leg and dressing the neck-wound tried to keep me for the night, but I managed to talk the doctor into letting me return to Lentini. The Walrus Air-Sea Rescue aircraft was a total wreck having been damaged in too many vital parts.

'Hunk' Humphreys had landed with Ives at Milazzo after escorting the Walrus back. He told me that 1 (SAAF) Squadron had got stuck into the 109s, which shot up the Walrus, and Hector Taylor had shot one of them down. However, Dick Charrington, one of the pilots in Mike Vialls's flight, had been shot down by a 109 as they came in to strafe the Walrus. This terrible piece of news chased away my happy thoughts at getting back to dry land once more. All I wanted to do was to get back to the Wing and thank the boys for all they had done, particularly 1 (SAAF), and Shand of 145, a Rhodesian, who had come along by chance and found me in the nick of time.

I pinched Ives's Spitfire and in bare feet (I'd lost my footwear in the sea) flew back with 'Hunk' Humphreys to Lentini.

Brian had laid on quite a party, but before it got under way, armed with a bottle of South African brandy I went in search of Shand. As far as I was concerned, my first drink had to be with him. When I found him I said:

'What made you fly over in my direction, when everyone else was searching so far away?'

'I got a funny feeling you weren't there,' he grinned. 'You're a restless sort of chap anyway, so I came to the conclusion you had probably gone for a swim; I was right – you are a restless swimmer, too.'

On the next day, 3 September 1943, in an olive grove near Syracuse, General Castellano signed the Italian surrender terms. Earlier the same morning 8th Army had established a bridgehead at Reggio, and British troops were pouring onto the mainland of Italy.

I was ordered to take forty-eight hours' rest, then told to report to DAF headquarters on my return, for a special assignment. My adventures in the sea had left me scorched and badly sunburned, even though I had a deeply tanned skin already. The old ear trouble had returned and was very painful. In a jeep loaded with extra rations, I set off for Taormina with 'Doc' Turner to stay at a hotel on the seashore that had lately been taken over as a leave centre.

Driving the jeep along the winding coast road I noticed a large notice painted on a wall. It read: 'Rest and be Thankful. The Highland Division passed this way afore ye!' I rested and was thankful and dreamed of my Highland hills.

One last thought stays with me. Though Anne Walker and I were not formally engaged at the time, we had an understanding that when I returned to England we would be married and live happily ever after. But it was not to be, due in part to my waywardness and also that absence did not make her heart grow fonder. So perhaps the loss of my Spitfire was a timely omen.

CHAPTER FIFTEEN

Foothold in Italy

When I returned to Lentini I was ordered to fly to Bizerta in the courier aircraft, and there join up with the airborne forces that were preparing to land at Taranto. My task was to recce for suitable airfields in the area once the landings took place, and, with the Army's help, get a landing ground ready to receive two Kittyhawk Squadrons of 239 Wing, and one of my Spitfire Squadrons from 244 Wing.

While the 8th Army chased the Germans up the narrow length of the 'foot' from Reggio, capturing in turn Pizza and Catanzaro before pushing on towards Potenza, I found myself en route for Taranto aboard a British warship in company with high-spirited formations of 1st Airborne Division. Six thousand men in all had to be transported by the Royal Navy because there were no transport aircraft or landing craft available for the operation.

As the Salerno landings were taking place on 9 September (the assault forces consisting of the 6th American Corps on the right, and the 10th British Corps on the left), the 1st Airborne Division were put ashore at Taranto. The naval units involved were covered by the fighters of Desert Air Force operating at extreme range.

Packed in a small landing craft full of tough paratroopers from the 1st Airborne Division armed to the teeth, I kept my fingers crossed as we made the run-in across the wide harbour. Apart from a cruiser that had been blown up by a mine, there had been no naval losses. Now as we ploughed through the water bathed in bright moonlight, I saw scores of bodies from the sunken cruiser floating around us, occasionally catching a glimpse of the distorted and grotesque features of dead men as they rocked past on the ripples, arms and legs sprawled, bloated and hideous.

A bit of sporadic rifle and light machine-gun fire greeted us on landing, but there was no serious opposition, as few Germans remained to defend the port and city. Finding a reasonably quiet spot in amongst the damaged buildings, I rolled myself up in a blanket and snatched a couple of hours sleep.

The next morning I linked up with a major from the Airfield Construction Group and got a lift out to Grottaglie, the nearest airfield to Taranto. The place was completely deserted: the bombing attacks had done much damage, but a part of the control tower was still habitable, and near the airfield there were a number of abandoned houses that would do as billets for the men. We noted that the landing area itself, though full of bomb holes, could be made serviceable quickly.

I had a stroke of luck. A small Italian communications aircraft, a Saiman 202, two- or three-seater monoplane, floated in and landed on the rough grass area. Out of it stepped a dapper Italian lieutenant, full of smiles and sporting a strong American accent. He introduced himself as 'Tino' and said he had flown over from the Macchi Wing at Brindisi. They had heard the RAF had taken over Grottaglie so he had come to offer his services as an interpreter. Now that Italy had surrendered he saw no reason why we could not all be friends.

His English was excellent and I could hardly believe I was not talking to an American. He was full of sparkling humour and asked a lot of questions. I subsequently discovered he had been living in the United States for some years and had returned to Italy on the outbreak of war to join the Air Force just for the hell of it.

I told him I was taking over his aircraft and ordered him to take myself and the major first to Lecce and then to Brindisi. A mixed bag of Macchi 202s and 205s were based at Lecce, also a few Re 2001/5s. The Italians were very friendly and agreed to keep out of the way and not fly their aircraft till we had got things sorted out.

At Brindisi I found a colonel in charge of the airfield and Macchi Wing, and he lost no time in surrendering his command to me. After making a touching speech with his staff drawn up behind him, he handed me his sword – I did not know what to do with it so kept it as a souvenir – then he promptly burst into

172

tears. His country's surrender and the uncertain future for himself and his men had broken his morale. I felt sorry for him and left as quickly as I could.

I returned to Lecce as this airfield was only slightly damaged and I thought it would do very well as a second string, in case Grottaglie became overcrowded. After a pleasant meal of spaghetti with the Italian pilots, I took the opportunity of inspecting the Macchi 205s and a couple of Re 2001/5s I found parked near the flight offices. The Re 2001/5s were fairly new to the Italian Air Force, and only a handful had been built. They had a wing shape very similar to the Spitfire, a powerful engine and were armed with four cannons. Having had a dog-fight with one of them, I am convinced we would have been hard pressed to cope in our Spitfires operationally, if the Italians or Germans had had a few Squadrons equipped with these aircraft at the beginning of the Sicily campaign or in operations from Malta. Fast, and with excellent manoeuvrability, the Re 2001/5 was altogether a superb aeroplane. Though I didn't get a chance to fly one I did manage to fly the Macchi 205 and the Me 109G. Neither of these aircraft measured up to the capabilities of the Re 2001/5 series in manoeuvrability or rate of climb.

The Reggiane 2000 series developed before the war was greatly influenced by American technology and in particular by the Seversky P–35, an aircraft flying with the USAAF. The prototype Re 2000 made its first flight in May 1939. By late 1941 the Re 2001 series entered service fitted with an Alfa Romeo RA 1000 RC41 Monsouie twelve-cylinder inverted-Vee liquid-cooled engine rated at 1175 hp. (It was a licence-built Daimler-Benz DB 601A.) The aircraft had a top speed of 339 mph at 17,000 ft and climbed to 22,965 ft in 8 minutes. Its service ceiling was 36,000 ft. The last in the series – the Re 2005 'Sagittario' – was a potent aircraft. After major design changes it underwent evaluation trials in July 1942 and entered production in February 1943 but not more than twenty aircraft were used in combat (mostly against Flying Fortresses) before the Italian surrender. The Germans were very interested in the Re 2005 and they flew some to Germany for trials. All Re 2005s were fitted with German-built DB 605 engines and propellers which gave them a maximum speed of 447 mph at 24,000 ft and reached 20,000 ft in 5½ minutes. It had a ceiling of 39,000 ft. Fitted with three 20-mm cannon and two 12.7-mm machine-guns, I think it was easily the best aircraft Italy produced.

I was most intrigued to learn after the war that a British Mission, led by Lord Hardwick with Air Ministry representatives, visited Italy in December 1939 to purchase marine engines, armaments, light reconnaissance bombers *and* 300 Re 2000 fighters! In January 1940 the Director of Aircraft Contracts confirmed the British order and in March 1940 the German Government gave the Italians its blessing for the sale, but withdrew it the following month. The British and Italian Governments then cooked up a scheme to complete the contract through the Italian Caproni company's Portuguese subsidiary. The whole scheme fizzled out, however, when Mussolini stabbed France in the back on 10 June 1940.

Reggiane pilots remember their aircraft with some affection. Italian fighter pilots were well trained and most of the organisation and operational procedures were copied from the Royal Air Force. Though there were some brilliant performers their attitude to aerial combat was somewhat old-fashioned for even when they held tactical surprise they could not resist indulging first of all in spectacular aerobatics with the hope, no doubt, of putting the wind up us rather than doing bloody battle and having lost the initiative lost the will to fight. It is a pity, however, that no Re 2001/5s survive to this day because they were fine examples of Italian engineering craftsmanship.

Getting my hands on a jeep I went off once more accompanied by the Army major to recce an airfield at Gioia, close to where the forward troops were operating in their advance on Bari. We found the place still rather hot, with enemy rear guards on the outskirts of the town. The airfield had been heavily mined by the retreating Germans and was quite useless until the engineers could clear it.

In the meantime, back at Grottaglie, Jackie Darwen flew in on 13 September leading 112 Squadron, followed by 3 (RAAF) Squadron, commanded by Brian Eaton. Soon afterwards 'Hunk' Humphreys arrived with 92 Squadron, the advance party of ground-crews having arrived in three Dakotas shortly before. The mobile radar control caravan (Mickey) was set up on some high ground close to the airfield, and the Air Formation Signals advance party laid the telephone lines. We were now ready to operate and control both tactical and air defence missions. As usual there had been no break in the continuity of operations. We used the partially bombed flying control tower on the airfield as our Mess.

Just before these events, on the night of 8/9 September, the Luftwaffe launched a large-scale attack on British warships covering the Salerno landings with torpedo-carrying He 111s and Ju 88s. The attack was unsuccessful and the Navy claimed some twenty enemy aircraft destroyed.

Following this, the Germans used a new weapon against ships – a glider bomb. Weighing over 3,000 lb it was a potent weapon, released by a high-flying bomber in a stand-off position onto the target. Some success was achieved, and HMS *Warspite* was hit astern. This weapon was followed later on with a bomb, which was guided after release by the bomb-aimer onto the target through radio control. Used mostly against merchant ships it had a limited success. Known as the Henschel Hs 293 it allowed the mother aircraft to remain up to ten miles from the target while the bomb-aimer 'flew' it with his radio control visually, making adjustments to its flight through the weapon's receiver. The system could be neutralised by a ship's radio jamming equipment so by the end of the year these weapons were seen no more.

A critical situation developed in the Salerno area on 13/14 September when the Americans were fiercely attacked by armoured units. The Germans pushed to within three miles of the beaches and the situation looked very grim. The American Army Commander, General Clark, called on General Montgomery for help, and in particular asked him to press on as quickly as possible and engage the enemy forces facing his 6th Corps. This he did, in the face of great difficulties, and by 16 September the 8th Army had made contact with the right flank of General Clark's forces. Montgomery's troops had fought and advanced 300 miles in twelve days over the most difficult country. Their task was made worse by extensive demolitions carried out by the retreating Germans, bringing in their wake the necessity to build many Bailey bridges.

Re-established at Grottaglie with adequate reserves of fuel, ammunition and bombs, Jackie Darwen set about attacking German transports and tanks along the roads leading to Salerno, across the mountains from the north and east. We escorted the Kittyhawks on these highly fruitful and successful missions, attacking any German trucks and other soft-skinned vehicles that were still left intact after the Kittyhawks had done their stuff. Not once did we meet the Luftwaffe during these operations, though one pilot of 92 Squadron was lucky enough to shoot down a Me 109 early one morning when it attempted to carry out a recce at Grottaglie.

On 16 September Brian Kingcome arrived leading the rest of the 244 Wing Squadrons, but after a couple of days we moved on to Gioia, which had now been cleared of mines

As September closed, it was apparent that all the main objectives of the invasion of Italy had been achieved. Naples had fallen, Bari had been captured, 8th Army had overrun the Foggia plain and were almost at the gates of Termoli on the Adriatic, while the 5th Army were holding a line along the Volturno river on the west coast. The only clouds on the horizon were literally bad-weather ones, for we had our first taste of rain.

Towards the end of October, the 5th and 8th Armies were holding a firm line on a front running from the Garigliano river in the west, and snaking its way across the Abruzzi mountains before joining the course of the river Sangro flowing into the Adriatic. The Desert Air Force Wings moved forward to the windswept plains of Foggia before leap-frogging onto the first all-weather strips which had been prepared for us by the airfield construction units close to the front line. During the month the Wing flew 1,400 sorties and destroyed five enemy aircraft, damaging two others; we were seeing enemy aircraft less and less by day, though their night-bombers continued to operate.

For the all-weather strips a very ingenious 'runway' was laid in pierced steel plates which were known (from the initial letters) as PSP. The sections hinged and were fitted together to form a continuous and highly efficient surface for aircraft. Each strip was laid out 40 yards wide by 1,200 – 1,500 yards long, and no matter how wet and muddy the ground became our Spitfires could move along the taxi tracks and take off and land without the risk of getting bogged down. It became a godsend to us during the wet and muddy Italian winter, and allowed us to have airfields in areas that otherwise would have been quite unsuitable.

Squadrons from the United States 15th Strategic Air Force quickly moved into the Foggia airfields and were able thus to extend the range of operations and penetrate to targets deep in southern Europe and the Balkans. The industrial areas of Silesia and Czechoslovakia, not to mention the highly important oilfields of Romania, now came under the hammer of the heavy bombers, protected by long-range fighter escorts provided by the Americans. At last our bomber offensive was able to co-ordinate with bombers already pounding Europe from airfields in England, extending the scope of operations to every corner of Hitler's empire. For the Germans it meant disaster, as there was no hiding place left that could not be hit by the combined forces of the United States 8th and 15th Air Forces and of Bomber Command.

244 Wing's move to Italy saw the end of our association with 1 (SAAF) Squadron. Number 7 (SAAF) Wing was now formed under the command of Doug Loftus, and No. 1 Squadron joined other SAAF Fighter Squadrons already operating in the Wing. I had a party with them at Gioia and said my good-byes, though I continued to see them from time to time in the months that lay ahead. I will always have a particularly warm place in my heart for these magnificent South Africans who were second to none when it came to courage, offensive spirit, and the will to win. Hannes Faure and his pilots always treated me as one of themselves. Vivian Voss, No. 1 Squadron's Intelligence Officer, known as 'Pop', had a special place in the affairs of the Squadron and in the affection of the pilots. Without 'Pop' guiding their fortunes, 1 Squadron would have lacked much of their distinctive character.

On 29 November I learned that I had been appointed to command 324 Wing with the acting rank of Group Captain. The Wing operated under the control of the US 12th Tactical Air Command on the 5th Army's front, though administrative control remained under Desert Air Force. They were currently based at Capodichino Airfield outside Naples. Apparently 'Sheep' Gilroy after a long and successful command was returning to England but 'Cocky' Dundas was to continue as Wing Leader.

An old friend and exceptional fighter-pilot, 'Cocky' Dundas had led 324 Wing with marked success. His attractive personality and discerning attitude to the problems faced by Squadron pilots, due to the unusual living and social conditions, helped me to appreciate more easily the situation in Naples. I soon found that my new responsibility, commanding a wing with over 1,200 officers and men, did not end with an ability to lead four Fighter Squadrons into battle.

Before leaving 244 Wing I handed over to Stan Turner, an ideal choice as Wing Leader. Parting company with Brian Kingcome, however, was difficult and sentimental. A loyal friend, he was also a most amusing companion with an old-fashioned appreciation of the ridiculous. An outstanding leader in every way, wounded in action during the Battle of Britain, Brian dealt in a most engaging way with everyday problems and difficult characters. With his lucid advice and sense of fun he put me straight many times when I got the bit between my teeth approaching a difficult fence. After I returned to the Wing from my swim in the sea, I remember I was rather upset because the rescue arrangements had not been up to scratch and said so to Brian. His reply:

'Ho-hum, m'dear chap, none of us thought you were going to make it – now you've put me in a difficult spot – I've disposed of your belongings to your keen admirers.'

I looked into our tent to find all my possessions, from my camp bed to my razor, gone. Then I heard Brian laugh. His well-conceived leg-pull was, of course, brilliant and just what I needed to feel right back at home again.

I found Naples in the grip of a typhus epidemic, with 'Doc' Russell, the Wing SMO, and the Squadron doctors being run off their feet by the Italians, who needed much help from our medical resources. Though the airfield was a good one, the living conditions for the officers and men left much to be desired, as billets and Messes were widely dispersed in civilian houses, some of them at great distances from the airfield, and the airfield itself overcrowded with American air force and army units.

The living conditions led me to believe that as commanding officer it was essential I should work and sleep on the airfield. One of the first things I did was to inspect the MT section and the area on the airfield where Italian motor-transport, caravans and equipment had been abandoned. It was here I found what I was looking for. A relatively new and quite undamaged Italian wireless trailer resting on four new low-pressure pneumatic tyres. I had it towed over to the MT section where I got the officer in charge, Flight Lieutenant Menzies, a Scot, to convert it into a caravan to house my office and sleeping quarter. He made a splendid job of it in next to no time, even getting some specialist Italians to carry out the carpentry work. The office part had a fair-sized desk, wall map, a couple of requisitioned easy chairs and some cupboard space for papers, books and writing materials. A sliding door divided it from my sleeping quarter in which there was a spring bunk-bed, a clothes cupboard for hanging uniforms and coats, wash basin and drawers under the bed for personal clothing etc. When the Wing was on the move, all that had to be done was to disconnect the telephone lines and electricity cables, close the windows and plug up the waste pipe under the basin. It could be hitched to any of the Wing's prime movers and was as steady as a rock. It went everywhere with me and it was a great wrench when I finally handed it over to my successor at Ravenna some sixteen months later.

The Squadrons consisted of 43, commanded by Parrott; 72, commanded by Daniels; 93, commanded by Westenra, a New Zealander I had known previously in 601 Squadron 244 Wing; and 111 Squadron, commanded by Matthews, an experienced ex-member of 1 Squadron RAF, who had served in the Advanced Air Striking Force in France in 1940. Day-to-day operations for 324 Wing were assigned by the 64th Fighter Wing, commanded by Brigadier-General 'Shorty' Hawkins, a Texan, who was a terrific personality and an experienced combat pilot.

On the night of 2/3 December, the Germans bombed Bari with a large force of Ju 88s and caused a lot of damage and casualties. The harbour was full of shipping at the time, and direct hits on two ammunition ships blew most of the installations to bits. When I heard the news, I remembered Lentini, and felt sure that Naples, and possibly Capodichino, would receive a similar pounding. Several sharp attacks did occur on Naples, but strangely, no attacks developed on our airfield which was closely packed with not only our Spitfires, but American aircraft as well. It was with a feeling of relief, therefore, that I heard early in January we were to move further north, to a newly prepared strip built with PSP at Lago, and close to the mouth of the Volturno river. This turned out to be a delightful place, the runway and dispersal area running through a belt of pines and mimosa trees, no more than a couple of hundred yards from a sandy beach.

CHAPTER SIXTEEN

Anzio patrol

The Army having come to a halt before Cassino, whose frowning heights guarded the entrance to the Liri valley and the road to Rome, it became obvious that sooner or later another assault landing on the pattern of Salerno must take place somewhere along the coast close to Rome, if we were going to be able to capture that city and finish off the war in Italy quickly.

It was noticeable that something was afoot. Our operations chiefly consisted of escort missions to Tactical and Strategic bombers which pounded centres of communication, military installations, and airfields north and south of Rome, operations typical of the prelude to a land offensive; in other words, the softening-up process to isolate the battleground. In between these operations we carried out fighter sweeps in search of a depleted Luftwaffe, and maintained constant standing patrols over the Army's forward positions.

On 21 January 1944 convoys sailed out of Naples Harbour en route for the Anzio beaches where, under cover of darkness that night, assault landings were made by the 6th US Corps consisting of the 3rd US and 1st British Divisions. The air effort on the 5th Army's front for defence and air support had been stiffened considerably by the attachment of DAF units, including 244 Wing who had taken up residence at Marcianise airfield near Caserta.

At the briefing held by the 64th Fighter Wing to tell us all about the plans, and to allocate tasks for the operation, it was explained that fighter cover over the beachhead area would be carried out from dawn to dusk. Protection for the convoys would be provided by Coastal Air Forces until the landing; thereafter 12th TAC would control the efforts of the fighters and fighter-bombers, through a headquarters ship lying off the beaches, and later from a command post on the beachhead itself.

The Spitfire formations were to be stepped in groups of four aircraft over the beachhead and ships, from 16,000 to 25,000 ft. We were to find later that patrols over 18,000 ft were a waste of time as the Luftwaffe usually ran in from the sea at 12,000 ft before delivering dive-bombing attacks and escaping inland at low level.

Leading 72 Squadron on patrol over the beachhead on the morning of 22 January, I spotted six Me 109s approaching us at the same height, flying in a long line-astern formation. Before I could get 72 into a good attacking position they avoided combat by rolling on their backs and diving inland. Other formations had better luck that day, and about ten enemy aircraft were destroyed. It was only that evening that I managed to shoot down a Me 109 trying to bomb the ships.

Fighter-bombers, on the other hand, were constantly engaging opportunity targets of lorried infantry, tanks and self-propelled guns, besides attacking pre-planned targets, and fulfilling the Army's requests for close support. In particular the 26th Panzer Division, trying to slip over to Anzio from in front of the 8th Army's position, came in for a fearful hammering. Though the Germans reacted quickly to the Anzio situation, the Air Forces stemmed the flow of reinforcements and it was not till the middle of February that the Germans built up enough strength to counter-attack.

In all the bitter fighting that took place, the action of our 24th Guards Brigade must rank as a great feat of arms. On the morning of 22 January, the Brigade, consisting of the 5th Grenadiers, 1st Scots and 1st Irish Guards, landed with the 1st Division. The bridgehead along the entire front, eighteen miles long and nine miles deep, was established with virtually no opposition for thirty-six hours, but the invasion force did not press on forward as expected. This fact has been considered by many to have been one of history's great missed opportunities. A bold thrust forward might have achieved spectacular successes as there were no enemy forces between Anzio and Rome. The American Commander, General Lucas, however, remembering some of the problems and bitter fighting at Salerno, decided to consolidate his base within the bridgehead before committing his forces to an advance and three days were to pass before he decided to press on, by which time it was too late. Eight German Divisions in the meantime had reached the perimeter and made contact with the Allied forces and more enemy formations were on the way.

In the bitter fighting during the next seven weeks, 24th Guards Brigade, though cut off and encircled, stood their ground and fought a magnificent action, thereby probably saving the whole expedition from being pushed back into the sea. Without sufficient supplies of food, water and ammunition they fought where they stood, until the situation was brought under control again. The Brigade was to lose 80 per cent of its strength, while the 1st Battalion Irish Guards were so severely engaged in the action they ceased to exist as a fighting force. On 25 January the Scots and Irish Battalions were beaten back trying to reach Campolene on the road to Rome and the battalion headquarters of the Irish Guards, overrun by the enemy and everyone captured. As they were being marched off the Irish turned on their German captors attacking them with anything that came to hand – a rifle, a spade, and even a petrol tin. Twenty Germans were killed and nine taken prisoner. What a performance!

A landing ground had been quickly made in the beachhead for emergency landings, and the use of casualty evacuation and communications aircraft. I happened to be there one day when some badly wounded guardsmen were being evacuated. They were all covered in bandages, but before getting into the Dakotas were interviewed by the BBC. It was Richard Dimbleby, who asked one Irish Guardsman how things had gone. The conversation went something like this:

'What was the toughest moment you had to face?'

'Well, it sure wasn't the Germans. We were being mortared and shelled – see – and all hell had broken loose – when suddenly, a crowd of our Spitfires came along – the next thing I knew they let fly all them petrol tanks, that looked like bombs – one of them whizzed past me and missed the top of me napper by a whisker. It frightened the life out of me, so I turned to the sergeant and said, "For God's sake, sergeant, spake to me and tell me if I'm still aloive".'

'Cocky' Dundas left the Wing for a well-deserved rest, and went on the Operations staff at Advanced HQ Desert Air Force, just before the Anzio show started. In his place I got Johnny Loudon, my old Squadron Commander, from the Hornchurch days. Of course, I had seen a lot of Johnny since Malta, as he had been on the staff at Desert Air Force, looking after the training of the fighter Squadrons. Unfortunately, he was lost on a fighter sweep north of Rome shortly after coming to 324, but baled out safely, though he dislocated his shoulders on landing. He was taken prisoner, but got home safely after the war.

In Johnny Loudon's place I got Dan du Vivier, a Belgian, a very experienced pilot who had served with 43 Squadron during the summer of 1940 in England.

With 72 Squadron on patrol one evening over Anzio, we intercepted a mixed formation of Me 109s and FW 190s. The 109s were stepped above, and as we dived to attack I turned behind one, and opened fire, seeing strikes on his wing root. Streaming smoke, he steepened his dive in a lazy turn to the left. Foolishly, I decided to follow him. I was at 18,000 ft when the engagement started, and at around 10,000 ft was engaged from behind by a solitary 109 and had to break off sharply. By this time 72 were completely split up, so with no sign of another Spitfire anywhere near, I ducked for our side of the lines hotly pursued by angry puffs of heavy AA. On landing I found 72 had destroyed two and two more damaged. One of the flight commanders, Sutherland, confirmed my Me 109 had caught fire and crashed.

At the height of all the Anzio activity, Sir John Slessor, the new Air Commander, Mediterranean Allied Air Forces, visited the Wing. I had heard a great deal about him. Unfortunately, his visit was marred by terrible weather, and my hopes of showing him high-intensity operations from Lago did not come off as planned. Sir John, a famous pilot of the First World War, had also seen much operational service between the wars in Iraq, the Middle East and on the north-west frontier of India. Two distinctive operations he planned, in particular, were highly successful: the support for Tito's partisans in Yugoslavia and the mining of the Danube. The mining operations prevented all movement of oil from Romania and proved a fatal blow to the Germans' war effort. Believing that we, at Wing level, should know what was going on, he visited us frequently to explain the aim of his broader strategy.

Ruggedly handsome, Slessor looked every inch the pugnacious, seasoned professional airman that he was, but at the same time radiated much charm and humour. He never seemed at a loss for the right thing to say to officer or airman, and his personal interest in discussing various activities with everyone he met was both refreshing and stimulating.

He was accompanied by Nigel Maynard, his personal staff officer, and we toured the squadrons, Sir John insisting on meeting the pilots and airmen though conditions underfoot were appalling, with thick mud everywhere.

Towards the latter part of February, we decided to keep a squadron overnight at Nettuno, the airfield on the Anzio beachhead. This was done to enable us to maintain standing patrols right up to dusk, and again at dawn the next morning. We rotated the Squadrons each day, but the airmen were left there for two weeks before being replaced. Pilots and groundcrews lived under pretty grim conditions, sleeping and eating in dug-outs because the landing ground came in for a lot of shelling from the German guns which were dug in across the hillsides overlooking the beachhead.

I did my share of duty at Anzio, and it was on one of these occasions that I saw a dog running around the airfield in rather a crazy fashion. Nobody seemed to know where the animal had come from, and we nicknamed him 'Blitz'. He was a large mongrel with a bushy tail and his favourite pastime was to chase and try to intercept bursting shells. As soon as the shelling started, 'Blitz' would dart about, rushing after the whistling shells, arriving, of course, on target after the explosion. He was a shy, elusive dog, and disappeared for days only to reappear to go through his routine. One day he finally caught one with devastating results.

111 Squadron was equipped unexpectedly with new Spitfire Mk IXs powered by Merlin 66 engines. These engines had been

developed by Rolls-Royce to give better performance in the 13,000–20,000 ft altitude bracket. Unfortunately, the first few operational sorties carried out proved disastrous due to engine failures. Some pilots were lucky enough to get down at Anzio, and others at Lago, but others had to either bale out or crash-land. We grounded 111, and in next to no time a Rolls-Royce team arrived from England, headed by Ronnie Harker, to look into the affair. In their usual efficient manner Rolls-Royce sorted out the trouble. It turned out to be nothing to do with the engine. The fault lay in the petrol that had been used. It was old stuff taken from drums, and full of rust or some similar foreign matter. This had the effect of smearing the sensitive plug-points when the engine developed maximum power for a lengthy period, resulting in a complete bank of cylinders cutting out. I cannot remember anything similar ever taking place before. The reliability of Rolls-Royce engines is legendary. Personally, I never gave a thought to the likelihood of my engine ever letting me down no matter how roughly I treated it on occasions. It was an integral part of the Spitfire, a hand-in-glove feeling, so that whether in combat or just fun flying, I knew instinctively the thoroughbred qualities of the aeroplane would enable me to reach peak performance whenever the need arose.

Soon afterwards the engineer officer of 111 Squadron, 'Spanner' Farrish, had a brainstorm; though he was not a pilot, and indeed had never soloed in an aircraft, he nevertheless took off in a Spitfire and headed for Anzio where he knew there were four Spitfires sitting on the ground out of commission.

Merlyn Rees, our Operations officer, nicknamed 'Dagwood', phoned this staggering news to me. The calm way in which he reacted to this rather delicate situation showed that he was politically minded and, in fact, after the war he did become a Member of Parliament. I raced after Farrish in my own aircraft in the hope of catching him. I thought I might persuade him back to Lago and then instruct him to bale out near the beach. There was no sign of him anywhere. In desperation rather than hope, I flew on to Anzio and hung about the circuit. There was some brisk shelling going on, and in the midst of this, Benny Osler, a South African commanding 601 Squadron, landed and promptly hit a shell-hole finishing up on his back, but unhurt. Right behind him came Farrish, and holding off at the right height he allowed the Spitfire to settle in a three-point attitude. I got this news over the R/T so landed at once, a bit flustered and not knowing what I should say to him. I discovered he carried out the entire flight with the aid of *Spitfire – Pilot's Notes*!

Farrish confessed to me he did it only because he wanted to get the unserviceable Spitfires at Anzio in working order again and back to Lago. He did not think he would be allowed to go to Anzio if he asked, so his keenness drove him to take the matter into his own hands. The fact that he might have killed himself did not occur to him. I let him stay and he worked on the aircraft till they were once more in a serviceable condition. Unfortunately, the affair did not end there. He was court-martialled but got away with it.

The first full-scale Allied attacks against the intricate German fortifications at Cassino failed to achieve a breakthrough. Against fortified positions dug into the sides of the hills surrounding the area, our fighter-bombers had little effect. The Germans put their heads down, waited for the danger to pass, then came out again ready to fight off any ground assault.

Our best efforts were concentrated on preventing enemy reinforcement supplies reaching Cassino by road. On one such occasion ninety-two Spitfires, forty-nine Kittyhawks and twelve Thunderbolts attacked an enemy convoy en route to Cassino, which had become snowbound near Sera. The Germans got hell from us and lost forty-six transports in flames; over fifty more were severely damaged.

One of the thorns preventing the plucking of the Cassino rose was the Benedictine Monastery of Monte Cassino rising above a most prominent and commanding hill feature. To destroy it, people said, would be an act of infamy. But what could we do about it? The Germans were using it for obvious reasons. To disregard its natural military value as an observation point, not to mention its safety as a shelter, would have been stupid. Monte Cassino became a German tower of strength and a visible symbol of German resistance, blocking the road to Rome.

The bombing of Monastery Hill was devastating in its completeness, reducing the Monastery itself to ruins. Leading 43 Squadron, I sat up above the stream of heavy bombers in my Spitfire overawed by the intensity of the onslaught. Could anything live under such bombardment? As the dust-clouds rolled away all that remained were a few walls with wide gaping holes, the whole area pock-marked with bomb craters. The ground assault that followed found the Germans still in possession, and the bombing had provided them with more cover for counter-attacks. To make matters worse, the Germans launched a fierce attack on our beachhead positions at Anzio that night, starting with a terrific artillery barrage, which was followed by two strong waves of bombers blasting our positions. The next day attacks continued, with enemy tanks and infantry trying to split our forces and drive us back into the sea.

Once again, as at Salerno, the Strategic and Tactical bombers were called in to bolster the land battle, and 950 tons of bombs were dropped in support of the Army. Throughout the next few days and nights, a further 600 tons blasted the German positions and communications, but by 3 March it was all over. Anzio had survived, due largely to the weight of air attack.

Next an assault was launched by our Strategic and Tactical bombers against Cassino itself, in the hope that this would pave the way to overcoming the obstacle. The bombardment went on from early morning till noon, with groups of bombers flying over every fifteen minutes. Meanwhile Spitfires and Thunderbolts maintained standing patrols and sweeps in the Viterbo-Rome area.

By the time the bombing attacks were over, Cassino was in ruins. As New Zealand troops, supported by tanks, tried to take over the heaps of rubble, they were surprised to find enemy troops using the ruins as fortifications. The devastation prevented our troops from operating. Bomb craters blocked the roads, and in every heap of rubble a hornets' nest lay concealed. It proved that under certain conditions the devastation left in the wake of air bombardment, instead of helping, hindered progress and was in fact an asset to the enemy. The Cassino stalemate was now complete. During the month, 324 Wing flew nearly 2,000 sorties in support of these operations and we destroyed nineteen enemy aircraft, damaging a further thirty-two. As March started to fade, bringing in its wake a sign of blue Italian skies and a promise of sunshine, Harry Broadhurst left Desert Air Force to go back to England, where he was to assume command of No. 83 Group in 2nd Tactical Air Force.

This news came as no surprise to us, for he was an automatic choice for senior command in the line-up for the invasion of France. All through the tough Desert war, then in Sicily and Italy, Broady had kept Desert Air Force on the crest of the wave, setting standards that became accepted principles of tactical operations amongst other air forces. He had guided DAF safely through tricky political issues involving centralisation and steered us away from any involvement, to the ultimate advantage and benefit of the 8th Army. He had established the RAF in the eyes of our Allies as a Service that could tackle any job, any time, any place without ever breaking down in operational continuity, whether in support of an army on the move, or an army bogged down by mud, fortified lines, or red tape.

The farewell party at Vasto for him was one to remember. All the Wing COs and their Wing Leaders were there, besides his own staff. One who was not there, sadly, was Jackie Darwen, for Jackie had been shot down by AA fire and killed a short time before. Tremendously courageous, no operation was ever too difficult for him, and he attacked the Germans whenever he could with a cold fury. There was a reason, of course. His beautiful bride was killed in his arms while they were dancing, when a bomb hit the Café de Paris in London one night during the blitz in 1941. He died as he would have wished – pointing straight at the enemy, his guns blazing.

CHAPTER SEVENTEEN

No audience with Il Papa

 The last days of March did not go out with blue skies and sunshine as I had hoped, nor in a downpour, but with an eruption. Vesuvius belched smoke up to a height of 16,000 ft, and the glow of lava creeping down the mountainside could be seen for miles.

One of the American bases close by suffered the fate of ancient Pompeii as molten lava and a rain of red-hot ash from the volcano descended in ever-thickening layers, eventually covering the whole airfield and burying the parked aircraft for ever.

During April we continued patrolling over Anzio and gave fighter protection to our tactical and fighter-bombers operating on the approaches to Rome in their attacks on interdiction targets – targets which were associated with specific areas affecting the land battle. The preparations for the spring offensive, starting with a breakthrough at Cassino, were at hand. We noted the movement of 8th Army units taking up positions alongside the American 5th Army facing the Cassino bastion. Desert Air Force Squadrons joined us in the Naples area with extra formations settling at Marcianise, while 244 Wing moved to a new airfield at Venafro.

On 20 April 1944, I was delighted to receive the following commendation from the General Commanding 12th Tactical Air Command:

'324 Wing (RAF) has served under 64th Fighter Wing, Tactical Air Command since 9 September 1943 to present date. During this period 324 Wing has destroyed 110 enemy aircraft, probably destroyed ten and damaged ninety-two. The pilots have also wrought great damage to the enemy by ground strafing. I take pleasure in commending 324 Wing for meritorious achievement. I particularly commend the ground-crews whose

190

devotion to duty made this enviable record possible.'

The Commendation was endorsed by the General Commanding, Mediterranean Allied Tactical Air Force.

One of the units taking part in the air offensive was the 79th American Fighter-Bomber Group operating with DAF. Amongst the squadrons was the 99th, all-Black Squadron, commanded by an exceptional officer, Major Davis. They flew Thunderbolts and we often saw and heard them during their strikes in the Anzio area. They were always very cheerful and chatty, and produced some devastating forthright comments on the R/T as they searched out their targets.

While on patrol one day I heard the voice of a flight leader:

'Red leader to red two – are youh with me?'

'Red leader, I say again, are youh behind me red two, if youh are, waggle youh wings man, cause youh shur look like a Focke-Wulfe.'

Silence.

'Oh – oh – you'se a Focke-Wulfe.'

On another occasion:

'Red leader callin' – target three o'clock below get ready to dive bomb – Blue leader go on down first – over.'

Silence.

'Red leader callin' Blue leader – ain't youh heard me – dive bomb – go.'

'Blue leader to Red leader – man look at all dat flak – youh all go on down – you'se got the Distinguished Flyin' Cross so let's see youh do some distinguished flyin'!'

Leading 72 Squadron on a fighter sweep north of Rome, I picked out a convoy of four German trucks heading north along the Viterbo–Orvieto road. We were on our way back and not having seen any enemy air activity I decided to go down and strafe. Leaving 'Duke' Arthur, CO of 72 Squadron, to cover me with his section I swooped down, intending to attack from the rear. As I started to ease out of my dive, I saw two Germans on motor-cycles turn onto the main road from a side road, followed by a staff car with its roof folded. Sitting in the back were two German officers looking very pleased with themselves. I was perfectly placed, and the first burst from my guns caught the car across the back. It went up in a sheet of flames, careered across the road and somersaulted into the ditch. I just had time to let the motor-cyclists have a burst before breaking away. We flew on and got two of the trucks in flames as well. I never discovered if the staff officers in the car were important or not.

Just before the Cassino offensive started, I missed a really exciting offensive sweep, north of Rome. I had arranged to lead 72 Squadron, but just before I was due to go round and brief them, two visiting staff officers turned up. I intended to leave them with 'Tiny' Le Petit, my senior administrative officer, though 'Tiny' seemed particularly keen I should remain and look after the visitors myself.

In the end 'Duke' Arthur rang me;

'We're all waiting – are you coming over for briefing?'

'I can't at the moment,' I said. 'You carry on and I'll meet you by my aircraft. You lead 72 and I'll fly as your number two.'

The discussion with the staff officers became too involved so I rang the Squadron and told them to go off without me.

Since I could not join them, 'Duke' dropped out the pilot who would have made up the eighth aircraft, and led a formation of six. The outward flight was uneventful, and sweeping round first Perugia, then Chiusi in the hope of seeing enemy fighters round the airfields in those areas, they headed south again via Rome. As they got to Lake Bracciano, 'Duke' saw eighteen Me 109s streaming across the dark blue water of the lake at 1,000 ft heading north. 72 lost no time in attacking the enemy aircraft, destroying nine Me 109s. 'Duke' Arthur, Hendry and Aspinall destroyed two Me 109s each and the other pilots destroyed one each. The whole engagement lasted less than five minutes.

Early in May I flew to DAF Advanced HQ, for a briefing on the new offensive, from our new Air Officer Commanding, Air-Vice Marshal W.F. 'Dickie' Dickson. Short and stocky, he had an infectious laugh. He also had a discerning eye and was extremely competent operationally. 'Dickie' Dickson had inherited an Air Force that was a going concern, but in addition he had strong views on the value of night-operations, and extended DAF's capabilities by increasing the night-intruding scale of effort. He was a great believer in personal contact and constantly visited his Wings, flying his own Spitfire.

No audience with Il Papa

A separate briefing was carried out by staff officers of the 64th US Fighter Wing to give us detailed information on the part my Spitfire Squadrons were to play in the offensive. At midnight on 11 May, 1,000 guns opened up on the German positions at Cassino, hammering them for a solid hour. Immediately the barrage lifted, the Polish brigade converged on Cassino and our 13th Corps attacked the Germans across the Rapido river. Meanwhile the French, including their Moroccan troops, spread-eagled the enemy across the Garigliano before attacking north to the Liri river and then on to Ausonia and San Giorgio. As dawn came the Air Forces joined the battle. While tactical bombers and fighter-bombers pounded enemy positions, transports, bridges and gun emplacements, Spitfires provided an impregnable air umbrella over the battle area and along the Liri valley to Rome. After seven days of the most bitter fighting our troops battled their way through the Cassino defences. Meanwhile, the Anzio offensive gained momentum, and while the Germans retreated from Cassino, our beachhead forces, helped by constant support from the air, turned the retreat into a rout. On 4 June we plucked the choicest rose in the Italian garden – Rome. The advance continued till it reached the Pisa-Rimini Line.

It was while the Cassino battle was at its height that I heard that Barrie Heath was coming to 324 Wing as Wing Leader. Dan du Vivier had gone back to England a short time before as the Belgians wanted him to take over a flying appointment for the invasion of Normandy. Barrie was an instant success with the Squadrons and he organised and led 324 Wing with tremendous skill and vision.

We were at Anzio together when Rome fell, and lost no time in chasing into the city on the heels of the advancing troops. In Rome the crowds spilled across the streets, throwing flowers into our vehicles and offering us great hospitality. Roman priorities did not seem to have changed, however. While Barrie was kissing a dark-eyed damsel a hand removed his camera from the jeep.

As 324 had recently moved to Anzio, we had several opportunities to visit Rome before we moved on 10 June to Tarquinia, about eighty miles north.

During that month we had flown 3,000 sorties and destroyed twenty-six enemy aircraft, damaging a further nine. For all these intensive operations 324 was awarded Field Commendations from HQ Mediterranean Allied Air Forces and from 12th Tactical Air Command.

One of the first people I met in Rome was 'Garry' Garrod-Cole, who had been shot down in the desert at the beginning of the war. He had made several spectacular escapes, but had been recaptured each time. His last escape about six months previously made him decide to wait for rescue. He joined up with Italian partisans and helped them in dangerous missions against the Germans. I took him to Caserta on his way back to England.

We also met a priest named O'Flaherty, who during the war years organised the escape from Italy of many of our aircrews that were shot down. Like so many Irishmen he loved danger, for in helping our men he took tremendous risks and thrived on the excitement. I feel sure he would have done the same for the Germans if the positions had been reversed. I asked him how he got in and out of the Vatican City with so many Germans about. With a twinkle in his eye he answered: ' 'Twas no trouble at all for Oie could get me boys in and out soideways.'

The Pope held a special blessing for the British forces and a number of pilots attended it. It was a very moving occasion. Unfortunately I was unable to attend because of my duties so Father Lewis, at that time based in Rome, promised to include me in an audience with the Pope later on. The following week and sooner than I expected, he telephoned me at Tarquinia, where we were then based, and said an audience had been arranged on a certain date. A few days later the AOC Air Vice-Marshal Dickson telephoned to say I was to attend an important conference at Desert Air Force headquarters and the date proved to be the same as my appointment with Father Lewis in Rome. The conversation thereafter went like this:

AOC: 'We are having the conference at ten o'clock and I hope you will stay to lunch with me.'

ME: 'I was wondering sir, could Wing Commander Heath attend instead?'

AOC (sternly): 'Why can't you come – what is more important than my conference?'

ME (a bit shaky): 'Well, an audience with the Pope has been arranged for me and I would like to go to Rome very much, sir.'

A deadly pause.

AOC: 'You are an obstreperous officer, Smithy, and I think that remark is in very poor taste – I'll see you on Thursday.'

There was a click and that was that. How could I explain it all to Father Lewis? Some years after the war Marshal of the RAF Sir William Dickson, as he was by then, came to realise that I hadn't been shooting a line. But will Father Lewis ever read my story and appreciate that an AOC's conference in war can be more important than an audience?

By the end of June, 324 were based at Grosetto, and on 4 July we moved to Piambino on the coast opposite Elba. It was a delightful spot, and my caravan was no more than a hundred yards from the sandy beach and inviting sea. A few days later we learned we were to move to Calvi, an established airfield on the north-west coast of Corsica, and just south of Ile Rousse. We were stood down from all operations till the Wing's advanced and rear parties had joined up again at Calvi.

As soon as the Wing was reassembled at Calvi, I heard from the AOC that Brian Kingcome and I were to go home to England and visit the Normandy beachhead for liaison purposes. 'Dickie' Dickson also added, with a chuckle, that Sir John Slessor had ordered that we were to take a week's leave in England at the same time. This was a most welcome piece of news. We left on 17 July in a Dakota for Algiers and Casablanca where I spent a most uncomfortable night in a bug-infested bed. We continued our journey the following day to England in an American Liberator. Boxed up in the bomb-bay in complete darkness, we arrived frozen stiff. My one hope during the journey was that there would be no malfunctioning of the landing-gear system as a wheels-up landing would surely have made a sandwich of us.

The visit to Harry Broadhurst's headquarters in Normandy proved most interesting. We were envious of 2nd TAF's equipment – we had not seen anything like it before – and particularly some of their newer types of aircraft. They were also dressed very smartly in blue uniforms that fitted properly. After the motley assortment of uniforms we wore in DAF everybody looked overdressed.

Broady wanted to hear about DAF's operations since he left, and also have news about the various personalities still serving in Italy. He was in good heart and was obviously enjoying the tight situation the Army faced in trying to break through at Caen. His choice remark: 'Unlike the old days with DAF/8th Army, when after an air strike the Army shot forward, here they are only prepared to advance as far as the furthest bomb-hole.'

This was a veiled reference to the first attack by Bomber Command in support of the Army on the German defences at Caen, on 7 July 1944. Though it had achieved a huge effect in lifting morale, it left the whole area covered in deep bomb craters which subsequently caused the Army many difficulties in its advance.

Following our visit to Normandy, Brian and I spent a few days in London, staying at the Berkeley Hotel. Checking our bank accounts with delighted managers, since our sojourn in foreign parts, we found ourselves well able to afford expensive living for a change and proceeded to do just that, to the astonishment of the Berkeley management and delight of our friends. It was just as well, perhaps, because London under concentrated 'doodle-bug' attack was frightening and depressing, to say the least. I was full of admiration for the Londoners who took it all with typical fortitude in much the same way as they had done during the blitz of 1940-1.

By the time I got back to 324 at Calvi on 6 August, the pre-invasion air assault for the invasion of the south of France was in full swing.

I had my caravan parked by a strip of mimosa trees close to the beach. My batman, a humorous and intelligent man, was standing by the shore gazing out to sea early one morning when I passed him on my way for a swim.

'You look pensive,' I murmured. 'Thinking about home and the girlfriend?'

'No sir,' he replied. 'I was thinking about my duchess.'

I did not get my swim immediately for he told me the

following story. Before the war, he had been a footman in the service of a well-known duke and duchess, popular with the national press for their renowned parties and extravagant ways. Cruising in their yacht off Corsica in the summer of 1938, he was duty barman one evening when their graces had a fearful row over the double martinis, resulting in the duke picking up and throwing his wife overboard still clutching a large dry martini in her jewelled hand.

'After her, lad,' the duke commanded, 'or she'll drown.'

Gallantly plunging into the sea and rescuing his mistress, getting a kick in the balls for his trouble, he was about to go below and change out of his wet uniform when the duke and duchess seized him and in no time flat had him over the side and back into the sea closely followed by themselves amid roars of laughter and cheers from the guests who had by this time lined the rail to see the fun.

'Never had so much fun in my life with them two,' he grinned. 'The duchess was a real lady, didn't half like a bit of fun and a good laugh. She always gave me a fiver after playing the fool with me. You know sir, that was the last time I was in these here parts.'

He was still gazing out to sea when I finished my swim.

CHAPTER EIGHTEEN

Maquis party

By the beginning of August the Normandy invasion was delicately poised ready to break the German defences at Caen and St Lo and capture Paris. But how far did the invasion of the south of France (Operation 'Anvil-Dragoon') support the Normandy battles and contribute to our final victory?

Though I had no means of knowing it at the time, there was a clash between the Americans and the British as to whether 'Anvil' was justified, or indeed necessary. The American view was that 'Anvil' was important to the success of the Normandy landings because it would contain German divisions in the south, which otherwise might be used as reserves against the Normandy beachhead. The British, on the other hand, did not want it to take place because the forces taking part would have to be bled from units in Italy so that our position would be weakened on the Italian front, and the campaign prolonged. This would inevitably mean delays in our advance and hinder a successful entry into Austria to capture Vienna before the Russians. As the invasion forces were to consist almost entirely of American and French divisions (three American and seven French), the French supported the American view, for political reasons. A mixed American and British Airborne division was employed as well during the assault stage.

The British argument put forward the conviction that if such a large force was to be of any assistance to Normandy, then instead of landing in the south of France it should cut through the Straits of Gibraltar and land at Bordeaux. This idea, however, was turned down by the Americans. For the landings in the south of France to be really effective it had been agreed by the Allies that 'Anvil' should take place within a week of the Normandy invasion. As events turned out, as a result of a shortage of landing craft for Normandy, the invasion was post-poned till 15 August, by which time the Normandy position was no longer critical, and in fact the breakout from the beach-head had succeeded. To support the operations the Navies provided six battleships, twenty-one cruisers and over one hundred destroyers. The Allied Air Forces were overwhelm-ingly superior to the enemy, in both fighter and tactical aircraft.

In the operations leading up to 'D' day, I led my Squadrons, alternating sorties with Barrie Heath, attacking targets along the beautiful Riviera coast. Our primary targets were the enemy radar installations hidden amongst the hilly features stretching from Toulon to Cannes. On one occasion of the many strikes, Barrie, leading 111 Squadron, attacked one of the more impor-tant radar sites at Cap Camarat near St Tropez, completely destroying the installation. Our troops informed us, after over-running it, that they found thirty dead enemy soldiers and technicians inside. By 'D' day, all but one of the enemy's radar sites had been liquidated. The remaining one was so severely damaged that it is doubtful if it was at all effective. Operations also included escorts to tactical bombers in their attacks against bridges, communications and airfields in the Marseilles area, and along the Rhone Valley.

On 3 August, Emanuel Galitzine, a flight commander in 72 Squadron while on a sweep with six aircraft, destroyed a He 117 seaplane over Lake Berre. Later the same day 93 Squadron found five He 117s moored on the lake and destroyed the lot.

The assault took place early in the morning of 15 August, when the US 7th Army landed between Hyères and Cannes. There were few casualties as opposition was slight, and after a token resistance the Germans fell back on the main road run-ning north through the Rhone Valley.

On 16 August, over the battle area, 72 Squadron intercepted a pair of FW 190s and damaged one of them. The next day I led 111, 72 and 93 Squadrons to act as escort to over twenty tactical bombers attacking the Pont d'Avignon. As the first bombs fell across the target, my pilots took up the famous French tune on the R/T giving short bursts of song here and there: 'Sur le pont d'Avignon, on y danse . . .'

By 28 August, the 7th Army had captured Valence and

Grenoble. They met stiff opposition from a Panzer division approaching Montelimar but after that swept on, reaching Lyons on 3 September. The Germans by this time were in full retreat.

Meanwhile, a landing strip had been prepared for us at Ramatuelle, a few miles from St Maxime and Fréjus. It had been hacked out of a vineyard and though adequate for our use was unpleasant because of its fine powder-like dust.

I landed at Ramatuelle on 19 August with Galitzine to check that the place was fit for use. 'Tiny' Le Petit and Bryant, my Signals Officer, who had been put ashore with our advance party on 'D' day, met me, both grinning like Cheshire cats. Obviously, the new-found hospitality of the local French was turning out to be too much for them. After consulting the CO of the American airfield construction unit I explained the dust problem and he promised to lay it with oil. Communications with 12th TAC and the 64th Fighter Wing were working, my trailer had been installed at the Wing site in a delightful glade amongst the pines, and the whole airfield was a hive of activity. The next day, the Wing flew in from Corsica and we continued operations without a break, giving cover to forward troops, and strafing German transports along the Rhone Valley and up in the mountains.

'Tiny' Le Petit, my jovial and kindly Senior Administration Officer, buttonholed me one morning to say that the Wing Padres, Rev(s) Scutt, Joyce and O'Donoghue (who had taken over from Father Lewis in April) were anxious to see me about a problem arising from their voyage from Naples to the beach-head. Inviting them to meet me in my caravan, I noticed Father O'Donoghue wink as he entered. Well, I thought, it can't be as serious as it looks. Scutt, the Church of England padre, explained that along with the Wing's ground officers they had all been shoved into the wrong ship, in the wrong convoy and, worse still, disembarked into deep water off the beaches with American combat troops on 'D' day when in fact they should have landed on 'D'+3 from a different convoy with other non-combatant forces. That was not all. They were issued with 'hard rations' in line with 'assault force' procedures and nobody had bothered to take note of their calling nor paid them due respect, for on opening the packages of rations they were amazed to find bundles of rubber contraceptives amongst the food and other items. He felt sure they had been deliberately insulted specially since they were British. He finished his heated report by saying: 'I feel sure you agree that a formal complaint must be made to higher authority for the way we have been treated.'

I looked at Father O'Donoghue: 'Do you also feel a formal complaint must be made, Father?' I said. 'After all, it must have been a great shock to you to find –'

'Not at all,' he interrupted. 'It was nothing at all, at all – as a matter of fact, I found the little gadgets came in very handy. You see – I er – we had to jump off the ship into thirty feet of water so I quickly popped me watch and me other knick-knacks into the little rubber gadgets and sure enough, they kept wonderfully dry all the way to the beach.'

I burst out laughing taking 'Tiny' and the others with me. End of meeting. More laughter and some sour looks but it really was a very funny ending to the assault on the beaches of the south of France.

A few days later I was summoned to 12th TAC for a briefing from the Commander, Major General House, on the next phase of operations. When I arrived, I was shown straight into the General's office. I saluted: 'I'm glad to report, 324 Wing have settled into Ramatuelle and operations are proceeding well. The communications are working fine, sir.'

'Waal', he eyed me critically, 'I've got noos for you – I want you to take 324 up to a landing ground at Sisteron, south of Grenoble.' He picked up some papers from his desk and moved to the wall map.

'Here,' he pointed, 'about a hundred miles, up near the mountains running along the Swiss border.' He glanced at the papers he was holding: 'I guess it's been liberated – but I can't tell – we haven't any army in the area, but Intelligence says it's O.K. and the Maquis are doing fine. You've got some RAF Regiment boys with you. I suppose they can protect the airfield.' He grinned, his eyes lighting up, and went on: 'Let's say you are going to be a "task force". We'll keep you informed and pass you the bomb-line position in the usual way. I'm giving you more range to get up and stay ahead of the Army. Things are moving so fast, we've got to keep on the ball. Call for anything you want. You guys are doing a swell job.'

As soon as I got back, I took off with 'Duke' Arthur and carried out a reconnaissance of Sisteron and the surrounding area. We did not see anyone on the airfield, but the strip looked fine. I discovered later it was called 'Thèze'. A few French waved to us, and suddenly near the town a big black Citroën pulled up beside the road in a cloud of dust, and four figures jumped out. I pulled my Spitfire round, with 'Duke' in long line astern, and swept past low over the spot. They were the Maquis all right, armed to the teeth with tommy-guns at the ready. They waved, and rocking my wings in answer, I turned and headed south.

That evening I called a Wing briefing and explained the situation. I told the CO of the RAF Regiment detachment to get off as soon as possible and secure Thèze airfield, explaining that he was to co-operate fully with the Maquis. I called for a flat-out effort from everyone and said we would have to depend on our own resources. Rations, petrol, oil, ammunition, supplies, equipment and mail, along with a host of other things, would have to be hauled by road each day from the coast. Before nightfall the first transports were on the move to our new location.

The days that followed were packed with action. As our convoy moved north it passed into territory that had not seen any British or Americans at all, and the welcome that awaited them was tremendous. This can be said also for the Riviera, for once the battle moved forward, the French population came down from the hills and life off duty was one long party. The champagne corks flew, the music blared from every bar and bistro. Hotels, such as the Carlton and Montana in Cannes, laid out the red carpet for us. Beautiful French girls took us to their hearts, vied with each other for our favours, and with typical French joie de vivre gave themselves over to entertaining us. I called it the 'Champagne Campaign' and somehow the name stuck.

Around the area we met our own kind – British civilians who had been caught up by the war in 1940 and never managed to get home. On one occasion while sitting outside the Café de Paris in Monte Carlo drinking a coffee and cognac, Barrie and I were amazed to see an elderly lady approaching along the pavement leading a bulldog with a Union Jack tied round his middle. She recognised our RAF uniforms and said: 'Well, thank goodness you've come at last – it's been an awfully long wait – I thought Britain had forgotten all about me.' It transpired she had been in Monte Carlo the whole war. Apparently the Germans went there for leave, so each day to annoy them she solemnly dressed her bulldog with the Union Jack and paraded in front of them while they sat at the cafés. Barrie asked her if she would have something to drink.

'No thanks,' she said, 'unless you've got some tea. I do miss my tea and I'd give anything for a cup right now.' That evening a jeep with tea, butter, coffee and other luxuries was sent to her.

From Sisteron we carried out patrols over our forward troops, and sweeps up as far as Dijon and Belfort. The best fun was strafing the roads, particularly along the Rhone Valley from Montelimar through Valence to Vienne. Today this road has been swallowed up by a motorway, but in 1944 it was very picturesque, twisting along by the river, following the hills and dipping through villages and hamlets. We chased the Germans along it, sharing with the US and French fighter-bombers the pickings of supply transports and lorried infantry, which were trying to escape the closing ring.

I had a message one night from the leader of the Maquis in Grenoble asking for a meeting. It had to do with some pockets of German resistance in his area of operations and he wanted us to beat up the targets with strafing attacks. Next morning I flew to Grenoble in our Fairchild light communications aircraft with Emanuel Galitzine. He spoke French fluently besides Russian, German and Italian and was always great company. A Russian prince related to the Romanovs, Emanuel's uncles, aunts and cousins seemed to stretch from one end of Europe to the other.

The meeting over and our maps suitably marked with the information needed to do the job, we repaired to a local bar for some champagne. Sitting at the next table were a couple of scruffy-looking characters and I noticed Emanuel paying particular attention to what they were saying to each other. Suddenly he jumped to his feet and spoke loudly in Russian where-upon the two men fell to their knees grovelling at his feet. Moments later, cringing like dogs, they rushed from the bar knocking over several chairs and a table on their way to the door.

'What was that all about?' I asked.

Grinning happily, he replied: 'Those two bastards are Russian Communists and were saying some very rude things about us and the French. I told them who I was and that when I became Tsar after the war I would hang them publicly from a scaffold in Red Square unless they mended their ways. Meanwhile the Maquis would be keeping an eye on them.'

Our Maquis friends thought this quite splendid and promptly ordered more champagne.

Leading eight aircraft of 72 Squadron at dawn one morning, I surprised a German convoy of ten vehicles a few miles south of Vienne. I dived on the bunched vehicles setting fire to two transports. Pulling away for a second attack, I saw the second flight of four aircraft get three more flamers. There was quite a lot of flak coming up from various points along the road, and as I turned for a second run in, I saw two transports close together partly hidden by a steeply banked bend in the road. As I went into attack, tracer streamed past, but I got a good burst at the vehicles.

As my shells splashed across the target, there was a sheet of flame followed by an explosion which blew me nearly over on my back. Half the hillside seemed to cave in, with debris and clouds of smoke erupting high into the air: I had scored hits on an ammunition truck and a lorry full of petrol.

Continuing past Vienne, and on the open road, I spotted a Tiger tank going as hard as it could towards Lyons. More in hope than in anger I gave it all my remaining ammunition. To my utter amazement it belched smoke and caught fire. When I gave my report to Tim Lucas, the senior Army Liaison Officer, he did not believe me, shaking his head and muttering that a Tiger was too tough for the shells of a Spitfire. I got my own back when I took him to the spot in my jeep, after we got to Lyons on 7 September, and showed him the tank. It was there I am pleased to say, burnt out, with 'Bravo RAF' painted on its blackened hull. To me the sight was worth a couple of Me 109s. Apparently some armour-piercing incendiary shells had ricocheted off the tarmac road into the oil tank and engine – pure luck, but very satisfying.

On another sortie leading 93 Squadron, to my great regret I fired on an ambulance; however, the Germans themselves were to blame. Along a straight piece of road leading north from Annonay, I saw a long column of German transports. I swung the formation in a wide arc eastwards, with the intention of attacking across the road. The flak, I knew, would be pretty stiff, and I thought that by this tactic we could take the enemy by surprise in the initial attack.

Putting 93 into line abreast, I dived for a large vehicle dead ahead of me. My opening burst caught it squarely along its side enveloping it in dust and debris. As I pulled up I saw the Red Cross on the roof. Realising I had attacked an ambulance I called off the attack. However, running my eye down the column as I swung round left in a climbing turn, I could see it was the only vehicle marked as an ambulance. The Germans did this quite often. They would put a few vehicles marked as ambulances in the midst of an armed convoy hoping we would not attack.

Later, when I went down the same road with Tim Lucas to look at the Tiger tank, I found this ambulance burnt out where I had strafed it, lying on its side in the ditch. Beside it was a communal grave with the names of twenty German soldiers fixed to the wooden cross. The spot where the petrol and ammunition trucks had blown up also had a communal grave with fifteen names. The ambulance incident was unfortunate, but unavoidable. I remembered a morning in England, during the summer of 1942, when I saw an FW 190 fighter-bomber strafe the main shopping area of Folkestone, which at the time was full of women; I couldn't do anything about it because I was unable to catch him. Looking at the names on the cross, I reckoned it was a just retribution.

On another occasion I strafed an open staff car and six trucks, destroying the whole lot with the help of the rest of my section. On the second attack, a German got up from the ditch, stood beside the road then levelled and fired his automatic pistol as I came for him. A few seconds later he disintegrated in a cloud of dust.

Normally pilots never see the results of their attacks at close quarters. In the 'Champagne Campaign', because of the speed with which the enemy retreated, we were able to check on the damage we did soon after the attacks took place. The carnage on the roads was awful. By the time we got to Lyons our air forces had destroyed and damaged over 3,000 transports, tanks, guns and horse-drawn vehicles.

324 Wing in the period 25 August to 13 September 1944 destroyed 156 vehicles, damaging a further 300; 182 horse-drawn vehicles, one tank, fourteen locomotives and a tracked howitzer gun were also destroyed, with many more vehicles, guns and railway wagons damaged. In the same period we flew 900 sorties.

All this intensive flying was not achieved without casualties. My old friend Griffiths, who had joined 43 Squadron in Corsica, and Simpson of 43, were killed. 'Griff' was shot down by flak during a bomber escort, and Simpson while strafing. The flak throughout had been intense and, strangely, most casualties occurred in 93 Squadron. About twenty Spitfires were destroyed or damaged in the Wing.

93 Squadron lost Sergeant Karck, killed by flak; Flight/Sergeant Wagstaffe shot down missing; Sergeant Hulse also shot down but taken prisoner; while Pilot Officer Fisher and Sergeant Loomes were wounded. Sergeant Fielding of 111 Squadron was shot down and wounded close to the enemy but, after crash-landing and before the Germans could get to him, an AOP Piper flown by a most gallant American officer swooped down and picked him up right under the Germans' noses. Fielding was back with his Squadron the same evening.

Nothing in the air would have been possible without great efforts being made by the specialist officers and ground-crews of the Squadrons and Wing personnel alike. Jim Evans, commanding the Engineering Squadron, Francis the equipment officer, Bryant and another Evans in charge of Signals, Perry my overworked armament officer, Menzies in charge of our MT, Croall and Van der Veen, the cypher officers, Ted Lewis my faithful, articulate spy in charge of Intelligence and 'Dag-

wood' Rees the Operations officer. They were a marvellous
team with 'Tiny' Le Petit, my senior officer in charge of
administration, pulling out all the stops under extreme conditions of improvisation and shortages. Then there were our
Army Liaison officers, Captains Tim Lucas, 60th Rifles, and
Peter Clay, Shropshire Light Infantry, who worked round the
clock to keep us informed about the land battle and in touch
with an ever changing bombline. And through the bustle and
hustle with a permanent smile for all to see 'Ackers' Moore, my
accountant officer, a most amusing and forthright Australian,
made sure we were never short of French francs to meet the
heavy demands made upon our pay-books in our off-duty
hours.

At Sisteron one day 'Tiny' said to me:

'We're out of tea – you know what that means – the men
won't put up with it and we'll come to a grinding halt.'

I sent a suitably worded signal to the Commanding General of
12th TAC: 'Out of tea period the war is about to stop period.'

Within six hours a Dakota landed with enough tea on board
to satisfy us for months. Attached to one of the chests was a
personal message for me: 'Keep the war going we are right
behind you period.'

This splendid reaction from the Americans seemed to me to
make up, in no small measure, for the Boston Tea Party!

We moved to Lyons/Bron airfield on 7 September, but between 13 and 20 September our operations were severely
restricted owing to the Germans having retreated beyond the
range of our aircraft. We hoped to move up to Besançon and
continue the fight, but due to heavy rain the airfield was unserviceable. I did get an advance party there but they had to be
recalled. In any case, on 29 September I was informed by 12th
TAC that we were to stand down from operations. The reason
became apparent the next day, when I received a signal from
Mediterranean Allied Air Forces saying we were to return to
Italy as soon as possible.

At the end of September 1944 John Cloete, a Rhodesian,
handed over command of 93 Squadron to Bertie Sachs, a South
African. I was sorry to see Cloete leave; he had done a splendid
job with the Squadron. However, Sachs was an old friend from

my time with 244 Wing, while he served in 92 Squadron. Sachs, fair and handsome, had German ancestry. This led to a personal problem because his younger brother decided, when South Africa went to war, to join the German Air Force. In Sicily he told me he had had a letter from his mother to say his brother had moved to Italy from France and was now serving in a Me 109 squadron. 'We are a house divided,' he laughed. 'She tells me if we meet in the air I am to remember he is my younger brother and I must not shoot him down. Can you beat that?' They survived the war. I would have dearly loved to have been present when the brothers Sachs finally met back home.

The move to Lyons brought in its wake an invasion of B24 Liberators of 15th USAAF in the form of an airlift of petrol, bombs and stores. This had become necessary because army and air force formations were running out of fuel for aircraft, MT and tanks while ammunition and bombs were also in short supply – all due to the rapid withdrawal of the Germans. Time was the essence of the problem so hauling vital stores by road all the way from ports in the south of France caused an unacceptable delay.

I had a meeting with the colonel in charge of the operation to organise the reception and turn-round of the Liberators. I was amazed to learn 200 aircraft would carry out the airlift, landing in batches of ten aircraft at intervals of one minute between them after arriving from their bases on the Foggia plain in Italy. The colonel went on to explain that the Americans would supply the ground party to unload the fuel and stores but I would be expected to provide the air traffic control, fire-fighting and medical facilities. As soon as the aircraft were unloaded (the fuel having been pumped direct from the Liberators' tanks into empty drums), they would taxi along the perimeter track and take off immediately to allow more aircraft to land. Each day they arrived and all went well, but on the last day a Liberator caught fire due to an auxiliary-pump motor overheating, nearly setting fire also to a Liberator in front and to another behind the burning aircraft. Luckily most of its fuel had been pumped into the drums so we were able to get the fire partially under control but we had a hell of a job clearing the bombs from under the burning aircraft in the nick of time before its wings collapsed in sheets of flame. No praise is too high for the way my officers and airmen responded to this highly dangerous emergency.

It was at Lyons that I ran across the first German atrocity I actually saw, soon after it had been committed. The French commandant of the airfield came to see me one morning in a very agitated frame of mind. He explained that a number of French workmen had been shot by the Germans, just before they pulled out of Lyons, and now lay buried in three bomb holes on the airfield. It appeared that one of them had escaped, and the Germans told the rest of them to find him otherwise they would all be shot. They had no idea where their comrade was, so the sentence was carried out. When the Germans evacuated Lyons, the escaped man reappeared and reported the incident.

Grimly we trooped off to the spot and dug up each bomb hole in turn. Sure enough we found the bodies, lying in a mass of arms and legs at the bottom of each hole. The murdered workmen had been forced to kneel at the bottom of the holes and had then been tommygunned, after which the holes had been filled in. It was a ghastly sight for, as it had happened shortly before we got to Lyons, all the corpses were still recognisable. There were about forty men in each hole.

CHAPTER NINETEEN

'Cab-rank' war

At the end of September Sir John Slessor flew to Lyons in his B25 Mitchell from Caserta and addressed the Wing, explaining why we were being pulled out of France back to Italy. The Italian front was proving an extremely tough nut to crack and he wanted every available aircraft in support of the Armies' operations. We were to move to Florence, and as soon as possible modify our Spitfires to carry bombs.

A day or two later we left Lyons for La Jasse, an airfield in the Marseilles area. We all hated the thought of going back to Italy with England now so close. We had made many friends among the hospitable French of Lyons, and the parting, when it came, was sentimental and emotional. As a farewell gesture on 23 September at the Athletic Stadium, we played a team from Lyons at rugger. There was a big turnout of the French population, and as many shouted for us as against us. Bill Creed, a flight commander in 43 Squadron and an ex-Gloucester player, captained our team, and 'Dendy' Lawton, a Springbok forward, led the pack, hurtling through the opposition like a tank. We lost by 9–13, but it proved important because it was the first meeting between teams from England and France for fifteen years. The French press gave it front-page coverage and the entire entrance charges were donated to Maquis charities.

With the 2nd Tactical Air Force now almost in sight over the horizon, I think we all hoped 324 Wing would ultimately come under its control. However, the decision to return to Italy was a sensible one in view of the tough struggle the 8th Army was facing against a well-disciplined and organised enemy on the Italian front. Close air support was going to be of vital importance in the final stages of the struggle. As the only British representatives in an otherwise entirely American/French operation we were thoroughly spoiled and fêted by the French population. I found that we British were still looked upon as France's major ally and memories of the 1914–18 conflict lingered on so that the affection was spontaneous, the liberation greeted with emotional thankfulness. We were being made to leave an attractive country and friendly people much against their will.

At La Jasse on the day of our arrival a terrific 'mistral' hit us in the middle of the night. On the airfield, the Spitfires strained and lifted on their wheels, but as they were all facing into the wind no aircraft suffered damage except my little Italian Saiman 202. It was the same one I had used at Taranto. I had kept it as a Wing communications aircraft and taken it with me when I moved from 244. Now the poor machine was lying on its back, smashed to pieces.

I flew over to Florence to have a look at our new home at Peretola before carrying out the move. It had a concrete runway and adequate dispersals but precious little else. One of the SAAF fighter recce Squadrons was based there, but there were no flying control or night-flying facilities. On the morning of 2 October, we sent off an advanced party of ground-crews and equipment in a Dakota to Florence. After lunch I took off for Corsica before proceeding to Florence. This procedure, I knew, would ease the refuelling problems en route and at the same time allow Squadrons to arrive at Florence in such a way as to make life reasonably easy for our small party of ground-crews.

I landed safely with 72, and after detailing 'Duke' Arthur to see to the rest of the Wing, I hurried off into Florence to check on the accommodation and messing for pilots and ground-crews, which had been organised during my previous visit.

Unfortunately, the refuelling stop in Corsica took too long and though 111 Squadron got down safely at Florence, 93 and 43 Squadrons arrived close behind each other at dusk with darkness fast approaching. 93 Squadron landed without incident, but 43 were caught in total darkness. There was no airfield ground-to-air control and no one was able to reach me by phone.

In desperation a makeshift flare-path was improvised with

the headlamps of a few trucks and jeeps by parking them on the edge of the runway and shining the beams along the landing run. Two aircraft got down safely, but the third crashed into one of the trucks and went up in flames. This blaze interfered with the vision of the next two pilots and they, too, crashed.

A pilot already on the ground, who was helping with the improvised flare-path, was killed when the first crash occurred – which also killed the pilot flying the aircraft and the driver of the truck. The other two pilots were injured. It was at this point that the remaining aircraft were diverted by the American sector control to Pisa where there were full night-flying facilities.

The series of accidents, and the sequence of events leading up to them, were shocking and quite unnecessary. The chaps on the ground had acted on the spur of the moment in good faith and if it had come off, they would have received high praise for initiative. As it was it had gone very wrong indeed, and in due course, after a Court of Inquiry, I was held to blame. It was a bitter pill, but as CO it was my responsibility.

After this we never really settled down properly at Florence. The weather was foul, with rain-squalls and mud. Nor did we relish the idea of hanging bombs on our aircraft.

Even though the weather seriously interfered with operations, we managed to carry out 105 offensive sorties during October and destroyed a Me 410 and a Me 109. Another Me 109 was probably destroyed and a further two damaged – all by 72 Squadron. In all, since February we had destroyed sixty-six enemy aircraft, probably destroyed six, and damaged fifty-six.

The 5th Army were held up by fierce fighting round Bologna, in fact the Germans fought harder here than at any time during the campaign, save possibly Cassino. Not even the terrific pounding from strategic and tactical bombers on the approaches of the town had any noticeable effect, and the bitter struggle continued.

We sat gloomily and waited for the mists and rain clouds to clear from the mountains. As my second winter in Italy stared me in the face, my thoughts turned homewards and I realised the strain was beginning to tell.

Barrie Heath was transferred to Air Vice-Marshal Dickson's

staff at Advanced HQ DAF much to my disappointment. Though I realised it was an important appointment, I argued with the AOC but he was adamant. I felt this was the last straw. I would miss him very much personally, but apart from that he was a key man in the Wing, and contributed a great deal towards the Wing's high morale and fighting spirit. In his place I got Bertie Wooten, an experienced and very likeable officer, but he, too, left almost immediately to go back to England having completed his overseas tour of duty. Before a replacement was nominated, I asked the AOC for Hannes Faure, the South African, and he agreed immediately. I was delighted, and it was under Hannes' guidance that we completed our conversion and training to the fighter-bomber role.

In the middle of November we moved back under the operational control of Desert Air Force and went to Rimini. I was thankful to see the last of Florence, with the frowning mountains standing guard over the city and the dirty-brown Arno river.

Since my Spitfires had been converted into fighter-bombers, we had to learn the Desert Air Force system of close air-support control. Though I had done some fighter-bombing in Malta I found these new systems vastly different. A new approach to the job was needed. Little had changed in the standard air-support system developed between DAF and the 8th Army since the Desert fighting. However, operations in the mountainous country of Italy called for a specialised application based on the old system. Two factors had influenced the new methods – greatly improved communications and complete air superiority above the land battle. This new system was code-named 'Rover David Cab-rank'. 'Rover David' was first introduced in North Africa for the battle of El Hamma. It consisted of putting an experienced fighter-bomber pilot in an Army Armoured Car with a Brigadier and all the necessary communications. 'Cab-rank' followed later when air superiority had been gained. Methods of identifying targets were constantly refined and the 'grid' system was introduced first in Sicily, where the close nature of the terrain made target identification more difficult than in the open country of the Western Desert.

The standard method developed in the Desert consisted of

forward tentacles (mobile controllers) broadcasting a series of code numbers and targets to the Air Liaison Sections at forward HQ Desert Air Force, the Mobile Operations Room Unit and all Wings. On receipt of the information the Air Liaison officers attached to the Wings would prepare maps, charts and photographs in light of the broadcast and would be ready to brief the Squadrons chosen for the various targets. No action was taken, however, till Army HQ had consulted with DAF and accepted or rejected the targets passed by the forward army units. Once accepted, HQ DAF needed only to send out a message: 'Signal code . . . accept.' On receipt the pilots would be briefed and the strikes would take place.

'Rover David Cab-rank' looked at the problem from quite a different angle. A mobile Army/Air Observation Post was set up and operated with the forward army units, which were in contact with the enemy. The air controller, being in R/T contact with orbiting aircraft in the area, was able to brief pilots immediately new targets were selected for attack. The key to the 'cab-rank' system was the use of a grid superimposed on a photograph, copies of which were in the possession of both pilots and controllers.

In the early stages the 'Rover' teams were located in armoured cars fitted with VHF radios. Later, because of the success of 'cab-rank' operations, the 'Rover' teams carried on their strength a truck, jeep and trailer, two Army and RAF wireless operators, and a radio mechanic. The controllers were experienced RAF pilots. To illustrate the system a reconstruction of a typical operation is necessary.

Let us say the time is nine o'clock in the evening and the place the Operations caravan at HQ DAF. A conference is about to start between the Army and Air Force. The RAF is represented by the Senior Air Staff officer, the Group Captain Operations, the Wing Commander Operations, and the Wing Commander Intelligence. The Army is represented by the Brigadier General Staff, the GI Operations (General Staff officer Grade 1) the GI Intelligence and the GI Air.

The BGS or GI Operations outlines what the Army has done during the day. The RAF states the effort and scale of the air operations that took place during the same period. The Army then tells the meeting what operations they intend carrying out the following day and may ask: 'Can we have "Rover" control for the forward units between nine and five in DZ area?' The RAF would reply: 'Yes – can you say what targets?' The Army might say: 'Various targets such as gun emplacements, strong-points and buildings in the battlefield area.' This information enabled the RAF to detail the correct types of armaments to be carried by aircraft.

After the conference a directive would go out to the Mobile Operations Room Unit (MORU) outlining the operations for the following day. MORU would sift the information and allot tasks to the Wings. Briefing at Wing became simple since the 'cab-rank' aircraft merely had to fly to an easily identifiable landmark and orbit until called by the 'Rover' controller. After half an hour's orbiting, if no targets came up, the controller would tell the formation to return to base.

The next day all sorts of requests would be passed by the forward units to the 'Rover' control-post. If the telephone lines were working well, the Army representative could check the priority of the targets by communicating with the units concerned. If for some reason this could not be done, he would be expected to use his experience to decide which requests to accept and state the priorities. The 'Rover' staff officers were capable of assuming full responsibility if the situation demanded, without further reference to HQ 8th Army or Desert Air Force.

The scene is now set for a typical 'cab-rank' operation. Imagine a rather shabby vehicle or battered house within a short distance of the forward troops. There is the sound of crackling electrics on the wireless sets and from outside the staccato rattle of rifle- and machine-gun-fire; the whine of shells and dull explosions; overhead the steady drone of aircraft. Two men wearing sheepskin coats and cord trousers splashed with mud are concentrating on the radio sets beside them. The moment has come for allotting the first targets of the day to the fighter-bombers. By the time the Kittyhawks, Mustangs or Spitfires are orbiting in the 'cab-rank' the RAF controller will have marked the first target on his map and worked out its grid reference. The radio set comes to life:

'Hello Rover David, Hotspur Leader calling – have you a target? – over.'

'Hello Hotspur Leader Rover David – have you a map of the Reno?'

Contact is thus established and as they are using a separate R/T channel the conversation will now proceed like a phone conversation:

'Look at square D4, at the top left-hand corner – have you got it?'

'Yes – I'm with you.'

'You will see a bend in the river just in front of a bombed bridge.'

'I'm still with you.'

'On the east bank above the bend there are two houses about two hundred yards apart – take the house nearest to you – the southerly one – that is your target.'

Hotspur Leader now rechecks the instructions with the 'Rover' controller, then clears the information with his pilots. They confirm they are on to the target.

'Rover David, thanks for your help, we are going down to attack – out.'

Hotspur Leader may now issue special instructions to his formation as he can clearly see the target, whereas the 'Rover' controller has only the grid photograph as a reference.

Theoretically targets could be attacked by our fighter-bombers at short notice after request. The only time-lag was the actual passing of calls for close support from Brigade via 'Rover' to the aircraft overhead. It must be remembered, however, that 'Rover David Cab-rank' would not have been feasible without complete air superiority in the battle area. The 'cab-rank' system developed by DAF was used extensively during the Normandy landings.

Shortly before Christmas 1944 Air Vice-Marshal 'Dickie' Dickson relinquished command of Desert Air Force, and Air Vice-Marshal Robert Foster took over from him. 'Pussy' Foster, as he was known, took over DAF at a very challenging time. An extremely calm person, I found him amazingly well informed on our current operations, and he was quick to spot weaknesses or inefficiency.

By all accounts the Germans should have been retreating, as they were doing in France and on the Eastern Front. Instead, in Italy they had lost very little ground in the preceding months and as winter closed in very firmly fixed in prepared defensive positions. Robert Foster was therefore faced with the task of dislodging the enemy from their positions under appalling conditions, and later, in the spring, of fighting the last battles of the campaign to final victory. Even after that his tasks would not be over, for it was going to be his responsibility to set the standard by which Desert Air Force would operate and maintain law and order in a conquered country. His deep understanding of the human aspects involved made him the ideal man for the job.

The Wing had become operational as fighter-bombers from the end of November onwards. Sometimes I let Hannes Faure lead, and I tagged on behind. It never ceased to surprise me that 'cab-ranks' could go on endlessly, providing almost dawn-to-dusk air support for the 8th Army. Nobody bothered any more to look behind or above in case a hostile Messerschmitt lurked in the sun. Whenever one saw other aircraft they were almost certain to be friends. We averaged around thirty aircraft sorties a day in these operations. The medium and small-arms return fire was intense. Three officer pilots were killed during this period.

Flying on my own one morning as the fifth member in Hannes Faure's section, I followed in an attack on a small farmhouse we had been told by 'Rover David' contained an enemy Battalion HQ. Being in long line astern I found myself flying through concentrated enemy medium and light flak but, undaunted, I lined up on the target and released my bomb. At that point no direct hits had been registered by the other aircraft though I saw a couple of near-misses, so I was pleased to see my bomb land and explode right on the house as I looked over my shoulder breaking out of the dive into a steep turn. Diving again to strafe, I picked out a machine-gun emplacement manned by four Germans and getting nicely into position fired my cannons and machine-guns straight into the middle of the nest. I followed this with a few short bursts at troops and transport hidden in a vineyard before diving to zero feet and making for our own lines hotly pursued by angry puffs of 40-mm flak.

On landing I discovered I had been holed by 40-mm shell splinters in a wing and a couple of bullets had gone through the spinner of the propeller. Exciting stuff but not unusual damage for the type of operation. It could have been worse.

On 18 February we moved to Ravenna and soon after the AOC had me along to DAF HQ to tell me that 'Barney' Beresford was going to take over 324 Wing in two to three weeks' time. I was being posted to command No. 1 Base Area in Naples for four months, after which I would be sent home to attend the Staff College at Bracknell.

So it had come at last. Somehow I felt no emotion; I suppose because I had been expecting it. The only regret I had was that I was leaving before the end of Italy. That end would surely come in a month or so. With the Germans pinned down between the River Po and the Alps, we would destroy them piece-meal. There would be no more escape. It would have been satisfying to have ended still in the thick of things.

The last large-scale fighter-bomber operation to take place before the end of the war in Italy was targeted against the harbour and ships at Venice.

It was code-named 'Bowler' and six Squadrons of 239 Wing, consisting of 100 Kittyhawks and Mustangs led by George Westlake, the Wing Leader, attacked and destroyed all the ships, anti-aircraft batteries and, as a bonus, the mini-submarine training school as well. The code-name was derived from a remark by the AOC, Robert Foster, at the planning stage of the operation when he informed the Wing Leader and the Squadron Commanders that any bombs landing in or near Venice itself would mean a 'Bowler Hat' not only for himself but everyone else too.

The whole operation went off very well considering the stiff opposition met from the defences, and only one aircraft – a Kittyhawk – was hit, but the pilot was picked up safely after baling out over the sea. Venice itself escaped all damage except for some broken windows caused by a terrific explosion on the quayside when a bomb scored a direct hit on top of a stockpile of mines. The explosion rocked even the Spitfires patrolling and taking photos at 20,000 ft. These pictures showed the hole caused by the explosion to be 100 ft across. Unfortunately, my Spitfires saw no enemy aircraft at all, returning to base rather chastened by the lack of action.

The time arrived. The next day I was to fly my Spitfire for the last time. I had flown her throughout my command of 324 Wing – Cassino, Anzio, the south of France, and also as a fighter-bomber after our return under the control of Desert Air Force. I never had any trouble with the airframe or engine. A few scars from flak, a cracked bullet-proof windscreen, the result of a direct hit while strafing, but these were of my making. I never had a stoppage from cannon or machine-gun nor a bomb hang-up. No praise was too high for my ground-crew, members of 72 Squadron, who looked after me and my Spitfire during this lengthy period. And I celebrated with them accordingly that cold blustery night at Ravenna.

The next morning I walked out to my Spitfire and climbed into the cockpit. A couple of slaps on my shoulders from the ground-crew. The farewells were over. Waving away the chocks I taxied out, the familiar crackle and snarl of the Merlin dulling my senses. I opened up the power and, easing my Spitfire into the air, turned in a wide arc, setting course across the mountains for Rome and Naples.

I had time to reflect on my long partnership with this unique fighting lady. A joy to fly, a sureness of robust qualities, a challenge to risk all.

CHAPTER TWENTY

Bravo Tommy!

 In command of No. 1 Base Area at Naples, my responsibilities concerned administering a host of large and small units. The largest unit was a Personnel Disposal Centre at Portici where officers and airmen assembled for repatriation to the United Kingdom.

I already knew my chief, Air Vice-Marshal John Whitford, AOC Mediterranean Allied Coastal Air Force, since he had previously been Air Officer Administration of Desert Air Force. He helped enormously in adjusting my outlook towards a better understanding of post-war problems. It was by no means easy as I had been attuned for so long to the hustle-bustle of an Operational command and to making snap decisions, which had to be the right ones.

It didn't take long to start enjoying the high standard of living in Naples with a well-furnished, comfortable, self-contained apartment I could call my own, after the rigours of life in the field. A splendid Officers' Mess, too, perched high on top of a modern building with a lovely wide terrace full of flowering shrubs and flower-beds. The Cocquimella Hotel, a rest and leave centre at Sorrento, came under my jurisdiction and I spent many happy week-ends relaxing there by the sea. Visits to Capri and Ischia were easy to arrange and I took full advantage of these opportunities.

The officer in charge of administration, 'Fergie' Ferguson, relieved me of much burdensome office work so I was able to spend more time visiting the various units in my parish. As a foretaste of the joys of peace, my time in Naples could not have been more pleasant.

I kept in touch with flying by visiting the Fighter Conversion Unit near Portici or by borrowing a Spitfire or a potent Mustang IV fighter-bomber from the Maintenance Unit at Capodichino.

Bravo Tommy!

When it came, the end of the war was too great an occasion to be absorbed all at once. It opened up a number of permutations and for the first time in my life I had to give serious thought to my own future. There was plenty of time for reflection but no close friend with whom I could discuss the shape of things to come. It was probably just as well, for it gave me a valid excuse to ignore ill-conceived plans that sometimes flashed in the inner windmills of my mind. The future could take care of itself. I was alive, that was the important thing and life was at hand to enjoy.

Air Vice-Marshal Robert Foster invited me in May to the celebration fly-past of his Desert Air Force squadrons and the party that was to follow. The fly-past proved spectacular with squadron after squadron sweeping across the saluting base bringing back memories of the glory that was Desert Air Force. My own 324 Wing, now led by Barney Beresford, in immaculate formation, thundered over, while I remembered Cassino, Anzio, Rome, Corsica, the south of France, Florence and Ravenna, one after the other and each a definite memory. Above me the wings, while beside me the other part of the great team, those without wings but without whose magnificent contribution the victory could not have been forged.

The garden of the AOC's house at Brazzaco near Venice that night was turned into a fairyland; the branches of the trees bedecked with coloured lights, a flare-path marking the driveway, floodlights pin-pointing the array of cocktail bars and tents full of food while the DAF Band filled the air with stirring music. Guests from other commands and the Army, who had been present at the fly-past, were there to meet the pilots, squadron commanders and wing leaders. The evening was to prove the last great occasion in which the veterans of the fighting – from North Africa, Sicily and Italy – met the new boys, old friends and soldiers – soldiers who knew all about the accuracy of fighter-bomber strikes no more than 100 yards from their positions and above them skies that had been swept clear of the Luftwaffe.

Though the Desert Air Force was soon to pass into history, its tradition and methods lingered on to be admired and copied by other commands in the Royal Air Force. Its capabilities in mobility, communications and principles of close air support, developed during the fighting in the Western Desert, through Tunisia and Sicily to Italy, had been accepted long since and, reapplied to the requirements of the Allied Tactical Air Forces in France, Germany and elsewhere. Forged into a unique brotherhood with the 8th Army, Desert Air Force operated beyond the reach of traditional and accepted Service regulations when it came to dress and a way of life but this in no way detracted from the efficiency and operational capability of its members. It was a happy family which grew in stature with every success until by the end it had become a legend in its own time.

The extent to which DAF's fighter-bombers helped to bring about the final capitulation of the Germans in Italy is best illustrated by the comments of a captured German Corps Commander:

'. . . the fighter-bomber pilots had a genuinely damaging effect. They hindered practically all essential movement at the focal points . . . even tanks could not move during the day. The effectiveness of fighter-bombers lay in that their presence alone over the battlefield paralysed every movement. . . .'

To have been part of this great victory made me feel humbly proud.

A short time before I returned to England, I flew to Klagenfurt, Austria, in a borrowed Spitfire to visit 324 Wing. Somehow my map-reading was adrift after I changed course over Udine and, cruising at 15,000 ft, I crossed into Yugoslavia, as I discovered later, near a place called Bovec. It was just as well I had been searching an arc of sky behind me because presently I spotted two 'Jugland' Yak fighters peel off and dive in my direction. The Yugoslav Air Force did not like any intrusion over their country and there had already been several incidents and engagements. I therefore quickly rolled onto my back and diving steeply turned due west and scampered out of the way. If I had been caught I could not have defended myself because my guns were not loaded. The incident made me wonder what could have gone wrong with our relationship with Tito and his partisans. After all the help we had given them in so many ways to beat the common enemy, losing many gallant pilots in the process, their hostility seemed very strange to say the least. I could only guess that the inviolability of the Communist state was more important now that the fighting had ceased, than recognising a friend trying to mind his own business.

At Klagenfurt, reunited with old friends, I spent three wonderful days sailing on the lake, picnicking in the mountains and partying in the Mess. There was no fraternising with Austrian civilians, so in the evening we stayed on our airfield and the Army remained in their camps. Austria was a gloomy place that summer, its people glum and uncompromising, so different from my previous visits before the war when it was difficult to keep up with the extrovert exuberance of the people one met. I tried one day to give some chocolate and an apple I had on me to a couple of fair-haired, blue-eyed attractive children I met by chance. They looked at me as if I were something the cat brought in and turning away muttered: 'Engländer – Schweine.' I found the remark more hurtful than a slap in the eye. I recognised hate for the sake of hate but also that adjustments in my feelings towards our recent enemies needed revising. These were proud people, much like ourselves in looks and character and, in the normal way, full of fun. The barriers of hate and distrust would have to be overcome through respect and understanding, time the healing factor. With the Italians it was different. The long-standing friendship between our countries reaching back to Garibaldi and beyond, seemed not to have suffered at all from the war; in fact it had grown stronger, from the Italian view at any rate, because we had rid them of Mussolini and his fascist followers for which they were sincerely grateful. A bribe, therefore, in the shape of a bar of chocolate and an apple was not accepted as a peace offering but as a gift.

Besides, Italian partisans, using guerrilla tactics, had caused endless disruption to supply lines, transport and communications through the systematic use of explosives and armed attacks upon the Germans wherever they were to be found. Furthermore, partisans had saved many Allied airmen from capture or death by rescuing them, often in populated areas, tending to their needs and eventually passing them back to safety through enemy lines.

I could not help admiring the courage of the Germans for,

even in defeat, their cold efficiency and professional outlook never wavered. Their fighting spirit was inexhaustible. In the latter stages of the war in Italy, with the Luftwaffe a spent force not able to support their land battle, army formations fought for every inch of ground and, although battered and bleeding to death, never broke and ran. The prisoners I saw carried most of their personal equipment, their bearing still disciplined. Round the square in Klagenfurt one morning were grouped several truck-loads of German prisoners on their way to prison camps. They were held up because in the centre, the fifes and drums of the Grenadier Guards were entertaining the considerable crowd of people watching the display. The band marched and counter-marched playing traditional military tunes of glory and, in the final flourish, Bud Flanagan's 'We're going to hang out the washing on the Siegfried line'. Immediately the music stopped the Germans exploded with cheering, laughter and shouts of 'Bravo Tommy!' Quite marvellous.

Soon after my return to England, the first atomic bomb exploded over Hiroshima on 6 August 1945, followed three days later by the second on Nagasaki. I was staying at the Wheatsheaf in Virginia Water, having collected my joining instructions from the Staff College at Bracknell, when I heard the news of Japan's surrender on 15 August. Even though it was a foregone conclusion that Japan was finished after Hiroshima, the end came as something of a shock. I found it difficult at the time to grasp the fact that the whole complexion of war had changed radically in the space of a few days. Before the bomb, the prospect of Japan surrendering seemed remote. The final assault, I felt, on the Japanese mainland would be long drawn-out and very costly in lives since the Americans were still several hundreds of miles from their objective. My inner thoughts had encouraged me to think – rather foolishly – that after Staff College I might get a posting to the Far East and somehow get back to Operations. It never occurred to me that it could be otherwise. Earlier that day the BBC's news broadcast mentioned that Royal Navy Seafires had been in action in Toyko bay during escort operations and had shot down eight Japanese Zeros. Suddenly it was all over.

Bravo Tommy!

My companionship with the Spitfires, the companionship of exceptional men, the flying with its moments of intense application while attacking the enemy in the air or on the ground and all the suspense of the moment, the blood racing, the sudden changes in fortune and triumph, the cut and thrust in beating the enemy man to man.

On very rare occasions I hear the evocative music of a Rolls-Royce Merlin and search the sky to find the familiar elliptical wing shape: once again the controls respond to my touch, my heart beats faster.

The fact is I enjoyed the war. This may seem strange and shocking, but it became my driving force because it had a purpose and I accepted the risks, the excitement of combat, survival and retrospect in that context. We all did. A dangerous game played with no rule-book, it rested on the individual – individual responsibility in leadership with faith and courage, so that the sense of belonging to a great Service in its hour of triumph lifted the spirit above the horror and bestiality of war.

Notes on Allied and German combat claims in Second World War

Over the years there has been discussion among fighter-pilots of Second World War vintage and others, interested in what appears to be the exaggerated claims of certain German fighter 'aces'. I use the word 'exaggerated' guardedly because I have never been able to get at the whole truth. Consequently, the following observations are made without prejudice and after studying various records and documents in the hope they may be of general interest. The victories in aerial combat credited to the German 'aces' Hartmann (352), Neumann (302), Nowotny (258) and Marseille (158) appear fantastic by any standards.

There is no doubt the Germans destroyed in the air and on the ground hundreds of near-obsolete Soviet aircraft such as the I1-15 Chata, I1-16 Rata and the I1-2 Shturmovik ground-attack aircraft during the summer and winter of 1941. In assessing individual combat claims, it has been suggested by some knowledgeable people on the subject that leaders of German fighter formations were credited with enemy aircraft claimed as destroyed by pilots in the formation and these were included in the leader's running total. There is some doubt also about the facts relating to aircraft shot up on the ground during strafing attacks and whether or not these, too, were added to individual victories.

Discussing these matters with some German fighter pilots after the war got me nowhere because they hotly denied, not surprisingly, that combat claims were ever fiddled. Be that as it may, there is the interesting if perplexing case of Hans-Joachim Marseille. Fighting over the Western Desert he is reported to have shot down sixty-one RAF aircraft in the period 1-7 September 1942 with seventeen British aircraft downed in a single day (1 September). RAF records show that there were no losses

226

that day in the areas the claims were made. Marseille was killed in a flying accident (as reported from German sources) on 30 September 1942. His total score by then was 158; 150 of them claimed over the Western Desert. It appears that his claims were accepted at face value and forwarded to the German High Command by the *Jagdgeschwader* (fighter-squadron) concerned.

It is true that German fighter pilots had many more Allied aircraft to shoot at from June 1941 onwards, particularly on the Eastern Front. Major Mölders, an exceptional pilot and leader who fought against the RAF with great distinction in the Battle of Britain as commander of JG 51 (fighter squadron) was the first fighter pilot to claim 100 aerial combat victories and, I think, there is little doubt that his individual claims were quite genuine. On the Eastern Front, JG 51 were credited with 1,350 Soviet aircraft destroyed in the period 22 June to 10 September 1941. A further 300 were apparently destroyed on the ground by strafing attacks. By the end of the first week in July 1941, following the invasion of the Soviet Union, the German Air Force had destroyed about 5,000 Soviet aircraft for the loss of less than 200 GAF fighters it was claimed. Werner Mölders died in a flying accident on 22 November 1941. Some responsible Germans believe his death was no accident but deliberately planned on Hitler's orders because of Mölders's political views and his great popularity with the German nation, who accorded him a hero's welcome each time he returned to Germany.

British pilots had to have confirmation of any kills. This was usually provided by other squadron pilots, by assessment of ciné-gun camera film or an eye-witness on the ground. If none of these requirements were met, it became the responsibility of Squadron and Sector Intelligence Officers to assess pilots' claims from the details of combat reports and determine to which category the claim belonged, i.e. destroyed, probably destroyed or damaged. No claims were admissible for any aircraft destroyed on the ground as these fell into the category of ground targets.

In a fluid fighter-versus-fighter battle, there is little doubt that individual pilots were guilty sometimes in over-claiming, as a result of mistaken evidence or the fact that the pilot concerned could not follow his victim down because he was forced to disengage in a fast-moving situation. In fighter sweeps over France in 1941 to 1942, there were many occasions when absolute certainty of a kill became difficult to assess due to high altitude and lack of oxygen in the rarefied air preventing the enemy fighter from catching fire immediately. Spontaneous combustion could only take place at a lower altitude when the stricken aircraft found a wealth of oxygen by which time, more than likely, it had disappeared from view.

If comparisons must be made, it is interesting that the score credited to the leading 'ace' from each of fourteen Allied nations (excluding the Soviet Union) totals 352 which averages out at 25.14 aircraft destroyed. Pat Pattle of South Africa, 'Johnnie' Johnson of Britain and Richard Bong of the USA – three quite outstanding fighter pilots – destroyed 129 enemy aircraft *between* them.

Can there be such a wide differential between the relative performances of top German and Allied fighter pilots even allowing for the huge number of aircraft German pilots engaged over the Eastern Front and Germany itself in the months following the Allied landings in Normandy? And what about the leading Soviet 'ace', Colonel Ivan Kozhedub under the circumstances, with his modest claim of sixty-two German aircraft destroyed? Even if the best Soviet pilots were not up to the standard of the best Germans, which I doubt, surely Soviet fighter pilots flying some superb aircraft by that time could not have been as ineffectual as the figures suggest.

Index

229

Index

Index

Index

Hube, Gen., 149
Hughes, AVM Desmond, 161
Hugo, G/Capt Peter, 104, 106, 133, 154, 155
Hulse, Sgt, 206
Humble, Bill, 82
Humphreys, S/Ldr P., 154, 169, 174
Hunter, Gen. 'Monk', 97–8, 104
Hutley, P/O Ralph, 3, 4, 9

identification marks, aircraft, 31
Innes, F/Lt 'Chumley', 81
instructors, flying, 23–5
instrument flying, 14
Intelligence, Military, 11, 161–2
Italian pilots, 150–1, 172–3, 174
Italy: attacks over, 212, 217–18; Germans in, 217; invasion of, 163, 171–80, 181–9, 190–7, 210, 217–19; planes, 143–4, 172–4; relations with, 223; and Sicily invasion, 159; surrender, 169, 172, 173

Jackson, S/Ldr 'Jacko', 136, 140–1
Jameson, Air Commodore P.G., 124–5
Jansen, Mishe, 89
Japan, surrender, 224
Johns, F/Lt 'Johnny', 99
Johnston, P/O Alan, 29, 75
Jones, G/Capt J.I.T. 'Taffy', 23–4
Joyce, Rev., 200
Jubilee, Operation, 105–12
Junkers aircraft: Ju 52: 154; Ju 86P: 118; Ju 87: 159; Ju 88: 24, 31, 32, 33, 44

Kayll, W/Cdr Joe, 63
Kenley Wing, 86–7, 130
Kent, G/Capt Johnny, 133
Kent, Tyler, 11
Kingaby, W/Cdr D.E., 86, 91, 102, 105, 107, 109
Kingcome, G/Capt C.B.F. 'Brian', 130, 132, 133, 142, 151, 153, 156–7, 160, 163, 169, 176, 178, 195
Kittyhawks, 155, 171, 187
Klagenfurt, 222, 223, 224

Lago airfield, 180, 184
La Jasse airfield, 210, 211
Landry, Col. Bob, 133
Lawton, F/Lt 'Dendy', 210
Lea, S/Ldr Robert, 109

leadership skills, 46, 53, 104, 128; training in, 130–1
Leather, G/Capt Jack, 30, 31
Lecce airfield, 172–3
Leicester, gifts from, 62
Leigh-Mallory, ACM Sir Trafford, 33, 34, 40, 62, 67–8, 95, 97, 124, 133
Lentini airstrips, 155, 156–8, 160, 171, 180
Le Petit, S/Ldr 'Tiny', 192, 200, 201, 207
Le Touquet airfield, 82–3
Lewis, S/Ldr Fr., 194, 195, 200
Lewis, F/Lt Ted, 206
Liberator aircraft, 208
Licata, capture, 149
Link training machines, 9–10
Lock, F/Lt Eric S., 69, 74–5, 78, 84
Loftus, Col. Doug, 177
London: bombing, 19–20, 36–7, 42; social life, 19, 39, 68, 196
Loomes, Sgt, 206
Lott, AVM G.E., 99, 106, 112–14
Loudon, W/Cdr J.M., 79, 80, 81, 133, 184
Low Countries, attacks over, 40, 41, 47, 63, 67
Lucas, Gen., 182–3
Lucas, W/Cdr P.B., 130
Lucas, Philip, 82
Lucas, Maj. Tim, 204, 205, 207
Luftwaffe: bombing attacks, 56, 156–7, 158, 175, 179–80; captured pilot, interviews, 161–2; morale, 162, 224; planes, 16, 80–1, 143–4, 159; re-connaissance, 139–40; tactics, 16, 36, 40, 49, 68, 74, 129, 153, 156, 161–2, 175, 182
Luqa: Malta, 138–9, 146; Wing, 133, 135–45, 147–8
Lyons, 204, 206, 207, 208–9, 210

Macchi 202 aircraft, 149–50, 151–2, 172–3
McComb, S/Ldr James, 29, 30, 33
McEvoy, ACM Sir Theodore, 127
McIndoe, Sir Archie, 62, 69
McKelvie, Sgt, 81
McQuaig, Sgt, 109
Magister monoplanes, 3, 49–50
Maidstone, D.S. patrols over, 36, 37
Malaya, service in, 124
Malta, 95, 135, 136, 141–2, 145; German

232

Index

Index

Index